HOW TO
COOK
STEP-BY-STEP

THE AUSTRALIAN Women's Weekly

HOW TO COOK
STEP-BY-STEP

acp books

CONTENTS

Introduction	6
Knives	8
Equipment	10
Beginnings	14
Middles	88
Sides	184
Ends	222
Glossary	304
Conversion chart	313
Index	314

INTRODUCTION

Whether you're an experienced cook or just starting out, there's always a new tip or trick to improve your kitchen knowledge.

Knives & equipment A selection of different knives for specific tasks is the starting point for everyone who's serious about cooking. For a range of essential knives and cutting implements see pages 8 and 9. Some jobs require specific tools for the best results. Stay away from gadgetry and stick with the tried and true. See pages 10 to 13 for a good range of useful kitchen tools.

Creating flavour Herbs and spices can elevate a meal from every day to exceptional. Always add leafy herbs such as basil, coriander, parsley and dill to a dish at the last moment to maintain their freshness and vibrancy. Hardier herbs such as thyme, rosemary and sage, can withstand longer periods of cooking in slow-cooked sauces and stews. When it comes to spices, where possible, buy them whole and grate them fresh as needed. You will notice the difference in freshness and strength of flavour compared to pre-ground spices.

A good stock can add an extra flavour dimension to a soup or stew, and while there are very good store-bought options available, there is nothing quite like making it yourself. Keep leftover beef bones and chicken carcasses, and make big batches of stock. Store stock in the freezer in 1-cup portions (or smaller) and simply remove as much as you need at the time.

Using ingredients to their advantage
Seasonal produce seems to be the catch-cry these days and for good reason. Fresh fruit and vegetables are at their very best for taste, flavour and appearance when harvested in their right season. Using meat to its advantage, means matching the cut to the most appropriate cooking method. Primary cuts of meat such as filet mignon, should be cooked quickly over a high heat. Cheaper, secondary cuts require slow cooking at lower temperatures – perfect for all those slow cooker dishes.

Leftovers Freeze leftover soups, stews and pasta sauces in individual containers for perfect ready-made weeknight meals. Freeze unused egg yolks (or whites) and cream in ice-cube trays for future use. Stale bread can be turned into crumbs in a food processor or blender. Overripe bananas are ideal for banana bread while berries, apples and stone fruit that have past their peak, can be stewed.

KNIVES

1 CLEAVER This large rectangular knife is used for splitting (cleaving) meat from bone. A cleaver should be used with a swift, short stroke to cut cleanly through the meat, poultry or seafood.

2 CHEF'S KNIFE This all-purpose knife has a long broad blade that curves upwards to a point. The curve of the blade allows for a more precise cut, as the knife can be rocked across the chopping surface. The broad, heavy base of the blade can be used in place of a cleaver to chop bone.

3 CARVING KNIFE With its long, smooth blade, a carving knife is designed for taking slices off a roast in one continuous action. A carving knife can have either a pointed or rounded tip. The former is used for carving meats around a bone, and the latter for large, boneless pieces of meat such as ham or roast beef.

4 UTILITY KNIFE Midway between a paring and a chef's knife, its blade is 10–18cm (4–7¼ inches) in length. It is useful for chopping foods such as celery and onions, and julienning carrots.

5 PARING KNIFE With a small blade (5–9cm/2–3¼ inches), this knife is made for close, intricate work such as peeling, trimming and coring. It is the best one to use when working with small ingredients like garlic, ginger and chilli.

6 STEEL When used properly a steel will keep knives sharp and in top condition. Strike the knife against the steel with short, sharp strokes to smooth and straighten the blade. Always use a steel that is at least as long as the blade you are sharpening – ensure you buy a steel that is as long as your largest knife.

7 SERRATED KNIFE A long, sturdy serrated knife is a kitchen must-have. A serrated blade is designed for cutting ingredients that are hard on the outside and soft on the inside, like bread and tomatoes. Commonly used for cutting bread, a good serrated knife cuts through a heavy crust without compressing the loaf.

8 KITCHEN SCISSORS Also known as kitchen shears, these sturdy scissors are an all-purpose utensil for food preparation. They are most commonly used to cut a whole chicken into pieces, or to cut out the backbone of a quail or small chicken.

9 MEZZALUNA Meaning "half moon" in Italian, this curved, crescent-shaped blade is designed for chopping quickly and safely. The curved blade is rocked back and forth over the chopping surface, and is ideal for mincing fresh herbs. Special chopping boards can be purchased that mimic the curve of the blade.

EQUIPMENT

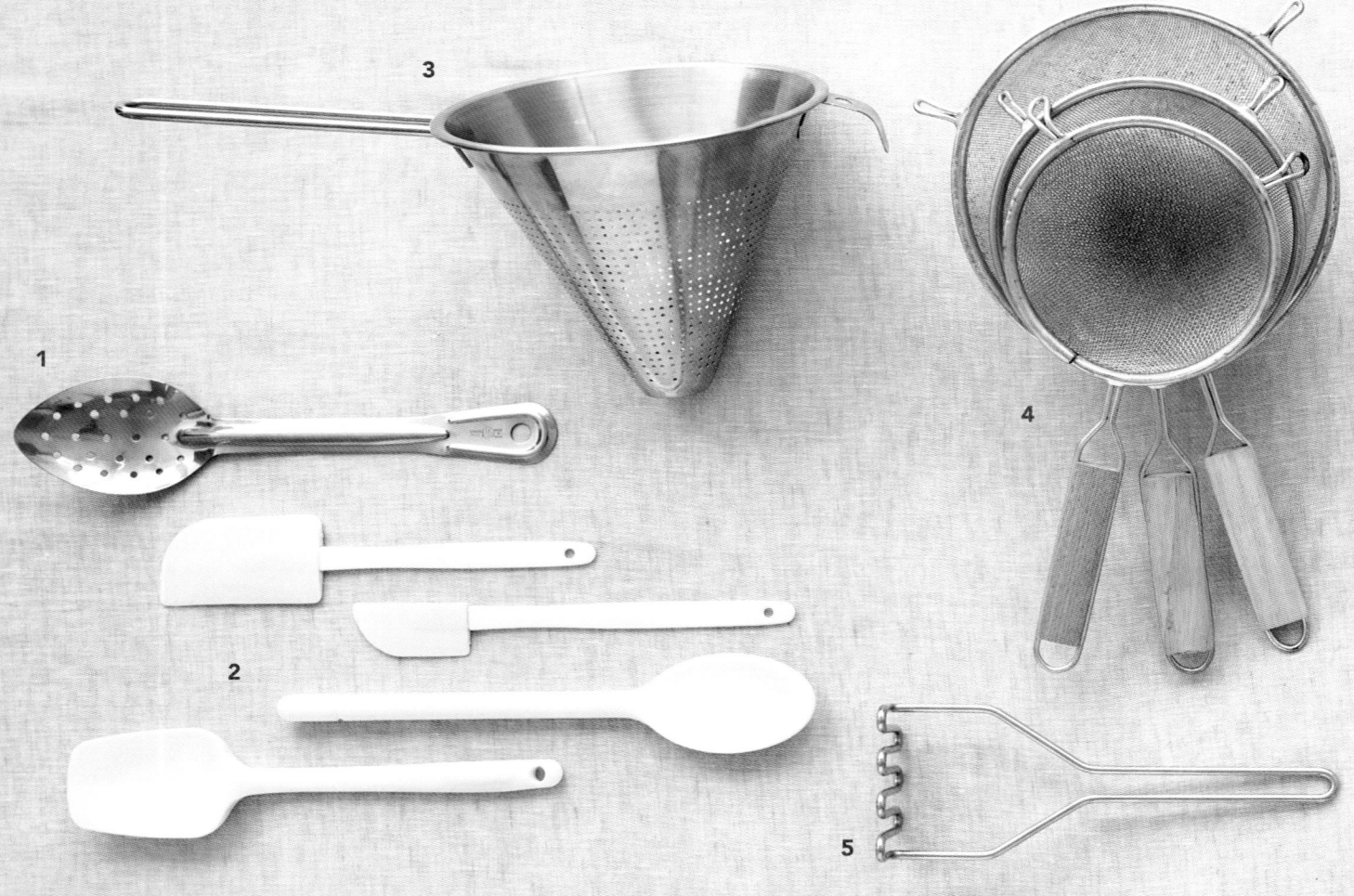

1 SLOTTED SPOON Any large spoon with holes or openings in it, a slotted spoon separates solids from liquids. It allows the liquid to pass through while solid foods sit on top.

2 SPATULAS Has a broad, flat, flexible 'blade' and available in a wide variety of sizes. It is designed to mix, spread, lift and turn food making it a multi-purpose utensil. It is worthwhile having a least two differently sized spatulas.

3 CONICAL STRAINER With an extremely fine mesh, it is used when you require a very smooth, lump-free mixture. Also called a chinoise, it is used to strain purees, soups and sauces.

4 SIEVES/STRAINERS Extremely useful for straining liquid from solids, sifting flour and turning pieces of food into a smooth puree by rubbing them through the mesh. They come in many sizes and degrees of coarseness/fineness.

5 POTATO MASHER Is used to mash, crush or break down any soft vegetables or pulses. The handle is connected to either a plate with holes or slits in it or a thick wire in a rounded zig-zag shape.

6 KITCHEN SCALES These are essential when it comes to baking as measurements must be precise. Scales should be reset each time they are used to ensure accuracy.

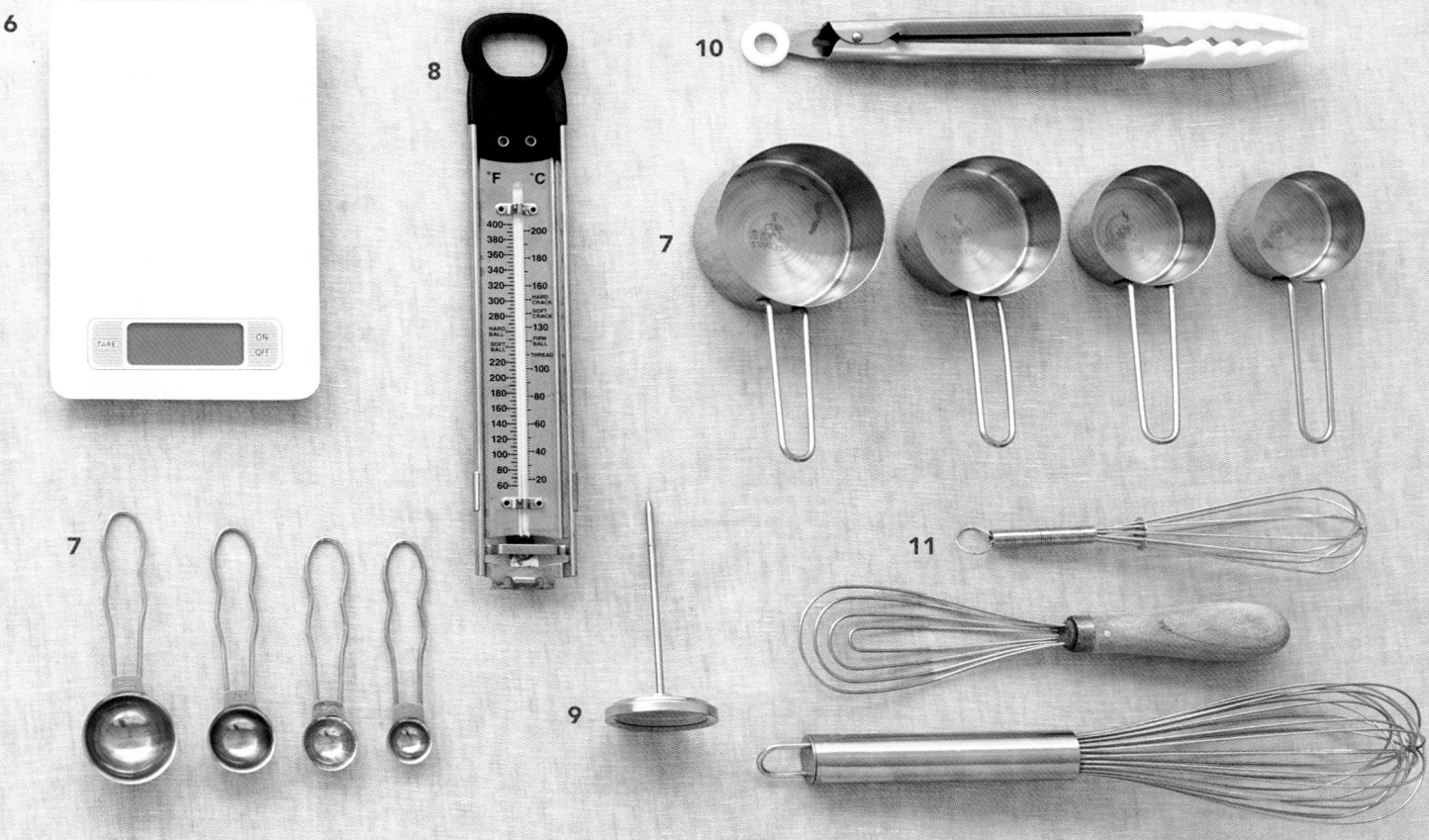

7 MEASURING SPOONS AND CUPS When using measuring cups and spoons you must be precise, make sure to use level not heaped quantities for true accuracy.

8 CANDY (SUGAR) THERMOMETER Takes the guesswork out of making jam, caramel and confectionery. It indicates at what stage the jam, or sugar syrup, is to be removed from the heat. It can also be used when deep-frying.

9 MEAT THERMOMETER A meat thermometer measures the internal temperature of meat. A sharp probe is inserted into the meat before cooking starts. The "doneness" of your meat (well-done, medium, medium-rare, rare) correlates with the internal temperature, allowing you to cook with precision.

10 TONGS They are used for gripping, moving and turning food. Look for tongs with long handles for outdoor barbecuing, and silicone tips to withstand high temperatures.

11 WHISKS Designed for blending, smoothing and aerating mixtures, a whisk has a long narrow handle that is connected to a series of wire loops. Available in a variety of shapes and sizes, the most common being the balloon whisk whose wide teardrop shape is best suited to mixing bowls. Used to whip egg whites and cream.

equipment ~ 11 ~ equipment

EQUIPMENT

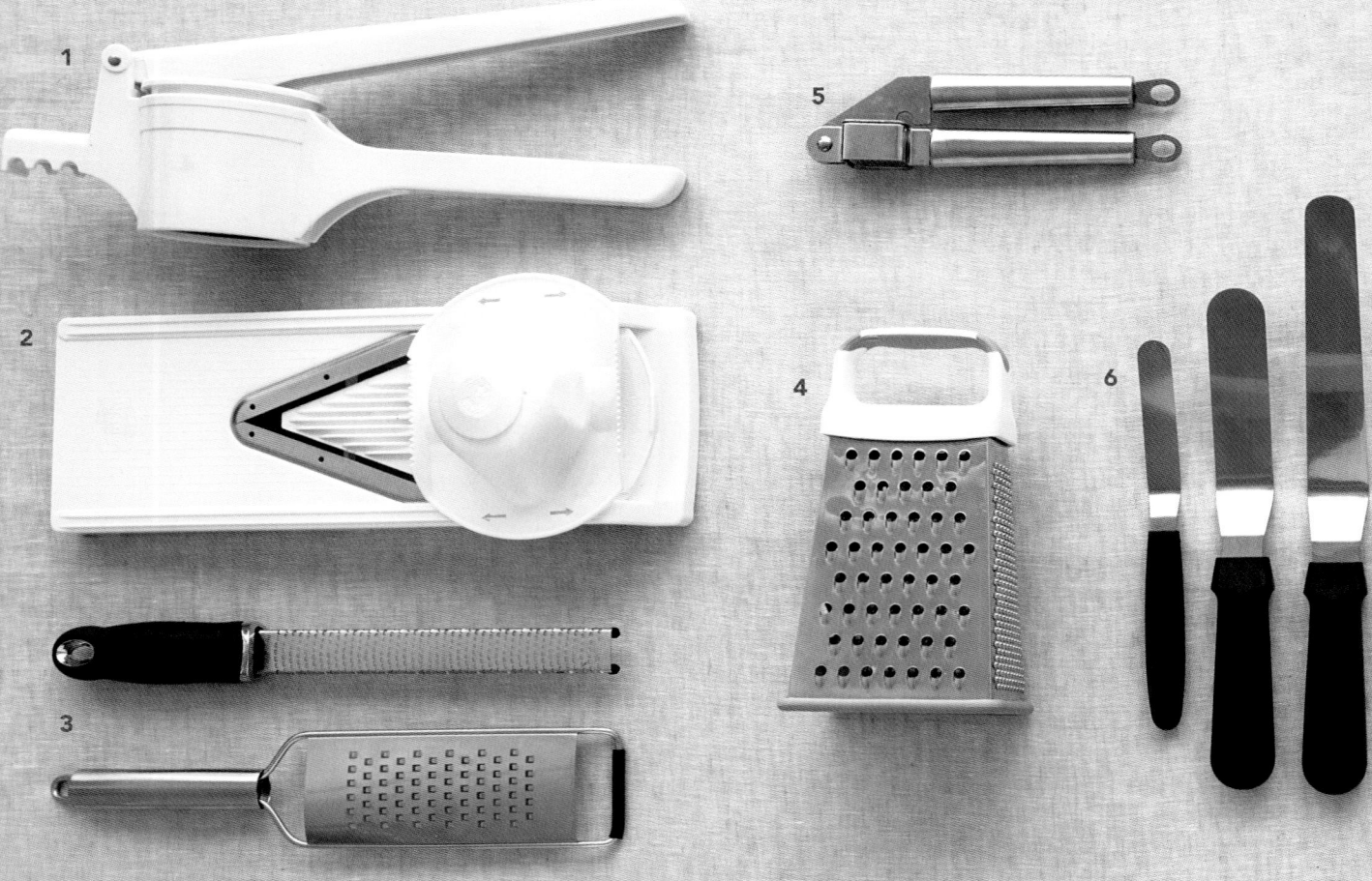

1 RICER Commonly called a potato ricer as it is often used to make lump-free mashed potato. Cooked potatoes or other foods are pushed through a sheet of holes usually no larger than a grain of rice and the result is a very light, fine, smooth mixture.

2 V-SLICER With razor-sharp, flexible thin blades V-slicers slice, dice, shred and julienne quickly and efficiently. It is deal to use for thinly slicing potatoes for bakes. Always use the guard to protect your fingers.

3 GRATERS Designed to shred food into pieces, graters are available in a variety of thickness options depending on how fine you want your food. Very fine graters are most commonly used for grating citrus rind or nutmeg.

4 BOX GRATER A box grater is useful for grating softer food, especially cheeses, as it is collected neatly inside.

5 GARLIC CRUSHER As the name suggests, a garlic crusher is designed to mince garlic for cooking. Being a key ingredient in many dishes and cuisines, a garlic crusher is a useful utensil to have on hand in the kitchen. Buy the most expensive one you can afford as this is a utensil you will use frequently.

6 PALETTE KNIVES Available in varying sizes with a blunt, flexible steel blade. They are handy for icing cakes.

7 DEEP-FRYING BASKET A wire basket is required when lifting food in and out of hot oil. The open weave of the basket also allows you to drain excess oil when you remove your food from the deep fryer.

8 WOK CHAN Its shovel-like shape makes a wok chan perfect for cooking in a hot wok with ease. Ingredients can be moved quickly, efficiently and easily due to the contour of the utensil which mimics the shape of a wok. Look for a wok chan with a wooden-tipped handle so it doesn't get too hot when cooking.

9 WOK LADLES A wok ladle has a long handle and a deep, round bowl. It is used for scooping liquid into or out of the wok. Available in different sizes.

10 WIRE MESH SKIMMER Commonly used in Asian cooking, this utensil has a long handle attached to a flat, mesh 'bowl'. Designed to skim food from cooking liquid, it is a versatile and inexpensive utensil, ideal for removing pasta, wontons or ravioli from boiling water or fried foods from hot oil.

11 BAMBOO STEAMER These inexpensive baskets are used regularly in Asian cooking. They sit in a wok (or on a saucepan of simmering water) and can be stacked on top of each other so meats and vegetables can be steamed at the same time.

BEGINNINGS

SCALLOPS WITH SAFFRON CREAM

prep + cook time 15 minutes (+ standing) ~ makes 12

12 scallops in half shell (480g)
1 teaspoon olive oil
1 small brown onion (80g), chopped finely
2 teaspoons finely grated lemon rind
pinch saffron threads
⅔ cup (160ml) pouring cream
1 tablespoon lemon juice
2 teaspoons salmon roe

1 Remove scallops from shells; wash and dry shells. Place shells, in single layer, on serving platter.

2 Cut scallop roe away from scallops; discard roe. Rinse scallops under cold water; pat dry with absorbent paper.

3 Heat oil in small saucepan; cook onion, stirring, until softened. Add rind, saffron and cream; bring to the boil. Reduce heat; simmer, uncovered, about 5 minutes or until mixture has reduced to about ½ cup. Remove from heat; stand 30 minutes. Stir in juice; stand 10 minutes. Strain cream mixture into small bowl then back into same cleaned pan; stir over low heat until heated through.

4 Cook scallops, in batches, on heated oiled grill plate (or grill or barbecue) until browned lightly and cooked as desired.

5 Return scallops to shells; top with cream sauce and salmon roe.

nutritional count per scallop
6.4g total fat (4g saturated fat); 288kJ (69 cal); 0.8g carbohydrate; 2.3g protein; 0.1g fibre

Using the tip of a small sharp knife, cut each scallop away from its shell. Wash and dry the shells well.

Cut the scallop roe away from the scallop, then discard the roe.

Pour the cream mixture through a sieve into a small heatproof bowl, then discard the solids. Return the cream mixture to the same cleaned pan.

Pull the head and entrails away from the body; remove the clear quill (backbone). Cut the tentacles from the head just below the eyes; remove the beak. Pull the membrane from the hood and wings; wash well.

Cut the squid hoods lengthways down the centre to open out.

Score the inside of the squid in a criss-cross pattern. Halve the squid lengthways, then crossways into thick strips.

SALT AND PEPPER SQUID

prep + cook time 45 minutes ~ serves 4

Tenderising squid in coconut milk with 1 tablespoon fish sauce will impart a wonderful flavour. Drain well and pat dry with absorbent paper before tossing it in the flour.

600g (1¼ pounds) squid hoods
¼ cup (35g) plain (all-purpose) flour
1½ teaspoons sea salt flakes
1½ teaspoons cracked black pepper
1 teaspoon dried chilli flakes
vegetable oil, for deep-frying
1 large tomato (220g), seeded, chopped finely
40g (1½ ounces) baby rocket (arugula) leaves

lemon aïoli
2 egg yolks
1 teaspoon dijon mustard
⅔ cup (160ml) extra light olive oil
⅓ cup (80ml) olive oil
2 tablespoons lemon juice
2 cloves garlic, crushed

1 Make lemon aïoli.

2 Clean squid. Cut squid down centre to open out; score the inside in a diagonal pattern. Halve squid lengthways; slice halves crossways into thick strips.

3 Combine flour, salt, pepper and chilli in medium bowl, add squid; toss squid to coat in flour mixture. Shake off excess.

4 Heat oil in wok; deep-fry squid, in batches, until tender. Drain.

5 Place tomato and rocket in small bowl; toss gently to combine.

6 Serve squid with tomato and rocket salad, and aïoli.

lemon aïoli
Whisk egg yolks and mustard in medium bowl. Gradually whisk in combined oils, in a thin, steady stream until thickened. Stir in juice and garlic.

nutritional count per serving
67.1g total fat (10.1g saturated fat); 3118kJ (746 cal); 8.2g carbohydrate; 28.6g protein; 1.6g fibre

tip For a quick way to coat squid, place the flour, salt and pepper in a strong plastic bag with the squid; grip the bag tightly closed, then gently shake. Remove the squid from the bag; shake off any excess flour mixture.

PRAWN AND GARLIC DUMPLINGS

prep + cook time 40 minutes ~ makes 30

800g (1½ pounds) uncooked medium prawns (shrimp)
1 egg white
4 green onions (scallions), chopped finely
2 cloves garlic, crushed
2.5cm (1-inch) piece fresh ginger (15g), grated finely
2 tablespoons finely chopped fresh chives
1 teaspoon chinese cooking wine (shao hsing)
2 teaspoons oyster sauce
30 gow gee wrappers
¼ cup (60ml) light soy sauce

1 Shell and devein prawns; chop prawn meat finely.

2 Beat egg white in medium bowl; stir in prawn meat, green onion, garlic, ginger, chives, cooking wine and oyster sauce.

3 Place wrappers on board; spoon rounded teaspoons of prawn mixture into centre of each wrapper. Brush edges with a little water; fold in half to enclose filling, press edges to seal. Trim rounded edge of dumplings using an 8cm (3¼-inch) round fluted cutter.

4 Cook dumplings, in batches, in large saucepan of boiling water about 5 minutes or until filling is cooked. Remove dumplings from water with a slotted spoon.

5 Serve dumplings with soy sauce.

nutritional count per dumpling
0.2g total fat (0g saturated fat); 130kJ (31 cal); 3.4g carbohydrate; 3.6g protein; 0.2g fibre

Spoon rounded teaspoons of prawn mixture into the centre of each wrapper. Brush edges with a little water; fold in half to enclose filling, press edges to seal.

Carefully trim the rounded edge of each dumpling with a round fluted cutter; don't cut too much off the dumpling or it may leak during cooking.

Cook dumplings, in batches, in a large saucepan of boiling water for about 5 minutes or until filling is cooked. Lift dumplings out of the water with a slotted spoon.

MIXED SASHIMI

prep time 45 minutes ~ serves 6

Finely shred the daikon using a mandoline or V-slicer. Place shredded daikon in a bowl of iced water until ready to use.

½ small daikon (200g)
300g (9½-ounce) piece sashimi tuna
300g (9½-ounce) piece sashimi salmon
300g (9½-ounce) piece sashimi kingfish
1 teaspoon wasabi paste
2 tablespoons japanese pink pickled ginger
⅓ cup (80ml) japanese soy sauce

1 Shred daikon finely; place in bowl of iced water. Stand until required.

2 Place tuna on chopping board; using sharp knife, cut 6mm (¼-inch) slices at right angles to grain of tuna, holding tuna with your fingers and slicing with the knife almost vertical to the board. Repeat with salmon and kingfish.

3 Divide drained daikon and fish among serving plates; serve with wasabi, ginger and soy sauce.

nutritional count per serving
7.7g total fat (2.4g saturated fat); 886kJ (212 cal); 1.6g carbohydrate; 33.5g protein; 0.7g fibre

tip It is important when slicing sashimi to have a very sharp, flat-bladed knife.

Place the knife at right angles to the grain of the tuna, holding the tuna with your fingers.

Cut through the tuna, slicing with the knife almost vertical to the board.

beginnings ~ 23 ~ beginnings

CHILLED CUTTLEFISH SPAGHETTINI WITH CHILLI AND HERBS

prep + cook time 1 hour 15 minutes (+ refrigeration) ~ serves 8

250g (8 ounces) spaghettini
½ cup (125ml) olive oil
500g (1 pound) cleaned cuttlefish hoods
2 cloves garlic, sliced thinly
1 fresh long red chilli, chopped finely
2 cups (500ml) dry white wine
½ teaspoon caster (superfine) sugar
½ cup firmly packed fresh flat-leaf parsley leaves
1 teaspoon finely grated lemon rind

1   Cook pasta in large saucepan of boiling water until tender; drain, reserving ¼ cup of the cooking liquid. Rinse pasta under cold water; drain. Drizzle pasta with 2 tablespoons of the oil and toss to coat. Spread pasta on baking-paper-lined tray. Cover; refrigerate.

2   Cut cuttlefish in half crossways.

3   Heat another 2 tablespoons of the oil in large frying pan; cook garlic and chilli, stirring, until fragrant. Add cuttlefish; cook, over high heat, 30 seconds, turning once. Add wine; bring to the boil. Using slotted spoon, transfer cuttlefish to a large bowl; cool.

4   Return wine mixture to the boil; boil, uncovered, about 5 minutes or until reduced to about ½ cup. Strain into small jug; discard solids. Blend or process wine mixture, adding remaining oil in a thin, steady stream until combined. Add reserved cooking liquid and sugar; process until combined. Refrigerate sauce until cold.

5   Slice cuttlefish thinly; coarsely chop parsley. Combine cuttlefish and parsley with pasta, sauce and rind in large bowl; season to taste.

nutritional count per serving
15.3g total fat (2.3g saturated fat); 1363kJ (326 cal); 21.9g carbohydrate; 14.2g protein; 1.4g fibre

tip Ask the fishmonger to clean the cuttlefish for you.

Add cuttlefish pieces to garlic and chilli in pan; cook for 30 seconds, turning once. Don't overcook as it will become tough.

Slice the cooked cuttlefish thinly before combining with the pasta and sauce.

Blend the oil with the reduced wine mixture to make the sauce. Here we show you how to slowly pour the oil into the mixture in a thin steady stream.

Thinly slice unpeeled apple into thin rounds. Cut the rounds into matchsticks.

Shape the crab mixture into 24 patties; coat the patties in breadcrumbs.

Heat ghee in large frying pan; cook patties, in batches, until browned lightly both sides.

CRAB CAKES WITH MADRAS AÏOLI AND APPLE SALAD

prep + cook time 45 minutes ~ serves 8

500g (1 pound) fresh cooked white crab meat
1 medium green-skinned apple (150g)
¾ cup (225g) whole egg mayonnaise
1 tablespoon sour cream
2 teaspoons lemon juice
1 tablespoon each finely chopped fresh chives and fresh flat-leaf parsley
2 teaspoons finely chopped fresh tarragon
1½ cups (110g) panko (japanese breadcrumbs)
60g (2 ounces) ghee (clarified butter)

madras aïoli
¼ cup (75g) whole egg mayonnaise
2 tablespoons sour cream
1 clove garlic, crushed
1 teaspoon madras curry powder

apple salad
3 medium green-skinned apples (450g)
2 tablespoons white wine vinegar
⅓ cup (80ml) olive oil
1 teaspoon dijon mustard
6 green onions (scallions), sliced thinly
2 cups loosely packed fresh coriander (cilantro) leaves

1 Make madras aïoli.

2 Make apple salad.

3 Drain crab meat on absorbent paper. Coarsely grate unpeeled apple; drain on absorbent paper.

4 Combine mayonnaise, sour cream and juice in medium bowl; stir in crab, apple and herbs. Season. Shape mixture into 24 patties; coat patties in breadcrumbs.

5 Heat ghee in large frying pan; cook patties, in batches, until browned lightly both sides. Drain on absorbent paper.

6 Serve crab cakes with aïoli and apple salad.

madras aïoli
Combine ingredients in small bowl. Cover; refrigerate until required.

apple salad
Cut unpeeled apple into matchsticks. Whisk vinegar, oil and mustard in medium bowl until combined. Add apple, green onion and coriander; toss gently to combine, season to taste.

nutritional count per serving
50.6g total fat (13.2g saturated fat); 2472kJ (591 cal); 20.5g carbohydrate; 13g protein; 2.4g fibre

Dip one rice paper round in a bowl of warm water for about 15 seconds until soft and pliable. Shake off any excess water before transferring to a tea-towel-covered board.

Place the noodle filling at the end of the rice paper round closest to you, then top with a little of the prawn meat. Leave a border at both ends to tuck in and avoid overfilling.

Fold the side of the rice paper closest to you over the filling, rolling to cover the filling. Fold in the sides of the rice paper; continue rolling to completely enclose.

VIETNAMESE PRAWN RICE PAPER ROLLS

prep + cook time 20 minutes ~ makes 12

These rolls can be made ahead of time and refrigerated for up to 3 hours. Cover with a damp tea towel to keep the rice paper moist.

50g (1½ ounces) rice vermicelli noodles
¼ small wombok (napa cabbage) (175g), shredded finely
½ cup loosely packed fresh mint leaves, torn
2 teaspoons light brown sugar
2 tablespoons lime juice
500g (1 pound) cooked medium king prawns (shrimp)
12 x 21cm (8½-inch) rice paper rounds

hoisin dipping sauce
½ cup (125ml) hoisin sauce
2 tablespoons rice vinegar

1 Soak noodles in bowl of water; drain. Roughly chop noodles.

2 Place noodles in medium bowl with wombok, mint, sugar and juice; toss to combine.

3 Shell and devein prawns; finely chop meat.

4 Make hoisin dipping sauce.

5 Dip one rice paper round in a bowl of warm water until soft; place on board covered with clean tea towel. Spoon some noodle filling on rice paper, leaving enough room on either side; top filling with some prawn meat. Fold rice paper up to cover the filling, roll to just cover filling. Fold in the sides, then roll to completely enclose. Repeat with remaining rice paper, noodle filling and prawn meat.

6 Serve rolls with dipping sauce.

hoisin dipping sauce
Combine ingredients in bowl.

nutritional count per roll
0.9g total fat (0.1g saturated fat); 326kJ (78 cal); 10.8g carbohydrate; 5.5g protein; 1.7g fibre

beginnings ~ 28 ~ beginnings

Cut across the head, under the eyes to separate the tentacles from the head.

Clean out heads and remove the beaks from tentacles; remove the eyes.

Combine the octopus, garlic, juice, oil and rigani in a medium bowl. Refrigerate, covered, for 3 hours or overnight.

BARBECUED BABY OCTOPUS
prep + cook time 25 minutes (+ refrigeration) ~ serves 6

Rigani is a dried Greek oregano; it is a stronger, sharper version of the familiar herb we use in Italian cooking and is available from good delicatessens and Mediterranean food stores.

1kg (2 pounds) baby octopus
2 cloves garlic, crushed
⅓ cup (80ml) lemon juice
⅓ cup (80ml) olive oil
2 teaspoons dried rigani
1 medium lemon (140g), cut into wedges

1 Clean octopus, remove eyes and beaks.

2 Combine octopus with garlic, juice, oil and rigani in medium bowl. Cover; refrigerate 3 hours or overnight.

3 Drain octopus; discard marinade. Cook octopus on heated oiled barbecue (or grill or grill plate) until tender.

4 Serve octopus with lemon wedges.

nutritional count per serving
13.4g total fat (1.7g saturated fat); 982kJ (235 cal); 1g carbohydrate; 27.6g protein; 0.2g fibre

tip Baby octopus should not need tenderising but if in doubt, freeze overnight then thaw, this partially breaks down the structure of the flesh and makes it more tender.

OYSTERS WITH MIRIN AND CUCUMBER

prep time 10 minutes ~ serves 6

Cut cucumber in half lengthways, then remove seeds with a spoon.

Thinly slice the trimmed green onions on the diagonal.

Spoon mirin dressing on each oyster, then top with a little green onion and cucumber.

1 lebanese cucumber (130g)
3 green onions (scallions)
48 oysters, on the half shell

mirin dressing
2 tablespoons mirin
1 tablespoon salt-reduced soy sauce
1 tablespoon lime juice

1 Make mirin dressing.

2 Halve cucumber lengthways; remove seeds. Finely dice cucumber. Slice the onions thinly on the diagonal.

3 Position oysters on serving platter. Drizzle dressing on oysters; sprinkle with cucumber and onions. Season with freshly ground black pepper.

mirin dressing
Combine ingredients in small bowl.

nutritional count per serving
4.8g total fat (1.8g saturated fat); 666kJ (159 cal); 2.1g carbohydrate; 24.8g protein; 0.3g fibre

Process the butter, flour and salt until crumbly, then add egg yolks, oil and the water; process until ingredients come together.

Cut 48 rounds from rolled pastry using a 7.5cm round cutter, re-rolling pastry scraps, as required.

Place rounded teaspoons of the chicken mixture in the centre of each pastry round, then fold in half to enclose the filling. Pinch the edges to seal.

CHICKEN EMPANADAS WITH TOMATO JAM

prep + cook time 2 hours (+ refrigeration) ~ makes 48

1 litre (4 cups) water
1 chicken breast fillet (200g)
1 medium potato (200g), chopped
1 tablespoon olive oil
1 small brown onion (80g), chopped finely
2 cloves garlic, crushed
1 teaspoon finely chopped pickled sliced jalapeño chillies
2 teaspoons ground cumin
½ cup (60g) frozen baby peas
¼ cup loosely packed fresh coriander (cilantro) leaves, chopped finely
¼ cup (60ml) lemon juice
1 egg, beaten lightly

pastry
3 cups (450g) plain (all-purpose) flour
100g (3 ounces) cold butter, chopped
2 teaspoons sea salt flakes
2 egg yolks
½ cup (125ml) vegetable oil
½ cup (125ml) iced water

tomato jam
2 tablespoons olive oil
1 medium red onion (170g), chopped finely
1 fresh long red chilli, chopped finely
½ cup (125ml) red wine vinegar
½ cup (110g) firmly packed light brown sugar
400g (12½ ounces) canned diced tomatoes

1 Make pastry. Make tomato jam.

2 Meanwhile, bring the water to the boil in medium saucepan; add chicken, return to the boil. Reduce heat; simmer, covered, about 10 minutes or until chicken is cooked through. Cool chicken in poaching liquid 10 minutes. Remove chicken from pan; discard liquid. Halve chicken horizontally, then shred finely.

3 Meanwhile, boil, steam or microwave potato until tender. Drain; mash in medium bowl until smooth.

4 Heat oil in medium frying pan; cook onion and garlic, stirring, until onion softens. Add chilli and cumin; cook, stirring, 1 minute. Transfer onion mixture to potato; add chicken, peas, coriander, juice and egg. Mix well, season.

5 Preheat oven to 200°C/400°F. Line oven trays with baking paper.

6 Roll each pastry half, separately, between sheets of baking paper until 3mm (⅛ inch) thick; cut 48 x 7.5cm (3-inch) rounds from pastry, re-rolling pastry scraps as required.

7 Place rounded teaspoons of chicken mixture in centre of each round; fold in half to enclose filling, pinch edges to seal. Place empanadas on trays.

8 Bake empanadas about 20 minutes or until browned lightly. Serve with tomato jam.

pastry
Process flour, butter and salt until crumbly. Add egg yolks, oil and the water; process until ingredients combine. Knead dough on floured surface until smooth. Divide pastry in half, wrap in plastic wrap; refrigerate 30 minutes.

tomato jam
Heat oil in medium saucepan; cook onion and chilli, stirring, until onion softens. Add vinegar and sugar; cook, stirring, until sugar dissolves. Stir in undrained tomatoes; bring to the boil. Reduce heat; simmer, uncovered, stirring occasionally, about 30 minutes or until very thick. Cool; season to taste.

nutritional count per empanada
5.8g total fat (1.7g saturated fat); 435kJ (104 cal); 10.1g carbohydrate; 2.5g protein; 0.7g fibre

CHICKEN LIVER PARFAIT WITH SOURDOUGH WAFERS

prep + cook time 1 hour 45 minutes (+ standing & refrigeration) ~ serves 10

It is best if the sourdough baguettes are a day old before slicing for this recipe. Sourdough wafers can be stored in airtight container for up to 3 days.

1 small brown onion (80g), chopped finely
1 clove garlic, sliced thinly
8 sprigs fresh thyme
¼ cup (60ml) red wine vinegar
½ cup (125ml) brandy
1 cup (250ml) port
500g (1 pound) chicken livers
200g (6½ ounces) ghee (clarified butter)
2 teaspoons finely chopped fresh oregano
2 eggs
100g (3 ounces) ghee (clarified butter), extra
1 teaspoon fresh thyme leaves
1 cup (180g) drained cornichons
2 cups firmly packed trimmed watercress sprigs

sourdough wafers
60g (2 ounces) ghee (clarified butter)
3 small 'petite' sourdough baguettes (360g)
2 teaspoons sea salt flakes

1 Combine onion, garlic, thyme sprigs, vinegar, brandy and port in small saucepan; bring to the boil. Reduce heat; simmer, uncovered, about 10 minutes or until reduced by about three-quarters. Strain port mixture into small jug (you will need ¾ cup strained liquid); discard solids. Cool.

2 Meanwhile, discard sinew from livers; pull lobes away from connecting tissue.

3 Preheat oven to 160°C/325°F. Grease thick metal 1.6-litre (6½-cup), 13cm x 23.5cm x 6cm (5-inch x 9-inch x 2.5-inch) loaf pan or glass or china loaf-shaped dish. Line base and sides with baking paper, extending paper over sides.

4 Melt ghee in small saucepan.

5 Blend or process livers, port mixture, oregano and eggs about 3 minutes or until smooth. Gradually add warm ghee in a thin, steady stream; blend until combined, season. Strain mixture through a very fine sieve into a large jug, pressing down on solids; discard solids.

6 Pour liver mixture into pan, place pan in tea towel-lined large baking dish; pour in enough boiling water to come halfway up sides of pan.

7 Cook parfait, in oven, about 20 minutes or until top is firm and temperature of parfait is 70°C/160°F. Remove parfait from baking dish; stand 1 hour.

8 Melt extra ghee in small saucepan; stir in thyme leaves. Pour mixture over parfait. Cover; refrigerate.

9 Make sourdough wafers.

10 To unmould parfait, rub sides of pan with a hot cloth; run a hot knife around sides of parfait. Invert parfait onto board, remove lining paper. Cut parfait into thick slices. Serve with sourdough wafers, cornichons and watercress.

sourdough wafers
Preheat oven to 200°C/400°F. Melt ghee in small saucepan. Slice bread thinly on an angle. Brush one side of bread with ghee; place on oven trays, sprinkle with salt. Bake about 3 minutes or until browned lightly and crisp.

nutritional count per serving
40g total fat (24.8g saturated fat); 2332kJ (558 cal); 22.8g carbohydrate; 14.1g protein; 2.5g fibre

Cut and discard any sinew from the livers; pull lobes away from connecting tissue.

Strain the liver mixture through a fine sieve into large jug, pressing down on the solids.

Place loaf pan in a tea-towel-lined baking dish; pour enough boiling water into the dish to come halfway up sides of pan.

Line the base and sides of the loaf pan with prosciutto, overlapping the slices and allowing them to overhang the sides of the pan.

Spoon the chicken mixture into the prosciutto-lined pan, pressing the mixture into the sides and corners.

Pour enough boiling water into the baking dish until the water comes halfway up the side of the foil-covered loaf pan. Bake 1 hour.

CHICKEN TERRINE

prep + cook time 1 hour 20 minutes (+ refrigeration) ~ serves 8

18 slices prosciutto (270g)
600g (1¼ pounds) chicken thigh fillets
600g (1¼ pounds) chicken breast fillets
¼ cup (35g) unsalted pistachios, chopped coarsely
3 teaspoons dijon mustard
1 teaspoon finely grated lemon rind
¼ cup coarsely chopped fresh flat-leaf parsley

1 Preheat oven to 200°C/400°F. Oil 1.25-litre (5-cup), 8cm x 20cm (3¼-inch x 8-inch) loaf pan; line base and two long sides with baking paper, extending paper 5cm (2 inches) over sides.

2 Line base and sides of pan with prosciutto, slightly overlapping the slices and allowing overhang on long sides of pan.

3 Chop chicken into 2cm (¾-inch) pieces. Process half the chicken until minced finely. Combine minced chicken, chopped chicken, nuts, mustard, rind and parsley in large bowl.

4 Spoon chicken mixture into pan, pressing firmly into sides and corners. Fold prosciutto slices over to cover chicken mixture. Fold baking paper over prosciutto; cover pan tightly with foil.

5 Place pan in medium baking dish. Pour enough boiling water into dish to come halfway up side of pan.

6 Bake terrine 1 hour. Remove pan from water; carefully drain juices from pan. Cool, then weight with another dish filled with heavy cans. Refrigerate 3 hours or overnight.

7 Turn terrine onto plate; slice thickly to serve.

nutritional count per serving
17.9g total fat (5.4g saturated fat); 1346kJ (322 cal); 0.9g carbohydrate; 39.5g protein; 0.6g fibre

tip You can make the terrine up to two days ahead of time.

CHICKEN TERIYAKI BROWN RICE SUSHI

prep + cook time 1 hour 20 minutes (+ cooling) ~ serves 4

1 cup (200g) brown short-grain rice
2 cups (500ml) water
1 tablespoon rice vinegar
3 sheets toasted nori (yaki-nori)
1 lebanese cucumber (130g)
20g (¾ ounce) snow pea sprouts, trimmed
2 tablespoons salt-reduced soy sauce

sushi vinegar
1 tablespoon rice vinegar
2 teaspoons white sugar
¼ teaspoon fine salt

chicken teriyaki
120g (4 ounces) chicken breast fillet, sliced thinly
1 clove garlic, crushed
1 tablespoon teriyaki sauce

1 Wash rice in large bowl with cold water until water is almost clear. Drain rice in strainer for at least 30 minutes.

2 Meanwhile, make sushi vinegar then chicken teriyaki.

3 Place rice and the water in medium saucepan, cover tightly; bring to the boil. Reduce heat; simmer, covered, about 30 minutes or until water is absorbed. Remove from heat; stand, covered, 10 minutes.

4 Spread rice into a large, non-metallic, flat-bottomed bowl (a wooden bowl is good for this). Using plastic spatula, repeatedly slice through rice at a sharp angle to break up lumps and separate grains, gradually pouring in sushi vinegar at the same time.

5 Continue to slice and turn the rice mixture with one hand; fan the rice with the other hand about 5 minutes or until it is almost cool. Cover rice with damp cloth to stop it drying out while making sushi.

6 Add rice vinegar to medium bowl of cold water. Place one nori sheet, shiny-side down, lengthways across bamboo mat about 2cm (¾-inch) from edge of mat closest to you. Dip fingers of one hand into bowl of vinegared water, shake off excess; pick up a third of the rice, place across centre of nori sheet.

7 Wet fingers again, then, working from left to right, gently rake rice evenly over nori, leaving 2cm (¾-inch) strip on far side of nori uncovered. Build up rice in front of uncovered strip to form a mound to keep filling in place.

8 Cut cucumber in half lengthways; remove seeds and cut into matchsticks. Place one-third of the cucumber, sprouts and chicken in a row across centre of rice, making sure the filling extends to both ends of the rice.

9 Starting with edge closest to you, pick up mat using thumb and index fingers of both hands; use remaining fingers to hold filling in place as you roll mat away from you. Roll forward, pressing gently but tightly, wrapping nori around rice and filling.

10 Working quickly, repeat process to make a total of three rolls. Cut each roll into four pieces. Serve with sauce and wasabi, if you like.

sushi vinegar
Combine ingredients in small jug.

chicken teriyaki
Combine chicken, garlic and sauce in small bowl. Cook chicken mixture in heated oiled small frying pan, stirring, until cooked through. Cool.

nutritional count per serving
2.3g total fat (0.5g saturated fat); 1058kJ (253 cal); 43.1g carbohydrate; 12.8g protein; 3.4g fibre

Slice the rice in a non-metalic dish with a spatula to break up any lumps and separate grains; gradually pour in the sushi vinegar, continuing to slice the rice as you go.

Dip your fingers in a bowl of vinegared water, pick up a third of the rice and place across the centre of the nori sheet.

Pick up mat with thumb and index fingers, holding filling in place with remaining fingers, and roll mat away from you. Press gently, wrapping the nori around the rice and filling.

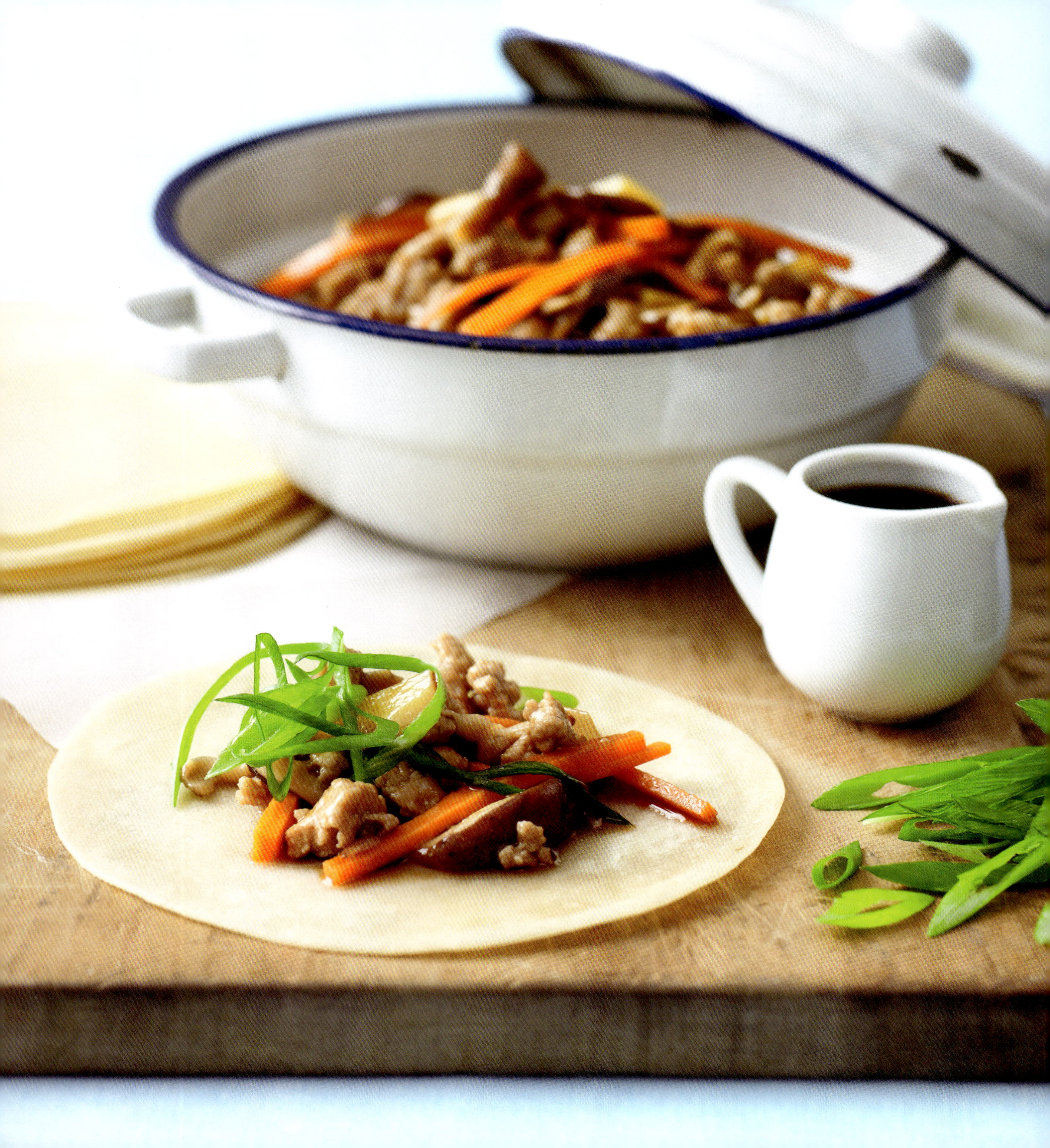

PORK AND VEGIE PANCAKES

prep + cook time 25 minutes ~ makes 12

Peking duck pancakes are small, round crêpes or pancakes made with plain flour; they are available from Asian food stores.

12 peking duck pancakes (230g)
1 tablespoon peanut oil
250g (8 ounces) minced (ground) pork
1 tablespoon chinese cooking wine (shao hsing)
1 tablespoon japanese soy sauce
1 tablespoon oyster sauce
1 small carrot (70g), cut into matchsticks
100g (3 ounces) fresh shiitake mushrooms, sliced thinly
4 green onions (scallions), sliced thinly
½ x 225g (7 ounces) canned sliced bamboo shoots, drained, rinsed
1 teaspoon sesame oil

1 To heat pancakes, fold each into quarters then place in steamer over large pan of simmering water until warm and pliable.

2 Meanwhile, heat half the peanut oil in wok; stir-fry pork until browned. Transfer pork to medium bowl; stir in combined cooking wine and sauces.

3 Heat remaining peanut oil in wok; stir-fry carrot and mushrooms until tender. Return pork mixture to wok with bamboo shoots and half the green onion; stir-fry until liquid is almost evaporated. Remove from heat; stir in sesame oil, season to taste.

4 Serve pork mixture with pancakes; sprinkle with remaining green onion.

nutritional count per pancake
26.9g total fat (8.1g saturated fat); 2224kJ (532 cal); 32.7g carbohydrate; 36.4g protein; 4.4g fibre

Fold each pancake into quarters, then place in a baking-paper-lined bamboo steamer over a saucepan of simmering water until warm.

Cut the peeled carrot in half crossways, then into thin slices lengthways; cut the slices into thin matchsticks.

Spoon pork mixture onto centre of each pancake and roll to enclose.

MONEY BAGS

prep + cook time 50 minutes ~ makes 12

1 tablespoon peanut oil
1 small brown onion (80g), chopped finely
1 clove garlic, crushed
4cm (1½-inch) piece fresh ginger (20g), grated finely
100g (3 ounces) minced (ground) chicken
1 tablespoon grated palm sugar
1 tablespoon finely chopped roasted unsalted peanuts
2 teaspoons finely chopped fresh coriander (cilantro)
3 green onions (scallions)
24 x 8cm (3¼-inch) square wonton wrappers
vegetable oil, for deep-frying

peanut dipping sauce
1 tablespoon peanut oil
1 small brown onion (80g), chopped finely
2 cloves garlic, crushed
10cm (4-inch) stick fresh lemon grass (20g), chopped finely
2 fresh small red thai (serrano) chillies, chopped coarsely
¾ cup (180ml) coconut milk
2 tablespoons fish sauce
¼ cup (55g) dark brown sugar
½ cup (140g) crunchy peanut butter
½ teaspoon curry powder
1 tablespoon lime juice

1 Heat oil in wok; stir-fry onion, garlic and ginger until onion softens. Add chicken; stir-fry until chicken is changed in colour. Add sugar; stir-fry about 3 minutes or until sugar dissolves. Stir in nuts and coriander.

2 Cut upper green half of each green onion into four long slices; discard remaining half. Submerge green onion strips in hot water for a few seconds to make pliable.

3 Place 12 wrappers on board; cover each wrapper with another, placed on the diagonal to form a star shape. Place rounded teaspoons of the filling mixture in centre of each star; gather corners to form a pouch. Tie green onion strip around neck of each pouch to hold closed, secure with toothpick.

4 Make peanut dipping sauce.

5 Just before serving, heat oil in wok; deep-fry money bags, in batches, until crisp and browned lightly. Drain on absorbent paper; remove toothpicks. Serve money bags with dipping sauce.

peanut dipping sauce
Heat oil in small saucepan; cook onion and garlic, stirring, until softened. Stir in remaining ingredients; bring to the boil. Reduce heat; simmer, stirring, about 2 minutes or until sauce thickens.

nutritional count per money bag
5.1g total fat (0.9g saturated fat); 435kJ (104 cal); 10.8g carbohydrate; 3.8g protein; 0.6g fibre

nutritional count per tablespoon dipping sauce
4.7g total fat (1.7g saturated fat); 251kJ (60 cal); 2.5g carbohydrate; 2.2g protein; 0.8g fibre

tip Freeze any excess dipping sauce for another use.

Cut the upper green section of each green onion into four strips using a sharp knife. Soften in hot water for a few seconds.

Place half the wrappers on a clean flat surface, position another wrapper on top forming a star shape.

Add teaspoonsful of filling to the centre of each wrapper and fold up sides to form a pouch. Pinch to enclose, tie with a green onion strip and secure with a toothpick.

Finely grate the peeled fresh ginger.

Finely chop the fresh shiitake mushrooms into small pieces.

Carefully spoon the pork mixture into the lettuce leaves then position on a serving platter.

SANG CHOY BOW

prep + cook time 30 minutes ~ serves 4

Sang choy bow is eaten with your fingers – the lettuce wrapped around the savoury mince filling. You can use chicken mince or a pork and veal mix instead; you can also serve the pork mixture in small witlof or betel leaves as cocktail food.

2 teaspoons sesame oil
1 small brown onion (80g), chopped finely
2 cloves garlic, crushed
2cm (¾-inch) piece fresh ginger (10g), grated finely
500g (1 pound) lean minced (ground) pork
100g (3 ounces) shiitake mushrooms, chopped finely
2 tablespoons light soy sauce
2 tablespoons oyster sauce
1 tablespoon lime juice
2 tablespoons water
4 green onions (scallions), sliced thinly
2 cups (160g) bean sprouts, trimmed
¼ cup coarsely chopped fresh coriander (cilantro)
12 large butter (boston) lettuce leaves

1 Heat oil in wok; stir-fry onion, garlic and ginger until onion softens. Add pork; stir-fry until changed in colour.

2 Add mushrooms, sauces, juice and the water to wok; stir-fry until mushrooms are tender. Remove from heat.

3 Add green onions, sprouts and coriander to pork mixture; toss to combine.

4 Spoon pork mixture into lettuce leaves to serve.

nutritional count per serving
11.5g total fat (3.6g saturated fat); 1112kJ (266 cal); 8.9g carbohydrate; 29.3g protein; 4.1g fibre

tip To keep the bean sprouts nice and crispy, trim them then place in a bowl of iced water for 5 minutes.

BEEF AND MUSHROOM OMELETTE

prep + cook time 25 minutes ~ serves 4

We used a combination of button, swiss brown and fresh shiitake mushrooms; you could also use enoki or oyster mushrooms.

2 tablespoons peanut oil
400g (14½ ounces) beef rump steak, sliced thinly
250g (8 ounces) assorted mushrooms, sliced thickly
2 cloves garlic, crushed
4 green onions (scallions), sliced thickly
2 tablespoons oyster sauce
8 eggs
2 tablespoons water
2 teaspoons japanese soy sauce
50g (1½ ounces) baby spinach leaves

1 Heat 2 teaspoons of the oil in wok; stir-fry beef, in batches, until browned. Remove from wok.

2 Heat another 2 teaspoons of the oil in wok; stir-fry mushrooms until browned lightly. Add garlic and green onion; stir-fry until fragrant. Return beef to wok with oyster sauce; stir-fry until hot, season to taste. Remove from wok; cover to keep warm.

3 Whisk eggs with the water and soy sauce in large jug. Heat 1 teaspoon of the oil in wok; pour in a quarter of the egg mixture, tilting the wok to make a 20cm (8-inch) omelette, cook until almost set. Slide omelette onto serving plate; top with a quarter of the beef mixture and a quarter of the spinach. Fold omelette to enclose filling; cover to keep warm.

4 Repeat to make a total of four omelettes.

nutritional count per serving
26g total fat (7g saturated fat); 1705kJ (408 cal); 4.3g carbohydrate; 38.5g protein; 2.2g fibre

Stir-fry the beef slices, in batches, over high heat until browned.

Pour a quarter of the egg mixture into heated oiled wok, tilting the wok to make a 20cm omelette; cook until almost set.

Slide the omelette onto a serving plate; spoon a quarter of the beef mixture onto half the omelette, top with a quarter of the spinach leaves. Fold the omelette over to cover the filling.

With motor operating, gradually add the olive oil in a thin, steady stream until the aïoli thickens slightly.

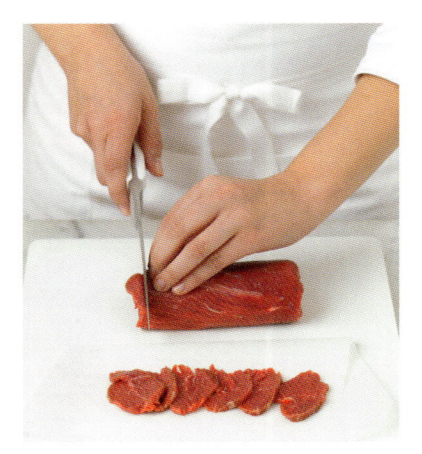

Using a sharp knife, cut the partially-frozen beef fillet into thin slices.

Place beef slices between sheets of baking paper, then roll until as thin as possible.

BEEF CARPACCIO WITH ROCKET, PARMESAN AND AIOLI

prep time 20 minutes (+ freezing) ~ serves 8

600g (1¼-pound) piece beef fillet, trimmed
150g (4½ ounces) parmesan cheese
100g (3 ounces) wild rocket (arugula) leaves

aïoli
2 eggs
1 clove garlic, chopped coarsely
2 tablespoons lemon juice
1 tablespoon dijon mustard
⅔ cup (160ml) olive oil

1 Wrap beef tightly in plastic wrap; freeze about 1 hour or until firm.

2 Meanwhile, make aïoli.

3 Unwrap beef; using sharp knife, slice beef thinly. Roll slices between sheets of baking paper until as thin as possible. Gently peel off top layer of paper. Turn bottom layer of paper, beef-side down, onto serving platter; carefully remove paper.

4 Using a vegetable peeler, shave cheese. Drizzle aïoli over beef; top with rocket and cheese.

aïoli
Blend or process eggs, garlic, juice and mustard until combined. With motor operating, add oil in a thin, steady stream until aïoli thickens slightly.

nutritional count per serving
28.9g total fat (8.2g saturated fat); 1509kJ (361 cal); 0.6g carbohydrate; 25.4g protein; 0.3g fibre

tip Freezing the beef first makes it much easier to cut into thin slices.

GOAT'S CHEESE SOUFFLE WITH SALT-ROASTED BEETROOT

prep + cook time 2 hours (+ cooling) ~ serves 6

60g (2 ounces) butter
1¼ cups (310ml) milk
1 teaspoon fresh thyme leaves
1 dried bay leaf
¼ cup (35g) plain (all-purpose) flour
2 egg yolks
4 egg whites
150g (4½ ounces) mild goat's cheese, crumbled
½ cup (125ml) pouring cream
⅓ cup (40g) finely grated gruyère cheese

salt-roasted beetroot
12 baby red beetroot (beets) (300g)
12 baby yellow beetroot (beets) (300g)
500g (1 pound) rock salt
4 sprigs fresh thyme
¼ cup (60ml) olive oil

1 Position the oven racks so you can bake the soufflés with the beetroot on the rack underneath.

2 Make salt-roasted beetroot.

3 Meanwhile, grease six ⅔ cup (160ml) soufflé dishes using 20g (¾ ounce) of the butter; line each base with baking paper. Place dishes in large baking dish.

4 Heat milk, thyme and bay leaf in small saucepan until simmering. Strain into medium heatproof jug; discard solids. Melt remaining butter in same pan, add flour; cook, stirring, until mixture bubbles and thickens. Gradually stir in hot milk; cook, stirring, until sauce boils and thickens. Transfer to large heatproof bowl; stir in egg yolks. Cover surface of sauce with plastic wrap; cool.

5 Preheat oven to 180°C/350°F.

6 Beat egg whites in small bowl with electric mixer until soft peaks form. Fold a quarter of the egg white into sauce. Fold goat's cheese into sauce, then remaining egg white. Spoon mixture into dishes. Add enough boiling water to baking dish to come half-way up sides of soufflé dishes.

7 Bake soufflés about 15 minutes or until well-puffed. Cool 30 minutes.

8 Unmould soufflés into small ovenproof dishes; place dishes on oven tray. Spoon a tablespoon of cream over each soufflé; sprinkle with gruyère cheese. Bake soufflés about 10 minutes or until browned lightly.

9 Meanwhile, return beetroot to oven, on rack below soufflés, until hot.

10 Serve soufflés with beetroot.

salt-roasted beetroot
Preheat oven to 200°C/400°F. Trim beetroot, leaving 2cm (¾ inch) of stems attached. Spread salt onto oven tray; top with beetroot, cover tray tightly with foil. Roast beetroot about 45 minutes or until tender. When cool enough to handle, peel beetroot. Place in shallow baking-paper-lined baking dish. Sprinkle with thyme; drizzle with oil, season.

nutritional count per serving
36.3g total fat (18.5g saturated fat); 1827kJ (437 cal); 14.5g carbohydrate; 12.9g protein; 3.3g fibre

Melt the butter in a small saucepan, stir in the flour; cook, stirring, until the mixture bubbles and thickens.

Fold a quarter of the beaten egg white into the sauce, then fold in the goat's cheese and remaining egg white.

Unmould the soufflés into small ovenproof dishes; place on oven tray. Spoon a tablespoon of cream on to each soufflé, then sprinkle with the gruyère cheese.

Remove and discard the stamens from the centre of the zucchini flowers.

Fill the flowers with the cheese mixture; twist the tips of the petals to enclose the filling.

Holding the tips of the petals, dip the flowers in the batter and drain off the excess.

GOAT'S CHEESE-STUFFED ZUCCHINI FLOWERS

prep + cook time 50 minutes ~ serves 8

75g (2½ ounces) goat's cheese
½ cup (120g) ricotta cheese
1 tablespoon roasted pine nuts
2 tablespoons fresh basil leaves, shredded finely
2 drained anchovy fillets, chopped finely
24 zucchini flowers, stems attached (240g)
vegetable oil, for deep-frying

batter
2⅔ cups (660ml) chilled sparkling mineral water
2 cups (300g) plain (all-purpose) flour
3 ice cubes
2 teaspoons sea salt flakes

watercress salad
2 cups firmly packed trimmed watercress sprigs
1 tablespoon olive oil
2 teaspoons red wine vinegar
½ cup (90g) seeded ligurian olives

1 Combine cheeses, nuts, basil and anchovy in medium bowl; season to taste.

2 Discard stamens from zucchini flowers; fill flowers with cheese mixture, twist petals to enclose filling.

3 Preheat oven to 160°C/325°F.

4 Make batter.

5 Heat oil in large saucepan. Working in batches, hold tips of petals and dip zucchini flowers into batter; drain off excess. Carefully lower flowers into hot oil. Deep-fry about 2 minutes or until browned lightly. Drain on absorbent-paper-lined oven tray; transfer to oven to keep warm.

6 Make watercress salad.

7 Serve zucchini flowers with salad.

batter
Whisk ingredients in medium bowl until barely combined (mixture should be lumpy). Use immediately.

watercress salad
Combine ingredients in small bowl; season to taste.

nutritional count per serving
10.6g total fat (3g saturated fat); 1066kJ (255 cal); 30.4g carbohydrate; 8.1g protein; 2.5g fibre

MARINATED MINI BOCCONCINI WITH PROSCIUTTO

prep time 20 minutes (+ standing) ~ makes 20

Cut the chilli in half, lengthways and remove the seeds. Finely chop the chilli into small pieces.

Cut each slice of prosciutto in half lengthways then in half crossways, trimming off the fat. You will need 20 pieces.

Wrap a piece of prosciutto around each bocconcini cheese and secure in place with a toothpick.

1 fresh long green chilli
200g (6½ ounces) baby bocconcini cheese
2 tablespoons olive oil
1 clove garlic, crushed
5 slices thin prosciutto (75g)
1 cup firmly packed fresh basil leaves

1 Halve chilli lengthways; remove the seeds, then finely chop.

2 Combine bocconcini, garlic, chilli and oil in medium bowl. Stand 30 minutes. Drain bocconcini; reserve marinade.

3 Halve prosciutto slices lengthways, then halve crossways. Wrap a piece of prosciutto around each bocconcini; secure with a toothpick.

4 Place bocconcini on serving platter, drizzle with reserved marinade and top with basil leaves.

nutritional count per piece
3.6g total fat (1.3g saturated fat); 176kJ (42 cal); 0.1g carbohydrate; 2.4g protein; 0.1g fibre

beginnings ~ 56 ~ beginnings

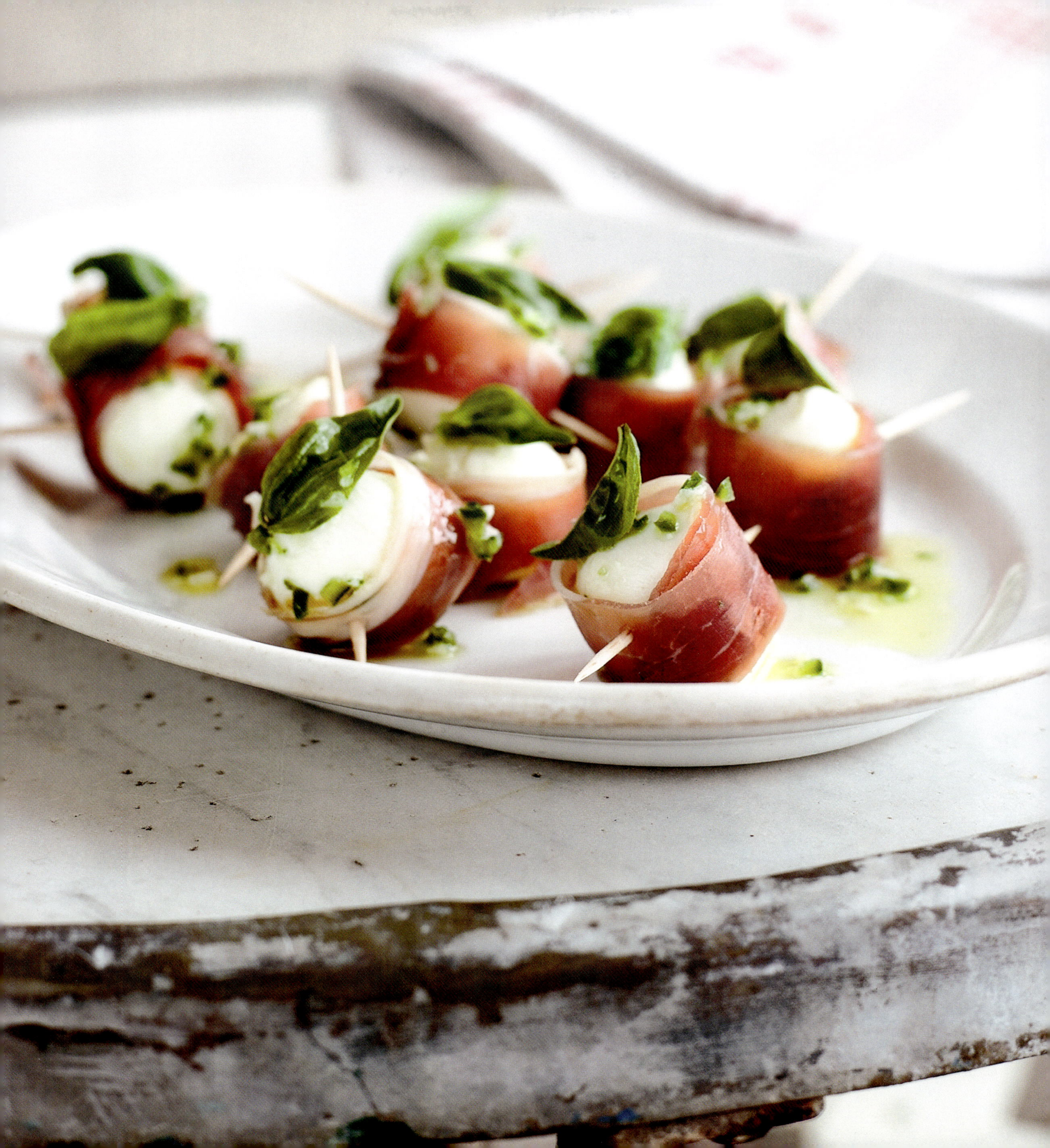

After the capsicum pieces have been roasted, peel away the skin.

Spoon cheese mixture into capsicum-lined pan holes, pressing down firmly into sides and corners. Smooth the surface.

Fold capsicum strips over the cheese mixture to completely cover the filling. Fold over the baking paper, overlapping the edges, to seal.

ROASTED RED CAPSICUM AND GOAT'S CHEESE TERRINE

prep + cook time 45 minutes (+ refrigeration) ~ makes 6

4 large red capsicums (bell peppers) (1.4kg)
500g (1 pound) ricotta cheese
375g (12 ounces) firm goat's cheese
1 clove garlic, crushed
⅓ cup finely chopped fresh chives
¼ cup (60ml) lemon juice

spinach and walnut pesto
100g (3 ounces) baby spinach leaves
1 clove garlic, chopped coarsely
¼ cup (25g) roasted walnuts
¼ cup (20g) finely grated parmesan cheese
¼ cup (60ml) olive oil
2 tablespoons lemon juice
1 tablespoon water

1 Preheat oven to 240°C/475°F. Grease six holes of 8-hole (½-cup/125ml) petit loaf pan. Line the base and two long sides of each hole with a strip of baking paper, extending 2cm (¾ inch) over sides.

2 Halve capsicums; discard seeds and membrane. Place on oven tray; roast, skin-side up, about 15 minutes or until skin blisters and blackens. Cover capsicum with plastic or paper 5 minutes; peel away skin. Cut each capsicum in half lengthways into 2cm (¾-inch) wide strips. Arrange strips, crossways, over base and two long sides of pan holes, extending 2cm (¾ inch) over edges.

3 Combine cheeses, garlic, chives and juice in medium bowl. Spoon cheese mixture into pan holes, pressing down firmly. Fold capsicum strips over to enclose filling. Cover; refrigerate 1 hour.

4 Meanwhile, make spinach and walnut pesto.

5 Carefully remove terrines from pan holes; serve topped with spinach and walnut pesto.

spinach and walnut pesto
Process spinach, garlic, nuts and cheese until chopped finely. With motor operating, gradually add combined oil, juice and water, in a thin, steady stream until pesto is smooth.

nutritional count per terrine (with pesto)
30.1g total fat (12.9g saturated fat); 1680kJ (401 cal); 11.9g carbohydrate; 21.1g protein; 3.2g fibre

SEA SALT MINI LOAVES WITH OLIVE OIL AND AGED BALSAMIC

prep + cook time 1 hour (+ standing) ~ makes 8

You will need to make the starter 12 to 24 hours (no longer) before making these loaves.

2 teaspoons (7g) dried yeast
2 teaspoons caster (superfine) sugar
¾ cup (180ml) warm water
2 tablespoons olive oil
2⅓ cups (350g) strong bread flour or plain (all-purpose) flour
2 tablespoons sea salt flakes
½ cup (75g) strong bread flour or plain (all-purpose) flour, extra
¼ cup (60ml) extra virgin olive oil, extra
2 tablespoons aged balsamic vinegar

starter
1 teaspoon (3g) dried yeast
1 teaspoon caster (superfine) sugar
1 cup (250ml) warm water
1 cup (150g) strong bread flour or plain (all-purpose) flour

1 Make starter.

2 Combine yeast, sugar and the water in small bowl. Stand in a warm place about 5 minutes or until frothy.

3 Beat yeast mixture, starter mixture, oil and flour in large bowl of an electric mixer with a dough hook, on low speed, until combined. Increase speed to medium; beat 2 minutes. Add half the salt; beat about 3 minutes or until dough is smooth and elastic. Scrape dough into oiled large bowl, cover with plastic wrap; stand in a warm place about 1 hour or until dough is doubled in size.

4 Meanwhile, line greased oven trays with baking paper; dust with a little extra flour.

5 Turn dough onto floured surface; knead until smooth. Divide dough into eight equal pieces. Shape each piece of dough into slipper shapes, place on floured oven trays. Brush loaves lightly with a little extra oil. Sprinkle with remaining salt. Dust tops of loaves lightly with a little sifted flour. Cover with absorbant paper; stand in a warm place about 1 hour or until loaves are almost doubled in size.

6 Meanwhile, preheat oven to 220°C/425°F.

7 Bake loaves about 20 minutes or until browned lightly and sounds hollow when tapped with fingers.

8 Drizzle balsamic into extra oil in serving bowl. Serve warm loaves with oil and balsamic mixture for dipping.

starter
Combine yeast, sugar and the water in medium bowl; stand in warm place about 5 minutes or until frothy. Add flour; beat with wooden spoon for 5 minutes. Cover with plastic wrap; stand 12 hours or overnight at room temperature.

nutritional count per loaf
11.9g total fat (1.7g saturated fat); 1258kJ (262 cal); 32.6g carbohydrate; 5g protein; 1.7g fibre

Combine yeast, sugar and the water in a medium bowl; stand in a warm place about 5 minutes or until the mixture is frothy.

Line greased oven trays with baking paper; dust with a little extra flour.

Shape each piece of dough into a slipper shape; place on the floured oven tray.

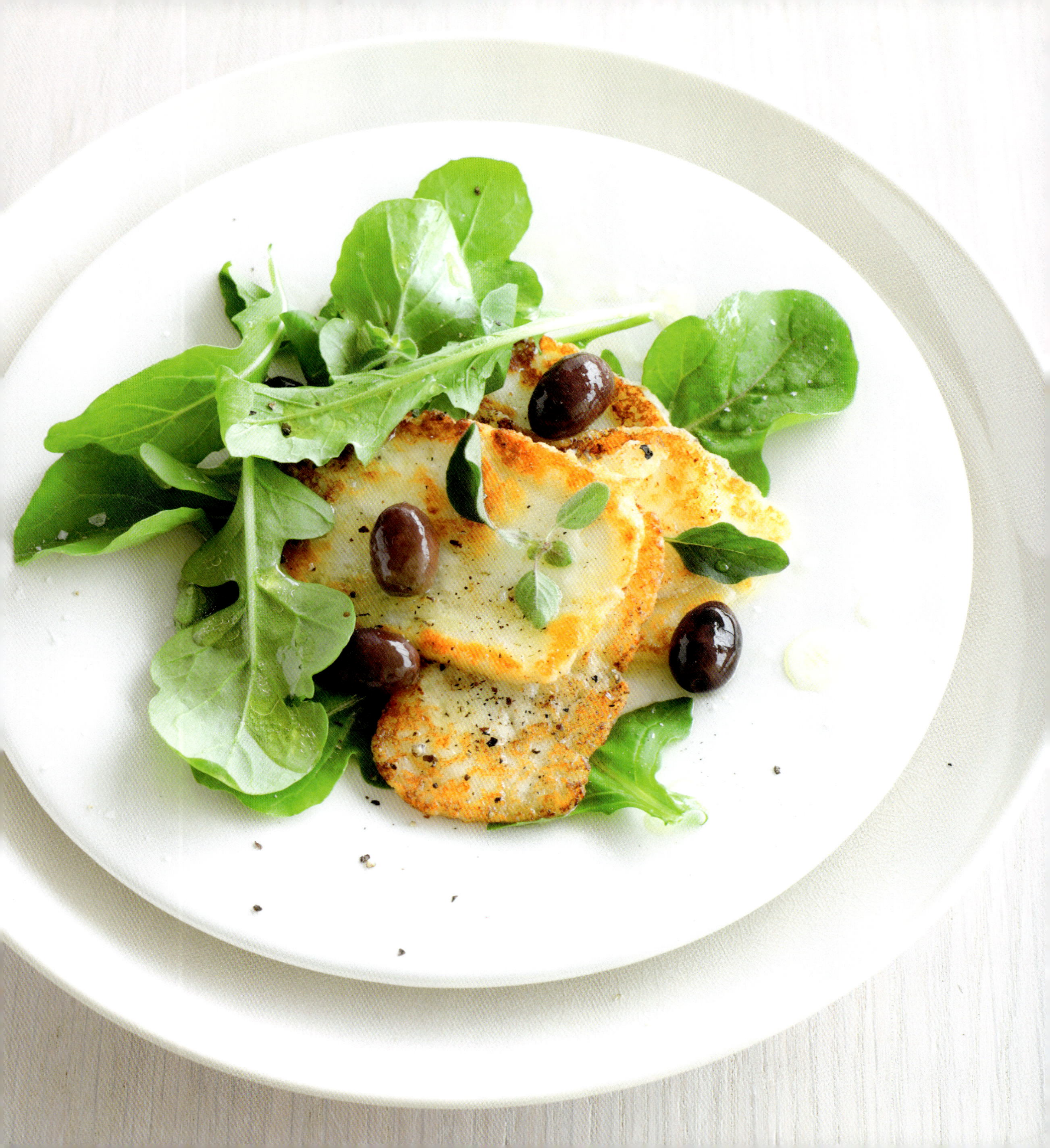

HALOUMI WITH LEMON, OLIVES AND OREGANO

prep + cook time 15 minutes ~ serves 6

500g (1 pound) haloumi cheese
½ cup (125ml) lemon juice
⅔ cup (160ml) olive oil
2 tablespoons finely chopped fresh oregano
200g (6 ounces) baby black olives
200g (6 ounces) rocket (arugula) leaves

1 Cut haloumi into 24 slices; place in a single layer in shallow dish. Combine juice and ½ cup of the oil in a small jug; pour over haloumi, stand 10 minutes.

2 Drain haloumi slices, reserve lemon mixture. Heat remaining oil in large frying pan; cook drained haloumi slices until browned both sides.

3 Add reserved lemon mixture to pan; add oregano and olives. Stir until heated through.

4 Divide rocket among serving plates; top each with four slices of haloumi. Spoon dressing over cheese.

nutritional count per serving
40.3g total fat (12.7g saturated fat); 1902kJ (454 cal); 3.2g carbohydrate; 19.5g protein; 1.6g fibre

tip Fried haloumi needs to be eaten as soon as possible after cooking as it becomes tough and rubbery as it cools. It only takes a few minutes to fry, so it is best to cook this dish just before serving.

Using a sharp knife, cut the haloumi into 24 slices.

Remove haloumi slices from lemon mixture with a fork, allowing mixture to drain. Reserve lemon mixture.

Cook drained haloumi slices in large frying pan until browned both sides, before adding the lemon mixture, olives and oregano.

GOZLEME

prep + cook time 1 hour ~ makes 6

You can't get much more traditionally Turkish than this combination of lamb, spinach and fetta. Try cooking these in a sandwich press – it works beautifully.

4 cups (600g) plain (all-purpose) flour
1 teaspoon coarse cooking salt (kosher salt)
1⅔ cups (410ml) warm water
2 tablespoons vegetable oil

lamb filling
1 tablespoon vegetable oil
3 cloves garlic, crushed
2 teaspoons ground cumin
½ teaspoon hot paprika
500g (1 pound) minced (ground) lamb
400g (12½ ounces) canned diced tomatoes
½ cup coarsely chopped fresh flat-leaf parsley

spinach and cheese filling
300g (11 ounces) spinach, shredded finely
1 small brown onion (80g), chopped finely
250g (8 ounces) fetta cheese, crumbled
1 cup (100g) coarsely grated mozzarella cheese
½ teaspoon ground allspice
½ cup coarsely chopped fresh mint

1 Combine flour and salt in large bowl. Gradually stir in the water; mix to a soft dough. Knead dough on floured surface about 5 minutes or until smooth and elastic. Return to bowl; cover.

2 Make lamb filling.

3 Make spinach and cheese filling.

4 Divide dough into six portions; roll each portion on floured surface into 30cm (12-inch) square. Spoon spinach and cheese filling onto dough squares, spreading filling across centre of squares; top each with equal amounts of lamb filling. Fold top and bottom edges of dough over filling; tuck in ends to enclose.

5 Cook gözleme, both sides, over low heat on oiled grill plate, brushing with oil, until browned lightly and heated through.

lamb filling
Heat oil in large frying pan; cook garlic and spices until fragrant. Add lamb; cook, stirring, until browned. Add undrained tomatoes; simmer about 15 minutes or until liquid is almost evaporated. Stir in parsley.

spinach and cheese filling
Combine ingredients in medium bowl.

nutritional count per gözleme
29.9g total fat (12.7g saturated fat); 3168kJ (758 cal); 75.8g carbohydrate; 41.8g protein; 7.1g fibre

Divide dough into six portions, then roll out each portion on a floured surface into a 30cm square.

Spoon spinach and cheese filling across the centre of each square, then top with the lamb filling.

Fold top section of pastry over filling, then fold bottom section up; tuck in the ends to completely enclose the filling.

Cut each pastry sheet into quarters; place squares on baking-paper-lined oven trays.

Fold in a 1cm border on all sides of each pastry square; prick the centre of the pastry with a fork.

Spread onion mixture onto baked pastry cases; top with two pieces of fig and crumbled cheese. Bake further 3 minutes.

CARAMELISED ONION, FIG AND PROSCIUTTO TARTS

prep + cook time 35 minutes ~ makes 8

Fetta or goat's cheese can be used in place of the blue cheese.

- 40g (1½ ounces) butter
- 2 large brown onions (400g), sliced thinly
- 1 tablespoon light brown sugar
- 2 sheets puff pastry
- 4 fresh figs (240g)
- 80g (2½ ounces) firm blue cheese, crumbled
- 4 thin slices prosciutto (60g), halved
- 1 tablespoon balsamic glaze
- 20g (¾ ounce) baby rocket (arugula) leaves

1 Preheat oven to 220°C/425°F. Oil oven trays then line with baking paper.

2 Heat butter in medium pan; cook onion, covered, over low heat, about 15 minutes, stirring occasionally, until onion is soft. Stir in sugar.

3 Meanwhile, cut pastry sheets into quarters; place on oven trays. Fold in 1cm (½-inch) borders; prick all over the centre with a fork.

4 Bake pastry about 15 minutes or until browned.

5 Cut figs into quarters. Spread onion mixture into pastry cases, top with figs and cheese; bake about 3 minutes or until cheese is softened.

6 Top tarts with prosciutto, drizzle with balsamic glaze then sprinkle with rocket.

nutritional count per tart
17.4g total fat (5.6g saturated fat); 1147kJ (274 cal); 22g carbohydrate; 6.8g protein; 1.9g fibre

tip The easiest way to slice onions is to first cut the onion in half through the root; peel, then place the flat side of the onion on the board and slice.

OREGANO-BAKED FETTA

prep + cook time 15 minutes ~ serves 6

Place fetta (one or two blocks, depending on how you buy it) in ovenproof dish.

Sprinkle olive oil all over fetta.

Sprinkle coarsely chopped fresh oregano onto cheese.

200g (6½ ounces) fetta cheese
1 tablespoon extra virgin olive oil
1 tablespoon coarsely chopped fresh oregano leaves
¼ teaspoon sweet paprika

1 Preheat oven to 200°C/400°F.

2 Place cheese in ovenproof dish; sprinkle with oil, oregano and sweet paprika. Season with pepper.

3 Bake, covered, about 10 minutes or until cheese is heated through. Serve fetta warm, with a sliced french bread loaf and seeded black olives.

nutritional count per serving
10.8g total fat (5.6g saturated fat); 502kJ (120 cal); 0.1g carbohydrate; 5.9g protein; 0g fibre

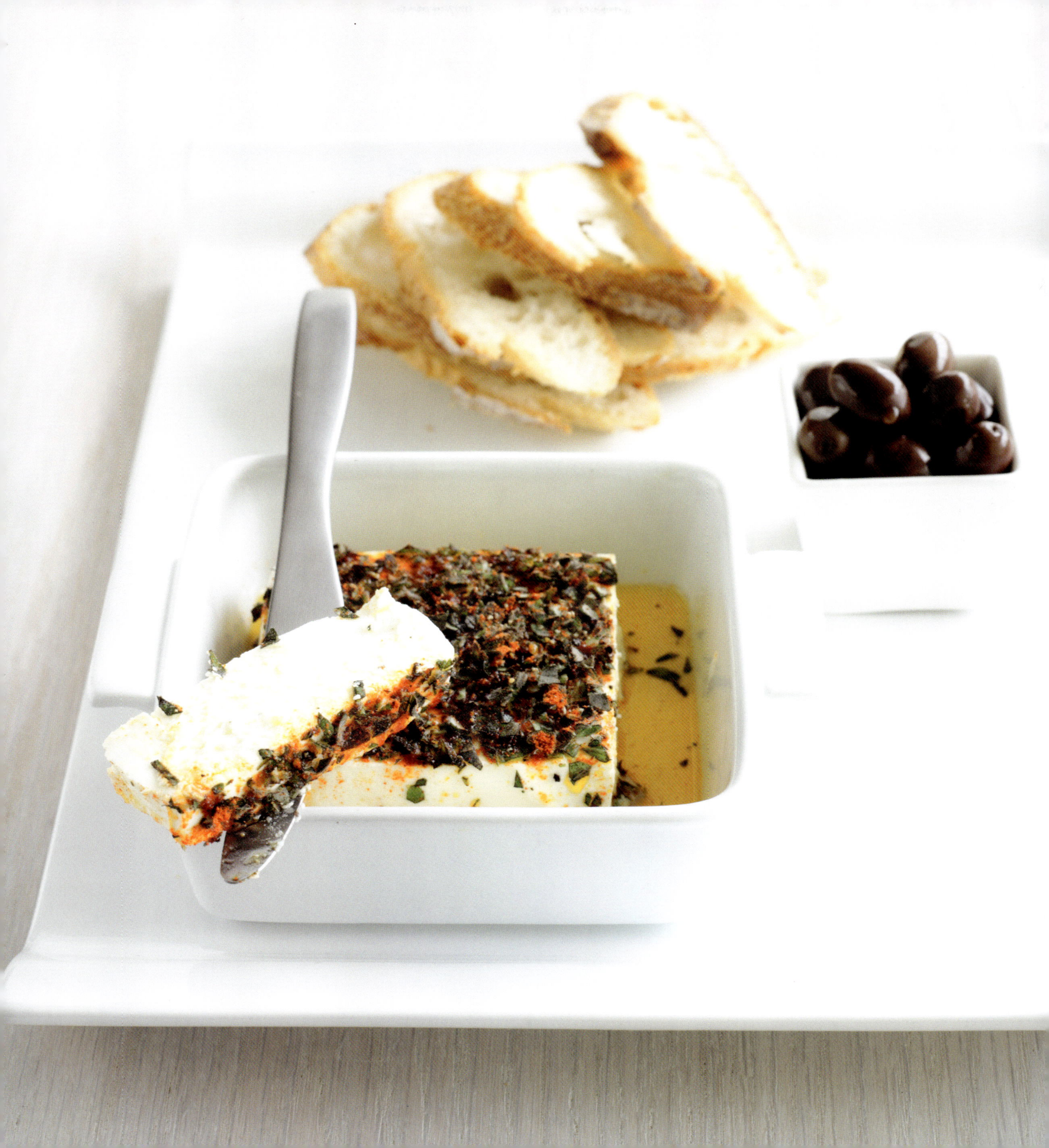

Cut french bread stick into 1cm-thick slices.

Rub the garlic, cut-side down, onto one side of each toasted slice of bread.

Top each crostini with the rocket mixture, then artichoke pieces and fetta cheese.

CROSTINI WITH FETTA, ARTICHOKES AND ROCKET

prep + cook time 20 minutes ~ serves 6

Ready-made crostini can be found in various flavours in most delicatessens and some supermarkets.

1 small french bread stick (150g)
1 clove garlic, halved
cooking oil spray
30g (1 ounce) baby rocket (arugula) leaves
1 teaspoon extra virgin olive oil
1 teaspoon red wine vinegar
5 marinated artichoke hearts, drained
100g (3 ounces) fetta cheese, crumbled

1 Preheat oven to 180°C/350°F

2 Cut bread into 1cm (½-inch) thick slices; spray both sides with oil. Place bread slices on oven tray; toast in oven. Rub one side of each crostini with cut side of garlic.

3 Combine rocket, oil and vinegar in medium bowl. Cut each artichoke into six wedges.

4 Top crostini with rocket mixture, then artichokes and cheese; season with freshly ground pepper.

nutritional count per serving
5.8g total fat (2.8g saturated fat); 535kJ (128 cal); 11.9g carbohydrate; 6g protein; 2g fibre

tip It is better to use day old bread, as it is easier to cut.

BABA GHANOUSH

prep + cook time 45 minutes (+ standing) ~ makes 2 cups

For an extra touch of the Middle East, top baba ghanoush with chopped mint, finely chopped pistachios or pomegranate pulp.

Pierce eggplants all over using a bamboo skewer or a fork.

Stand roasted eggplants for 15 minutes, then peel away the blackened skin. Discard skin.

Place chopped eggplant flesh in strainer over heatproof bowl to drain, pressing down on the eggplant to squeeze out the excess liquid.

2 large eggplants (1kg)
3 cloves garlic, crushed
2 tablespoons tahini
¼ cup (60ml) lemon juice
2 tablespoons olive oil
½ teaspoon sweet paprika

1 Preheat grill (broiler). Line oven tray with baking paper.

2 Pierce eggplants all over with a skewer or fork; place on tray. Grill about 30 minutes or until skin blackens and eggplant is soft, turning occasionally. Stand 15 minutes.

3 Peel eggplants, discard skin. Roughly chop eggplant, place in strainer over heatproof bowl. Press eggplant with the back of a wooden spoon; drain 10 minutes.

4 Blend or process eggplant, garlic and remaining ingredients. Serve sprinkled with a little extra paprika.

nutritional count per ¼ cup
8g total fat (1g saturated fat); 431kJ (103 cal); 3.6g carbohydrate; 2.5g protein; 3.7g fibre

tip This recipe can be refrigerated in an airtight container for up to a week.

serving suggestion Serve with crisp vegetables, pitta bread or rice crackers.

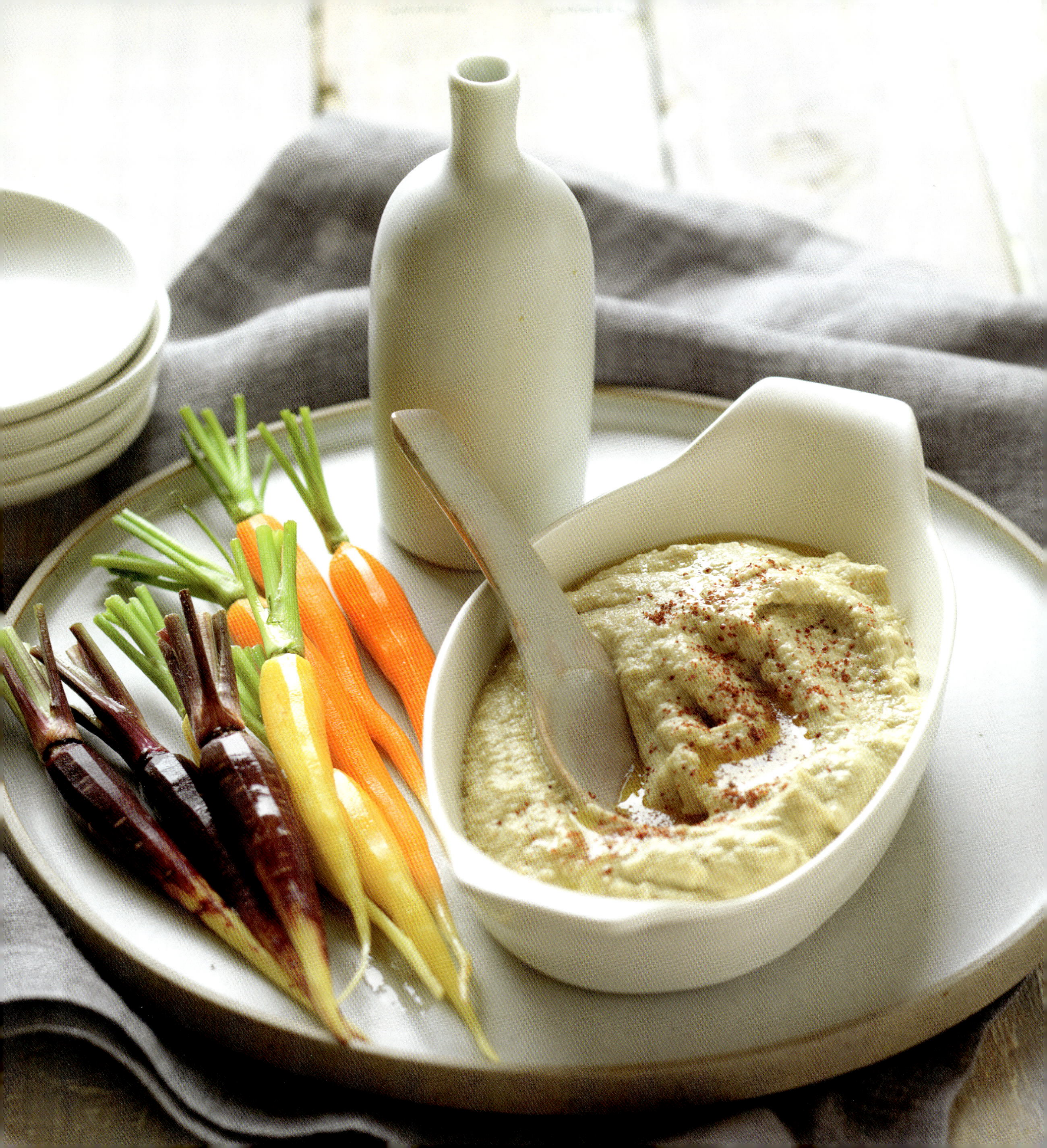

Make a well in centre of the flour; add oil and enough of the water to mix to a soft dough.

Use clean fingers to mix the oil and water into the flour. Add a little more water if required.

Roll each piece of dough into a long oval shape about 3mm thick.

PUMPKIN HUMMUS WITH GREEN ONION CRISPBREAD

prep + cook time 2 hours (+ standing) ~ serves 8

1 cup (200g) dried chickpeas (garbanzo beans)
500g (1 pound) butternut pumpkin, peeled, chopped coarsely
olive-oil spray
1.25 litres (5 cups) water
2 cloves garlic, quartered
⅓ cup (80ml) lemon juice
½ cup (140g) tahini
¼ cup (60ml) olive oil
2 tablespoons olive oil, extra

green onion crispbread
2 cups (300g) plain (all-purpose) flour
1 tablespoon (14g) dried yeast
2 tablespoons sea salt flakes
½ teaspoon caster (superfine) sugar
6 green onions (scallions), chopped finely
2 tablespoons olive oil
1 cup (250ml) hot water, approximately
1 tablespoon sea salt flakes, extra

1 Place chickpeas in medium bowl, cover with cold water; stand overnight.

2 Make green onion crispbread; reduce oven to 200°C/400°F.

3 Place pumpkin, in single layer, in baking-paper-lined large shallow baking dish; spray with oil. Roast pumpkin, uncovered, about 45 minutes or until tender. Cool.

4 Meanwhile, drain chickpeas, rinse well. Place chickpeas and the water in large saucepan; bring to the boil. Boil, uncovered, about 45 minutes or until chickpeas are tender. Drain chickpeas over a medium heatproof bowl; reserve cooking liquid.

5 Meanwhile, blend or process chickpeas with 1 cup reserved cooking liquid, roast pumpkin, garlic, juice, tahini and oil until smooth (add a little more of the reserved cooking liquid, if necessary, until hummus is a creamy consistency). Season to taste.

6 Drizzle hummus with extra oil, serve with green onion crispbread.

green onion crispbread
Combine flour, yeast, salt, sugar and onion in medium bowl; make a well in the centre. Stir in oil and enough of the water to mix to a soft dough. Knead dough on floured surface about 5 minutes or until smooth and elastic. Place dough in large oiled bowl, cover; stand in warm place about 1 hour or until dough doubles in size. Preheat oven to 220°C/425°F; oil oven trays, place in oven. Turn dough onto floured surface; knead until smooth. Divide dough into 16 equal pieces. Roll each piece into long ovals about 3mm (⅛-inch) thick; place on hot trays. Lightly coat with olive-oil spray. Sprinkle with extra salt. Bake about 5 minutes or until browned lightly and crisp.

nutritional count per serving
28.9g total fat (4g saturated fat); 2065kJ (494 cal); 40.3g carbohydrate; 13.8g protein; 7.9g fibre

SUMAC LABNE WITH COPPA

prep time 15 minutes (+ refrigeration) ~ serves 8

Muslin is an inexpensive, finely woven, undyed cotton fabric used in cooking, specifically for straining stocks and sauces.

Place a muslin-lined colander over a bowl; spoon the yogurt mixture into the colander.

After the yogurt mixture has drained for 24 hours, discard the liquid left in the bowl.

Using oiled hands, roll tablespoons of yogurt mixture into balls. Roll balls in oil, then sprinkle with sumac.

840g (1¾ pounds) Greek-style yogurt
3 teaspoons fine table salt
2 tablespoons olive oil
2 teaspoons sumac
24 slices mild coppa (360g)

1 Combine yogurt and salt in medium bowl; spoon into muslin-lined large colander or sieve placed over bowl. Gather corners of muslin together, twist then tie with kitchen string. Place a plate on top of the muslin, then weight with two or three heavy cans; refrigerate 24 hours.

2 Place yogurt in medium bowl; discard muslin. Using oiled hands, roll level tablespoons of yogurt into balls; roll in oil then sprinkle with sumac.

3 Serve labne with coppa.

nutritional count per serving
28.8g total fat 11g saturated fat); 1505kJ (360 cal); 10g carbohydrate; 15.5g protein; 0g fibre

tip Labne can be left to drain and thicken, still weighted, in the fridge for up to three days.

serving suggestion Serve with lavash crisps.

beginnings

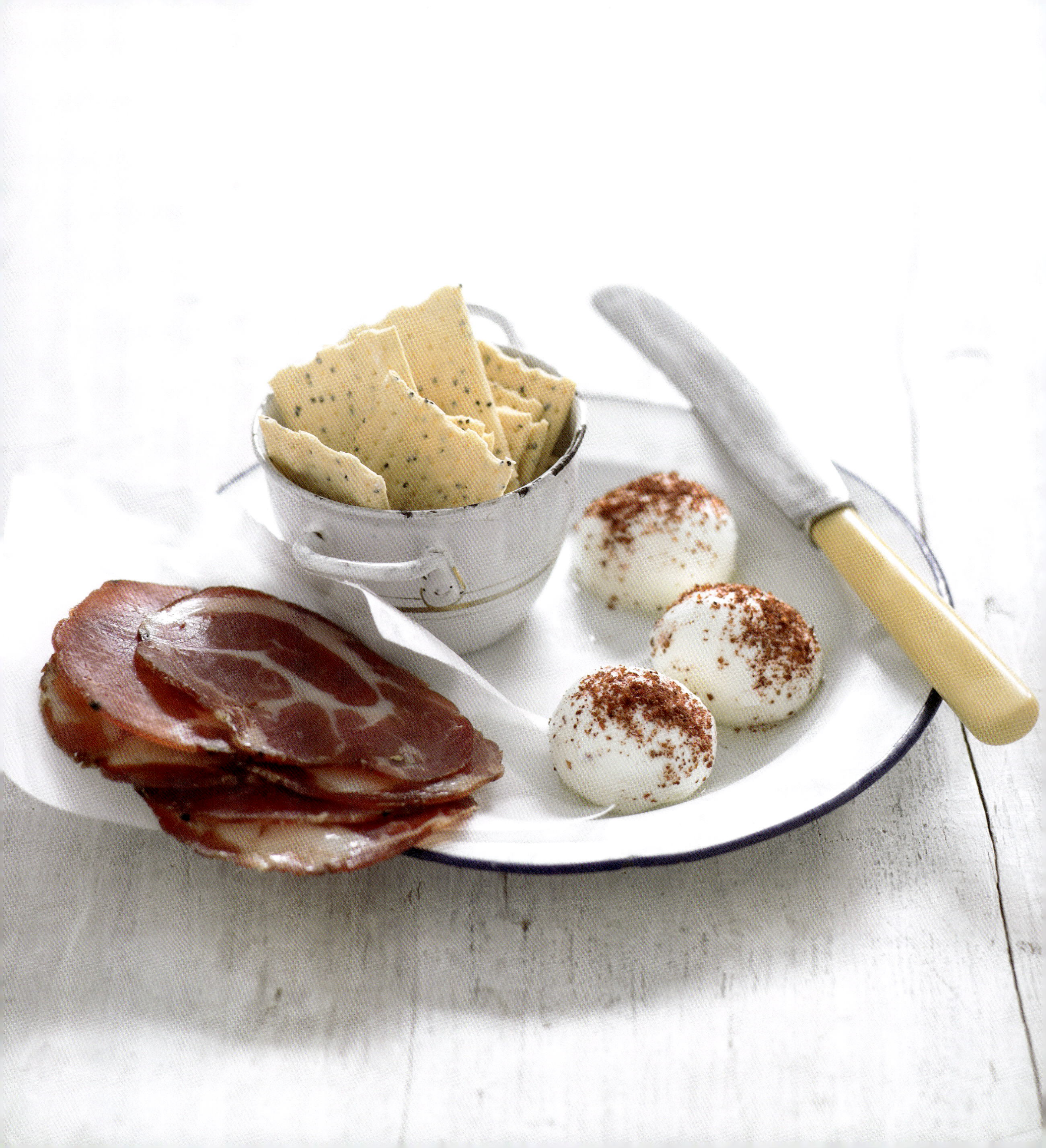

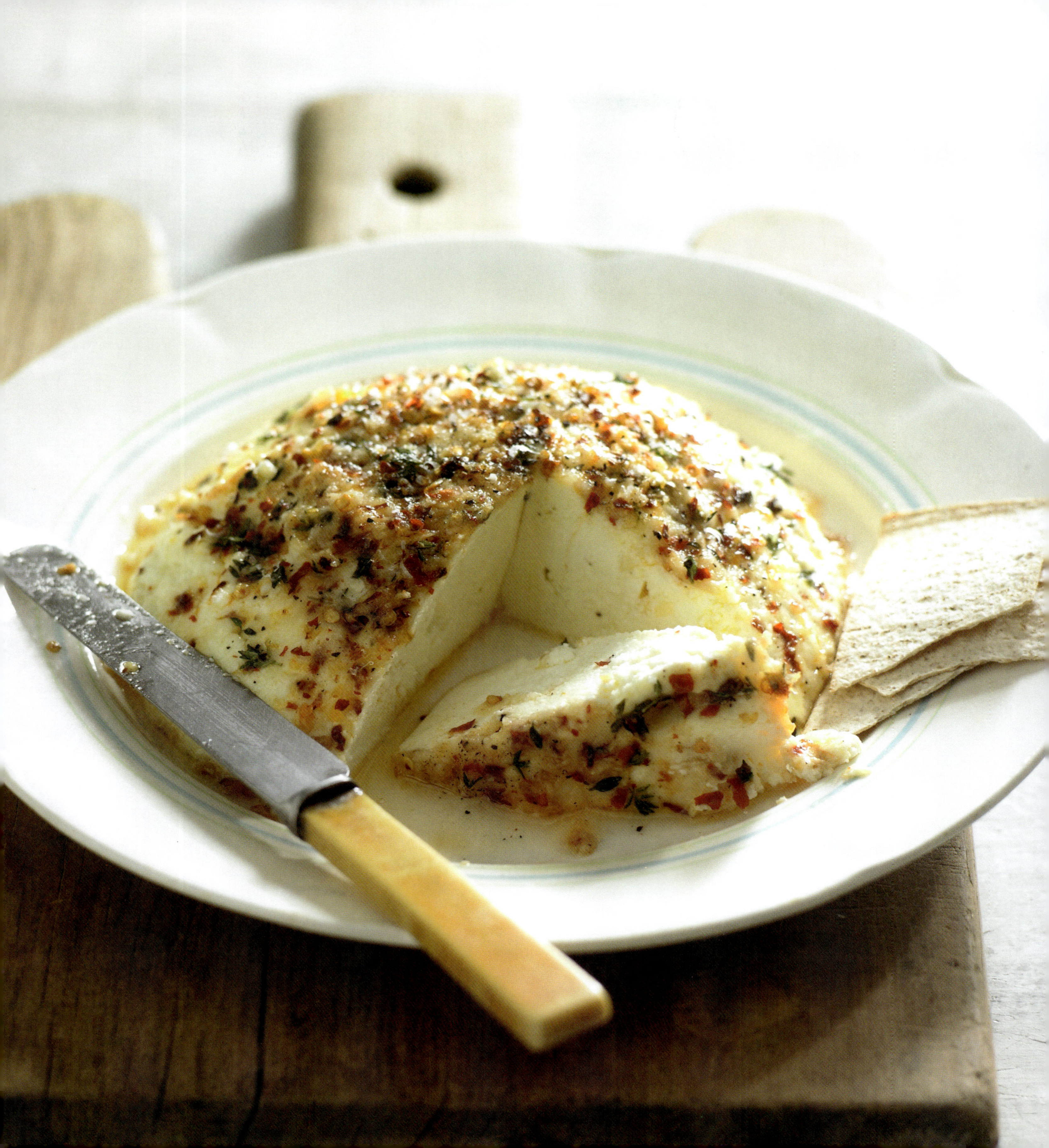

BAKED RICOTTA

prep + cook time 40 minutes (+ refrigeration) ~ serves 8

500g (1 pound) fresh ricotta cheese
2 cloves garlic, chopped finely
½ teaspoon dried chilli flakes
½ teaspoon fresh thyme leaves
2 tablespoons finely grated parmesan cheese
2 tablespoons olive oil
120g (4-ounce) packet flatbread
90g (3 ounces) bottled tomato tapenade

1 Press ricotta into 12cm (4¾-inch) sieve; place over bowl. Cover; refrigerate 4 hours or overnight.

2 Preheat oven to 180°C/350°F. Oil oven tray, line with baking paper.

3 Turn ricotta onto tray. Combine garlic, chilli, thyme and parmesan in small bowl; sprinkle over ricotta then drizzle with oil.

4 Bake ricotta about 30 minutes or until cheese is browned lightly. Cool. Serve ricotta with flatbread and tomato tapenade.

nutritional count per serving
17g total fat (6.5g saturated fat); 986kJ (236 cal); 10.7g carbohydrate; 10g protein; 0.9g fibre

tip This dish is best prepared and baked on the day of serving.

Spoon ricotta into sieve over a bowl, pressing down firmly to mould the ricotta into the shape of the sieve; smooth the surface.

Turn the moulded ricotta onto the baking-paper-lined oven tray.

Sprinkle combined garlic, chilli flakes, thyme and parmesan cheese over the ricotta, then drizzle with oil.

BEETROOT DIP

prep + cook time 50 minutes ~ makes 2 cups

It's always a good idea to wear gloves when handling and peeling cooked beetroot because the juice will stain your hands.

3 medium beetroot (beets) (500g), trimmed
1 teaspoon caraway seeds
1 teaspoon ground cumin
¼ teaspoon hot paprika
2 cloves garlic, crushed
¾ cup (200g) yogurt
½ cup loosely packed fresh mint leaves
1 tablespoon lemon juice

1 Cook beetroot in medium saucepan of boiling water, uncovered, about 45 minutes or until tender; drain. When cool enough to handle, peel beetroot then chop coarsely.

2 Meanwhile, dry-fry spices in a small frying pan until fragrant; cool.

3 Blend or process beetroot and spices with remaining ingredients until smooth.

nutritional count per tablespoon
0.3g total fat (0.2g saturated fat); 67kJ (16 cal); 2g carbohydrate; 0.8g protein; 0.7g fibre

serving suggestion Serve with pitta bread.

When cool enough to handle and wearing gloves (to prevent staining your hands), peel the cooked beetroot.

Stir spices in dry, small frying pan until they are fragrant. Remove from heat and cool.

Process the chopped beetroot, fresh mint, yogurt, garlic, spices and juice until the mixture is smooth.

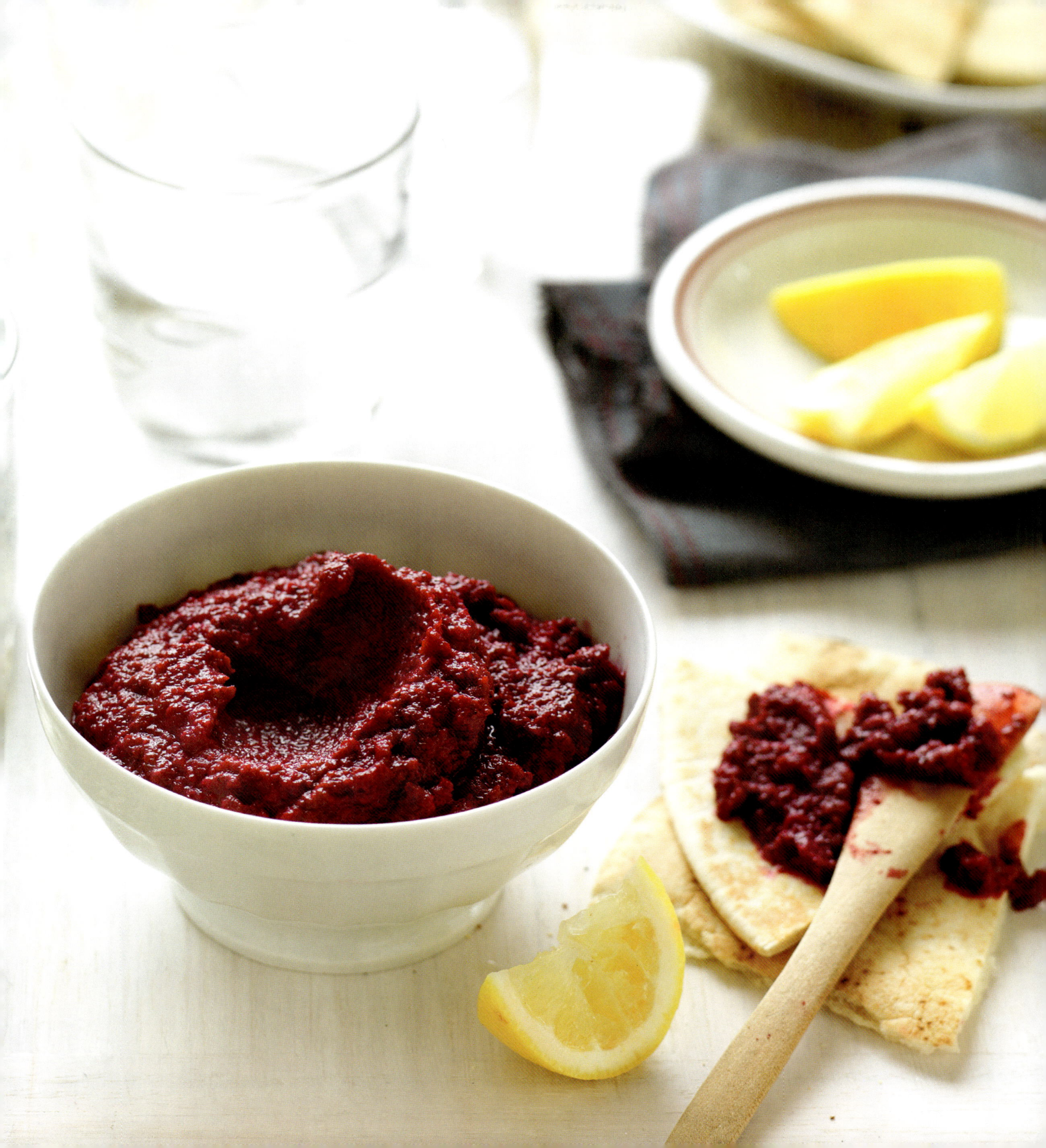

Roast nuts in a single layer, in a small dry frying pan, over low heat, until fragrant and just changed in colour. Remove immediately from the pan so they won't burn.

Cook the garlic, curry powder and parsnip, stirring occasionally, for about 15 minutes or until the parsnips are caramelised.

Strain the cooled, blended soup back into the same, cleaned pan.

CURRIED CARAMELISED PARSNIP SOUP

prep + cook time 1 hour 45 minutes (+ cooling) ~ serves 8

50g (1½ ounces) butter
2 tablespoons olive oil
1 large brown onion (200g), sliced thinly
2 cloves garlic, crushed
2 tablespoons curry powder
1.5kg (3 pounds) parsnips, chopped coarsely
2 large potatoes (600g), chopped coarsely
1 litre (4 cups) chicken stock
2¾ cups (680ml) water
½ cup (60g) roasted walnuts, chopped finely
1¼ cups (310ml) pouring cream
½ cup firmly packed fresh coriander (cilantro) leaves, shredded finely
1 tablespoon olive oil, extra

1 Heat butter and oil in large saucepan; cook onion, stirring, until soft. Add garlic, curry powder and parsnips; cook, stirring occasionally, about 15 minutes or until the parsnips are caramelised.

2 Add potato, stock and the water; bring to the boil. Reduce heat; simmer soup, uncovered, about 45 minutes or until vegetables are tender. Cool 10 minutes.

3 Blend soup, in batches, until smooth. Strain soup into same cleaned pan, add cream; cook, stirring, until hot. Season to taste.

4 Serve soup sprinkled with nuts and coriander; drizzle with extra oil.

nutritional count per serving
34.4g total fat (15.9g saturated fat); 1877kJ (449 cal); 25.9g carbohydrate; 7.5g protein; 5.5g fibre

tip You can use just one 300ml carton of cream for this recipe.

FRENCH ONION SOUP WITH GRUYERE CROUTONS

prep + cook time 1 hour 15 minutes ~ serves 4

A tablespoon of cognac, stirred into the soup at the last minute, is an excellent addition.

50g (1½ ounces) butter
4 large brown onions (800g), sliced thinly
¾ cup (180ml) dry white wine
3 cups (750ml) water
1 litre (4 cups) beef stock
1 bay leaf
1 tablespoon plain (all-purpose) flour
1 teaspoon fresh thyme leaves

gruyère croûtons
1 small french bread stick (150g)
½ cup (60g) coarsely grated gruyère cheese

1 Melt butter in large saucepan; cook onion, stirring occasionally, about 30 minutes or until caramelised.

2 Meanwhile, bring wine to the boil in large saucepan; boil 1 minute then stir in the water, stock and bay leaf, return to the boil. Remove from heat.

3 Stir flour into onion mixture; cook, stirring, 2 minutes. Gradually add hot broth mixture to onion mixture, stirring, until mixture boils and thickens slightly. Reduce heat; simmer, uncovered, stirring occasionally, 20 minutes. Discard bay leaf; stir in thyme.

4 Meanwhile, make gruyère croûtons.

5 Serve bowls of soup topped with croûtons and some extra thyme leaves.

gruyère croûtons
Preheat grill (broiler). Cut bread into 1.5cm (¾-inch) slices. Toast bread under grill on one side then turn and sprinkle with cheese; grill croûtons until cheese browns lightly.

nutritional count per serving
16.7g total fat (10g saturated fat); 1522kJ (364 cal); 31.1g carbohydrate; 13.4g protein; 3.9g fibre

Cook onions in melted butter, stirring, for about 30 minutes or until caramelised.

Once the onions have caramelised, add the flour; cook, stirring, 2 minutes.

Toast one side of the bread slices under the grill. Turn toasted slices over, then sprinkle with gruyère cheese. Place under hot grill until cheese browns lightly.

Roast ham hock and onion in a hot oven for about 30 minutes or until cooked.

Once the broth has been made, remove the hock and strain the broth through a muslin-lined sieve into a large heatproof bowl. Discard the remaining solids.

Remove the ham from the hock and, using two forks, shred the meat coarsely. Discard the bone, fat and skin.

MINESTRONE

prep + cook time 4 hours (+ refrigeration) ~ serves 6

1 ham hock (1kg)
1 medium brown onion (150g), quartered
1 stick celery (150g), chopped coarsely
1 teaspoon black peppercorns
1 bay leaf
4 litres (16 cups) water
1 tablespoon olive oil
1 large carrot (180g), chopped finely
2 sticks celery (300g), extra, chopped finely
3 cloves garlic, crushed
2 large tomatoes (440g), chopped finely
¼ cup (70g) tomato paste
1 small leek (200g), sliced thinly
420g (13½ ounces) canned white beans, rinsed, drained
1 cup (100g) small pasta shells
½ cup each coarsely chopped fresh flat-leaf parsley and fresh basil
½ cup (40g) flaked parmesan cheese

1 Preheat oven to 220°C/425°F.

2 Roast ham hock and onion in baking dish, uncovered, 30 minutes.

3 Place hock and onion in large saucepan with celery, peppercorns, bay leaf and the water; bring to the boil. Reduce heat; simmer, uncovered, 2 hours.

4 Remove hock from broth. Strain broth through muslin-lined sieve or colander into large heatproof bowl; discard solids. Allow broth to cool, cover; refrigerate until cold.

5 Remove ham from hock; shred coarsely. Discard bone, fat and skin.

6 Meanwhile, heat oil in large saucepan; cook carrot and extra celery, stirring, 2 minutes. Add shredded ham, garlic, fresh tomato and paste; cook, stirring, 2 minutes.

7 Discard fat from surface of broth. Pour broth into a large measuring jug; add enough water to make 2 litres (8 cups). Add broth to pan; bring to the boil. Reduce heat; simmer, covered, 20 minutes.

8 Add leek, beans and pasta to pan; bring to the boil. Reduce heat; simmer, uncovered, until pasta is tender. Remove from heat; stir in herbs. Serve soup sprinkled with cheese.

nutritional count per serving
7.2g total fat (2.4g saturated fat); 865kJ (207 cal); 19.6g carbohydrate; 12.7g protein; 6.1g fibre

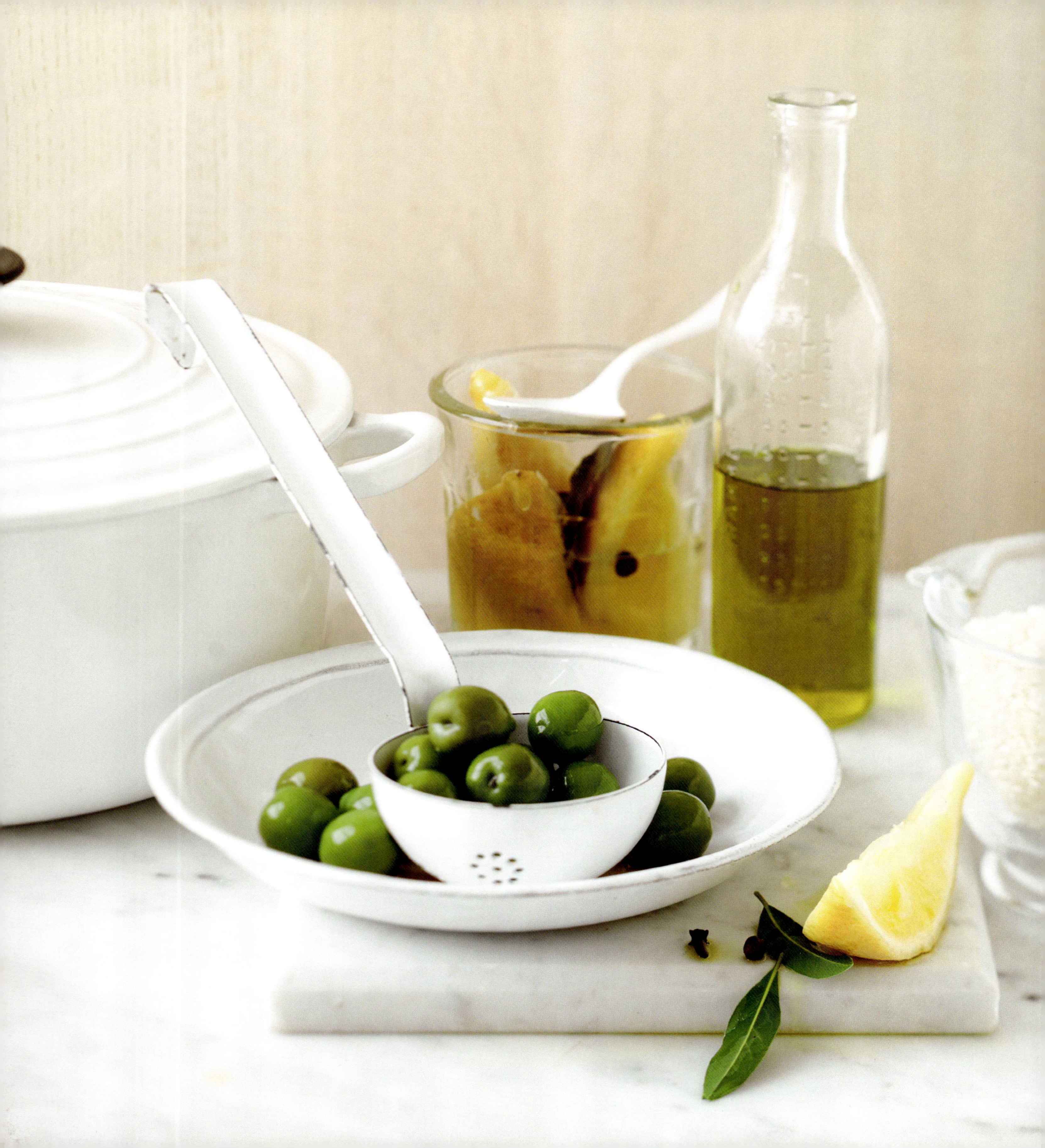

MIDDLES

RICOTTA GNOCCHI WITH RICH TOMATO SAUCE

prep + cook time 1 hour 45 minutes ~ serves 6

1 cup (150g) plain (all-purpose) flour
2 eggs, beaten lightly
700g (1½ pounds) firm full-cream milk ricotta cheese
1 cup (80g) finely grated parmesan cheese
½ cup finely shredded fresh basil leaves
½ cup small basil leaves
2 tablespoons olive oil

rich tomato sauce
2 tablespoons olive oil
1 small onion (80g), chopped finely
2 cloves garlic, crushed
4 drained anchovy fillets, chopped finely
½ cup (125ml) dry white wine
800g (1½ pounds) canned chopped tomatoes
2 cups (500ml) salt-reduced chicken stock

parmesan crisps
1 cup (80g) finely grated parmesan cheese
2 tablespoons pine nuts, chopped finely

1 Preheat oven to 200°C/400°F.

2 Make rich tomato sauce, then parmesan crisps.

3 Sift flour into medium bowl; make a well in the centre. Place egg, cheeses and basil in well and gradually stir in flour to make a firm dough. Do not over-mix dough.

4 Line a large oven tray with a piece of baking paper.

5 Bring a large wide saucepan or deep frying pan of salted water to the boil; reduce heat to a rapid simmer. Use a dessertspoon to scoop up a spoonful of the ricotta mixture; using a second dessertspoon, scoop under the mixture and gently push the oval-shaped scoop (quenelle) into the simmering water. Working quickly, repeat to make 10 gnocchi at a time. Cook gnocchi for about 2 minutes or until they float to the surface of the water. Remove gnocchi with a slotted spoon, place on tray. Repeat using the remaining mixture.

6 Serve gnocchi on the tomato sauce, topped with parmesan crisps. Scatter with basil leaves, drizzle with oil.

rich tomato sauce
Heat oil in large, deep, frying pan; cook onion and garlic, stirring, until onion softens. Add anchovy and wine to pan; bring to the boil. Add undrained tomatoes and stock; return to the boil. Reduce heat; simmer, uncovered, about 50 minutes or until sauce is thick.

parmesan crisps
Line an oiled 24cm x 32cm (9½-inch x 13-inch) swiss roll pan with baking paper. Combine cheese and nuts in small bowl. Scatter cheese mixture over pan, shake lightly from side to side to evenly spread mixture. Bake crisps about 3 minutes or until cheese is melted and browned lightly. Cool on pan. Break into small pieces.

nutritional count per serving
40.1g total fat (16.5g saturated fat); 2533kJ (606 cal); 26.1g carbohydrate; 31g protein; 3.3g fibre

for steps, see pages 92 & 93

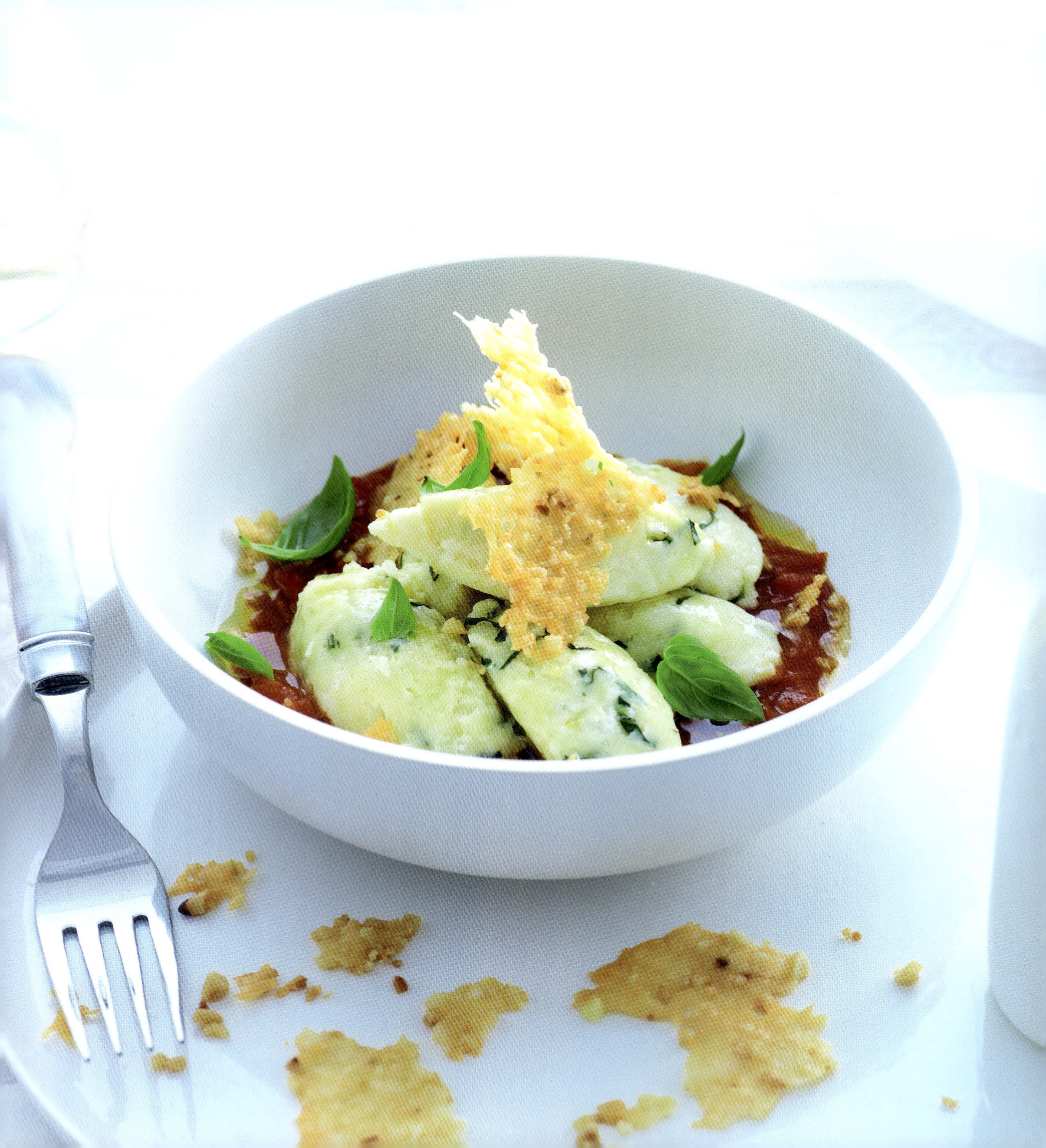

RICOTTA GNOCCHI WITH RICH TOMATO SAUCE

Scatter the cheese mixture over an oiled and baking-paper-lined swiss roll pan. Shake the pan lightly to evenly spread the cheese mixture.

Bake the cheese mixture 3 minutes or until the cheese is browned lightly and melted. Cool in the pan, then break into small pieces.

To finely shred (or chiffonade) the basil leaves, lay the leaves flat on top of each other, then roll up tightly and cut into thin slices. This results in long, fine strips.

To create the gnocchi shapes, use a dessertspoon to scoop up a heaped spoonful of the gnocchi mixture.

Use a second dessertspoon to scoop around the gnocchi mixture to make an oval-shaped scoop (quenelle); place on a baking-paper-lined tray. Repeat with remaining mixture.

Cook the gnocchi in boiling water. When they float to the surface, they are cooked; remove from the pan with a slotted spoon.

middles ~ 93 ~ middles

MUSHROOM RISOTTO

prep + cook time 40 minutes ~ serves 4

10g (½ ounce) dried chanterelle mushrooms
10g (½ ounce) dried porcini mushrooms
1 litre (4 cups) chicken or vegetable stock
2 cups (500ml) water
50g (1½ ounces) butter
100g (3 ounces) chestnut mushrooms, trimmed
100g (3 ounces) button mushrooms, sliced thickly
2 flat mushrooms (160g), halved, sliced thickly
4 shallots (100g), chopped finely
2 cloves garlic, crushed
2 cups (400g) arborio rice
½ cup (125ml) dry white wine
½ cup (40g) finely grated parmesan cheese
2 tablespoons finely chopped fresh chives

1 Combine chanterelle and porcini mushrooms, stock and the water in medium saucepan; bring to the boil. Reduce heat; simmer, covered.

2 Meanwhile, melt 30g (1 ounce) of the butter in large saucepan; cook chestnut, button and flat mushrooms, stirring, until mushrooms are tender and liquid evaporates. Remove from pan.

3 Melt remaining butter in same pan; cook shallots and garlic, stirring, until shallots soften. Add rice; stir to coat rice in butter mixture. Return mushrooms cooked in butter to pan and add wine; bring to the boil. Reduce heat; simmer, uncovered, until liquid has almost evaporated. Add 1 cup of the simmering stock mixture; cook, stirring, over low heat, until stock is absorbed. Continue adding stock mixture, in 1-cup batches, stirring, until absorbed between additions. Total cooking time should be about 25 minutes or until rice is tender. Stir in cheese and chives.

nutritional count per serving
15.4g total fat (9.4g saturated fat); 2391kJ (572 cal); 82.2g carbohydrate; 17.9g protein; 4.4g fibre

tip Unlike some other rice dishes, risotto does not require you to rinse the rice before you begin to cook. In fact, the starch is essential to the dish. The initial toasting of the rice loosens the starch in each grain. As liquid is added to the rice and stirred in, gently and almost constantly, more starch is released. This process will eventually leave you with a soft, creamy and evenly cooked risotto.

Using a sharp knife, cut both flat and button mushrooms into thick slices, then trim the ends of the chestnut mushrooms.

Add the rice to the shallot mixture; cook, stirring constantly, until each grain is coated in butter.

Add 1 cup of simmering stock mixture to the rice; cook, stirring, over low heat until stock is absorbed. Continue adding the stock mixture, in 1-cup batches, stirring, until absorbed between additions.

BRAISED DUCK RAGU WITH PAPPARDELLE

prep + cook time 3 hours ~ serves 6

Ragù is a staple of northern Italy. It is a meat sauce usually served with pasta.

- 4 duck legs with boneless thigh meat attached (1kg)
- 1 cup (250ml) dry red wine
- 2 cups (500ml) chicken stock
- 2 cups (500ml) water
- ¼ cup (60ml) sherry vinegar
- 1 sprig fresh rosemary
- 1 tablespoon olive oil
- 6 slices pancetta (90g), chopped finely
- 1 medium brown onion (150g), chopped finely
- 1 medium carrot (120g), chopped finely
- 2 sticks celery (300g), chopped finely
- 4 cloves garlic, crushed
- 800g (24 ounces) canned crushed tomatoes
- 1 cup (250ml) water, extra
- ¼ cup finely shredded fresh basil leaves
- 600g (1¼ pounds) fresh pappardelle pasta
- 1 cup (80g) shaved parmesan cheese

1 Place duck, skin-side down, in single layer, in large heavy-based saucepan or flameproof casserole dish. Cook duck, over medium heat, about 15 minutes or until fat has rendered; turn duck, cook 1 minute then transfer to a plate.

2 Discard fat from pan. Add wine; bring to the boil. Reduce heat; simmer 5 minutes. Add duck, stock, the water, vinegar and rosemary; bring to the boil. Reduce heat; simmer, uncovered, skimming occasionally, about 1 hour or until meat is falling off the bones. Using a slotted spoon transfer duck to a shallow bowl. When cool enough to handle, shred duck meat, discarding skin and bones. Strain stock through a muslin-line sieve into a large jug; discard solids.

3 Meanwhile, heat oil in saucepan; cook pancetta, stirring, until crisp. Add onion, carrot, celery and garlic; cook, stirring, until vegetables soften. Add undrained tomatoes and the extra water; bring to the boil. Reduce heat; simmer, uncovered, 15 minutes. Add duck, stock and basil; simmer, uncovered, about 15 minutes or until mixture is thick.

4 Meanwhile, cook pasta in large saucepan of boiling water until tender; drain.

5 Add pasta to sauce; mix gently. Serve sprinkled with parmesan.

nutritional count per serving
17.6g total fat (6g saturated fat); 2508kJ (600 cal); 62.1g carbohydrate; 37.4g protein; 6.6g fibre

for steps, see pages 98 & 99

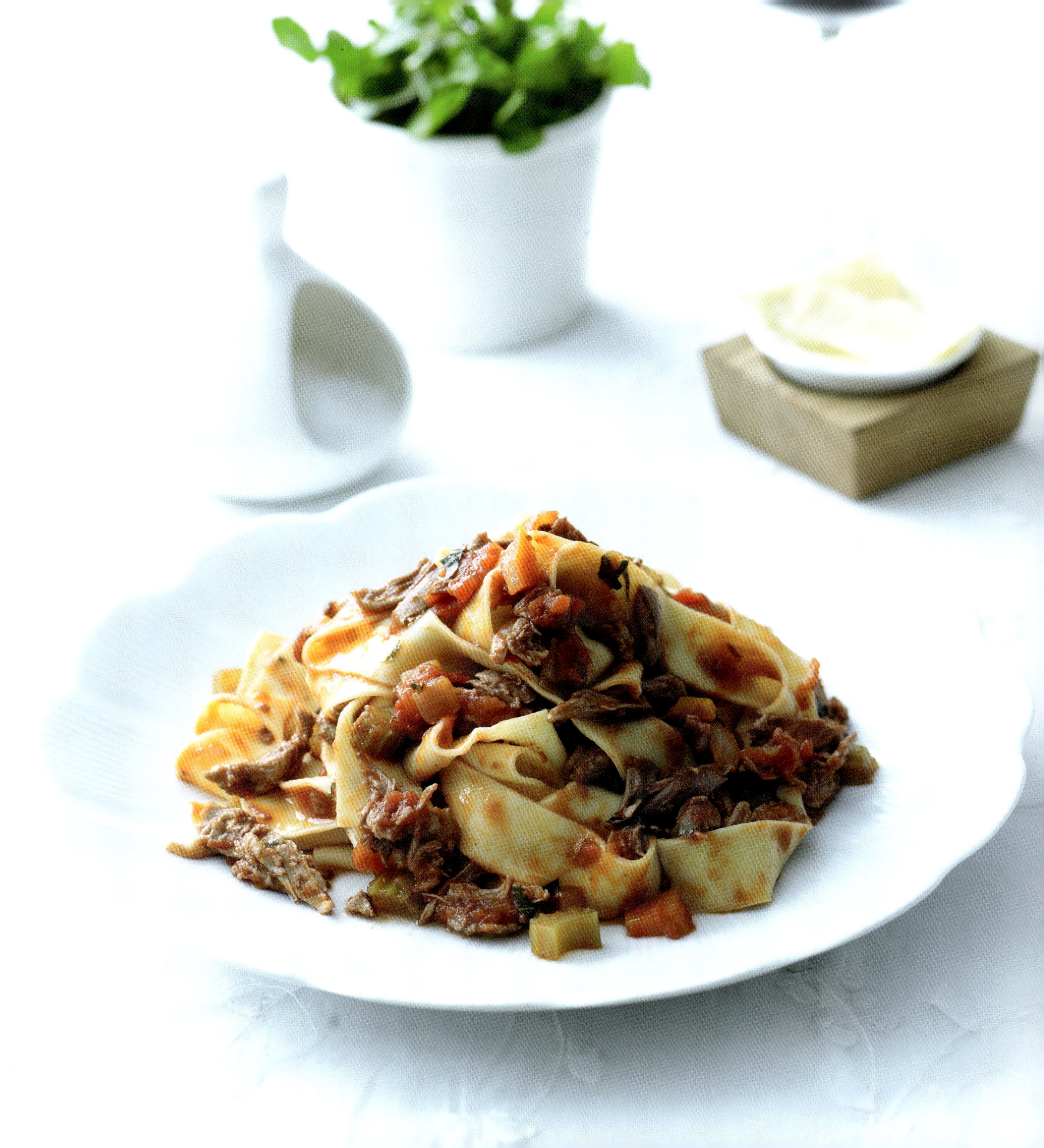

BRAISED DUCK RAGU WITH PAPPARDELLE

Cook the duck, skin-side down, until the fat has melted (rendered) and the skin is golden brown. Turn the duck and cook for 1 minute. Transfer duck to a plate.

Return the duck to the pan with the stock mixture. Simmer the stock, skimming the surface occasionally, to remove the fat.

Remove the duck using a slotted spoon, so that the braising liquid is left in the pan.

When cool enough to handle, shred the duck meat, discarding the skin and bones.

Strain the stock through a muslin-lined sieve into a large jug; discard the solids.

Add the shredded duck meat to the vegetable mixture; simmer, uncovered, for 15 minutes or until the mixture has thickened.

Spread ½ cup of the cheese sauce over the base of the ovenproof dish, then top with a layer of pasta sheets.

Spread half the cheese and spinach mixture over the pasta layer. Top with chopped sausages, 1 cup tomato sauce then half the remaining cheese sauce.

Top the final layer of pasta sheets with the mozzarella slices, then spread the remaining tomato sauce over the top.

ITALIAN SAUSAGE AND THREE-CHEESE LASAGNE

prep + cook time 2 hours 40 minutes ~ serves 8

This hearty lasagne can be assembled ahead of time and baked at the last minute, giving you more precious time with your guests.

500g (1 pound) italian sausages
250g (8 ounces) frozen chopped spinach, thawed, drained
250g (8 ounces) ricotta cheese
½ cup (40g) finely grated parmesan cheese
¼ teaspoon ground nutmeg
1 egg
9 sheets fresh lasagne (450g)
250g (8 ounces) mozzarella cheese, sliced thinly

tomato sauce
1 tablespoon olive oil
1 medium onion (150g), chopped finely
1 medium carrot (120g), chopped finely
1 stick celery (150g), chopped finely
5 x 8cm (3¼-inch) long parsley stalks, crushed
2 cloves garlic, crushed
½ cup (125ml) dry red wine
¼ cup (70g) tomato paste
700g (1½ pounds) bottled tomato pasta sauce

cheese sauce
50g (1½ ounces) butter
⅓ cup (50g) plain (all-purpose) flour
2 cups (500ml) milk
1½ cups (120g) finely grated parmesan cheese

1 Make tomato sauce, then make cheese sauce.

2 Preheat oven to 200°C/400°F.

3 Cook sausages in oiled large frying pan until browned all over; drain then slice thinly.

4 Combine spinach, ricotta and parmesan cheeses, nutmeg and egg in medium bowl.

5 Spread ½ cup of the cheese sauce over base of 20cm x 30cm (8-inch x 12-inch) ovenproof dish. Top with two pasta sheets then spread with half the spinach mixture. Sprinkle with half the sausage; cover with 1 cup of the tomato sauce then half the remaining cheese sauce.

6 Top with two more pasta sheets. Spread remaining spinach mixture over pasta; sprinkle with remaining sausage. Spread with 1 cup tomato sauce, then remaining cheese sauce.

7 Top with remaining pasta sheets, then half the remaining tomato sauce. Top with mozzarella slices; spread with remaining tomato sauce.

8 Bake, covered, 30 minutes. Uncover, bake about 10 minutes or until browned lightly. Stand 10 minutes before serving.

tomato sauce
Heat oil in large saucepan; cook onion, carrot, celery and parsley, stirring occasionally, until vegetables soften. Add garlic; cook, stirring, 1 minute. Add wine; cook, stirring, until almost evaporated. Discard parsley stalks. Add paste; cook, stirring, 3 minutes. Add sauce; simmer, uncovered, about 15 minutes.

cheese sauce
Melt butter in medium saucepan, add flour; cook, stirring, until mixture thickens and bubbles. Gradually add milk; stir until mixture boils and thickens. Reduce heat; cook, stirring, 1 minute, remove from heat. Add cheese, stir until melted.

nutritional count per serving
46.5g total fat (23.6g saturated fat); 2876kJ (687 cal); 27.2g carbohydrate; 38.7g protein; 7.2g fibre

tip After you have finished cooking the cheese sauce, cover the surface with plastic wrap to stop a skin forming.

PASTA PRIMAVERA WITH POACHED SALMON

prep + cook time 40 minutes ~ serves 4

300g (9½ ounces) fettuccine pasta
1.25 litres (5 cups) water
2 sprigs fresh dill
6 black peppercorns
2 teaspoons finely grated lemon rind
440g (14 ounces) skinless salmon fillets
2 teaspoons olive oil
1 medium red onion (170g), sliced thinly
2 cloves garlic, crushed
170g (5½ ounces) asparagus, halved crossways
150g (4½ ounces) snow peas, halved, trimmed
½ cup (60g) frozen peas
2 tablespoons lemon juice
2 teaspoons finely chopped fresh dill
2 tablespoons coarsely chopped fresh flat-leaf parsley

1 Cook pasta in large saucepan of boiling water until tender; drain.

2 Meanwhile, place the water, dill sprigs, peppercorns and half the rind in large saucepan then add fish; bring to the boil. Reduce heat; simmer, uncovered, 8 minutes, turning fish halfway through cooking time. Remove fish from poaching liquid; discard liquid. When fish is cool enough to handle, flake fish into medium bowl.

3 Heat oil in same cleaned pan; cook onion, garlic and asparagus, stirring, until asparagus is tender. Add snow peas, peas, juice, remaining rind, pasta and fish; stir until hot. Remove from heat; stir in herbs.

nutritional count per serving
11.2g total fat (2.2g saturated fat); 2015kJ (482 cal); 57.7g carbohydrate; 33.7g protein; 5.8g fibre

tip You may need a little more liquid in your final pasta dish. Just in case, reserve ½ cup of the pasta cooking liquid and add as required.

Combine the water, dill, peppercorns and half the rind in saucepan, then add the fish; bring to the boil. Reduce heat; simmer, uncovered, 8 minutes.

Once the fish has cooked, remove from the poaching liquid; discard liquid. When the fish is cool enough to handle, flake the fish.

Cook the onion, garlic and asparagus until the asparagus is tender. Add the snow peas to the pan along with the peas, juice, remaining rind, pasta and fish.

CRAB AND SCALLOP CANNELLONI WITH CAULIFLOWER PUREE

prep + cook time 2 hours (+ standing) ~ serves 4

Micro cress is a cress that has been harvested at seedling stage. It has small tender green leaves with a strong radish-like flavour and is available from specialty greengrocers.

200g (6½ ounces) cooked white crab meat
2 shallots (50g), chopped finely
60g (2 ounces) butter
⅓ cup (50g) plain (all-purpose) flour, plus extra for dusting
1¾ cups (430ml) hot milk
2 tablespoons brandy
1 tablespoon finely chopped fresh dill
500g (1 pound) scallops (without roe)
¾ cup (60g) finely grated parmesan cheese

pasta dough
2 cups (300g) plain (all-purpose) flour
½ teaspoon sea salt flakes
2 eggs
1 tablespoon olive oil
¼ cup (60ml) water

cauliflower puree
½ small (500g) cauliflower, cut into florets
¾ cup (180ml) milk
½ teaspoon sea salt flakes
90g (3 ounces) butter

1 Make pasta dough and cauliflower puree.

2 Drain crab meat, remove any small pieces of shell or grit.

3 Melt butter in medium saucepan, add shallots; cook, stirring, about 2 minutes or until soft. Add flour; cook, stirring, until bubbling. Gradually stir in combined milk and brandy; cook, stirring, over medium heat, until sauce boils and thickens. Cover surface of sauce with plastic wrap; stand 30 minutes. Stir in dill.

4 Cut pasta dough into four equal portions. Using the palm of your hand, fatten one portion into a rectangle. Dust pasta with a little flour, roll the dough through the widest setting of a pasta machine. Dust again with flour, repeat on the same setting.

5 Reduce the width between the pasta rollers by one, roll the dough through as before. Repeat the process, adjusting the roller width each time until the lowest setting is reached. Cut eight 10cm x 16cm (4-inch x 6½-inch) pieces from pasta sheets.

6 Preheat oven to 220°C/425°F. Oil two oven trays, then line with baking paper.

7 Cook pasta in large saucepan of boiling salted water about 2 minutes or until barely tender; drain. Refresh pasta in large bowl of iced water. Cover bench with a layer of plastic wrap, place pasta on top, then cover with another layer of plastic wrap to prevent drying out.

8 To make cannelloni, place one piece of pasta on a sheet of baking paper; place three scallops along one short end, then top with some crab meat and a tablespoon of sauce. Roll into a tube shape, trim ends. Repeat with remaining pasta, scallops, crab meat and sauce. Place cannelloni on trays in pairs for easy serving; top with remaining sauce and parmesan.

9 Bake cannelloni about 10 minutes or until heated through and browned.

10 Reheat cauliflower puree in medium saucepan, stirring, over low heat. Spoon puree onto serving plates, top with cannelloni; sprinkle with micro cress leaves, if you like.

pasta dough
Process ingredients until mixture forms a ball. Gently knead about 2 minutes or until smooth and elastic. Press into a flat rectangle, enclose in plastic wrap; stand 20 minutes at room temperature.

cauliflower puree
Process cauliflower until finely chopped. Combine cauliflower and milk in large saucepan; bring to the boil. Reduce heat; simmer about 10 minutes or until cauliflower is soft. Remove from heat, stir in salt and butter. Stand 10 minutes; blend until smooth.

nutritional count per serving
51.3g total fat (29.2g saturated fat); 4101kJ (981 cal); 75.1g carbohydrate; 47.7g protein; 5.8g fibre

tip Crab meat can be bought already cooked from some fishmongers. Alternatively, buy cooked crabs (about 600g/ 1¼ pounds in weight) and remove enough flesh from the shells and claws to weigh 200g. Well-drained canned crab meat could be used in this recipe.

for steps, see pages 106 & 107

CRAB AND SCALLOP CANNELLONI WITH CAULIFLOWER PUREE

To chop shallots, cut in half through the root then peel. Make horizontal, then vertical cuts in each half, but don't cut all the way through; chop each half finely.

Add flour to butter mixture; cook, stirring, until mixture bubbles.

Gradually stir combined milk and brandy into flour mixture; cook, stirring, until mixture boils and thickens. Remove from heat; cover surface of sauce with plastic wrap.

Flatten each pasta dough portion into a rectangle with the palm of your hand, then dust with a little flour. Roll each rectangle through the pasta machine on its widest setting; dust with more flour, then repeat on the same setting.

Reduce the width between the pasta rollers by one, roll the dough through as before. Repeat the process, adjusting the roller width each time until you reach the lowest setting.

To make the cannelloni, place one piece of pasta on a sheet of baking paper; place three scallops along one short end, then top with some crab meat and some white sauce. Roll into a tube and trim the ends. Repeat with the remaining pasta, scallops, crab meat and sauce.

FISH WITH MIXED VEGETABLES

prep + cook time 25 minutes ~ serves 4

500g (1 pound) firm white fish fillets, cut into 3cm (1¼-inch) pieces
2 cloves garlic, chopped finely
2½ tablespoons peanut oil
350g (11 ounces) broccolini, cut into 3cm (1¼-inch) lengths
1 large carrot (180g), cut into matchsticks
150g (4½ ounces) baby corn, halved lengthways
¼ cup (60ml) oyster sauce
1 tablespoon japanese soy sauce
1 tablespoon water

1 Combine fish pieces, garlic and 2 tablespoons of the oil in medium bowl.

2 Heat wok; stir-fry fish mixture, in batches, until browned. Remove from wok.

3 Heat remaining oil in wok; stir-fry broccolini, carrot and corn until tender. Return fish to wok with sauces and the water; stir-fry until hot, season to taste.

nutritional count per serving
15.1g total fat (3g saturated fat); 1388kJ (332 cal); 12.9g carbohydrate; 32.4g protein; 6.7g fibre

tip We used blue-eye fillets in this recipe, but you can use any white fish fillets.

serving suggestion Serve with steamed jasmine rice.

Add peanut oil to fish pieces and chopped garlic, then mix to combine.

Cut the peeled carrot in half crossways, then into thin slices lengthways; cut the slices into thin matchsticks.

Stir-fry broccolini, carrot and corn in heated oiled wok until vegetables are tender.

Place fish in large baking-paper-lined bamboo steamer over a saucepan of simmering water; steam, covered, 15 minutes.

Simmer the sugar syrup, without stirring, until the mixture is a light caramel colour.

Remove pan from heat; allow bubbles to subside. Stir in rind and juice; return to the heat and stir to melt any pieces of caramel. Remove from heat; stir in oil and vinegar.

STEAMED SALMON WITH BURNT ORANGE SAUCE

prep + cook time 30 minutes ~ serves 2

2 x 200g (6½-ounce) salmon fillets
¼ cup (55g) caster (superfine) sugar
1 tablespoon water
1 teaspoon finely grated orange rind
2 tablespoons orange juice
2 teaspoons olive oil
2 teaspoons rice wine vinegar
175g (5½ ounces) watercress, trimmed

1 Place fish in large baking-paper-lined bamboo steamer set over large saucepan of simmering water; steam, covered, 15 minutes.

2 Meanwhile, stir sugar and the water in small saucepan, without boiling, until sugar dissolves. Bring to the boil. Reduce heat; simmer, uncovered, without stirring, until mixture is a light caramel colour.

3 Remove pan from heat; allow bubbles to subside. Carefully stir in rind and juice. Return pan to low heat; stir until any pieces of caramel melt. Remove pan from heat; stir in oil and vinegar.

4 Serve fish with watercress, drizzled with orange sauce.

nutritional count per serving
9.6g total fat (1.9g saturated fat); 970kJ (232 cal); 14.7g carbohydrate; 20.8g protein; 1.7g fibre

tip Lining the bamboo steamer with baking paper makes it easier to lift the fish out after cooking.

SNAPPER WITH POTATO STACKS AND BEURRE BLANC

prep + cook time 1 hour 45 minutes (+ refrigeration) ~ serves 6

If your pan doesn't have an ovenproof handle, cover the handle well with several layers of foil.

6 x 220g (7-ounce) snapper fillets, skin on
1 tablespoon lemon juice
1 tablespoon olive oil
30g (1 ounce) butter

potato stacks
3 medium potatoes (600g)
1 shallot (25g), chopped finely
1 clove garlic, crushed
2 tablespoons olive oil
1 cup (250ml) fish stock
30g (1 ounce) butter

beurre blanc
¼ cup (60ml) dry white wine
1 tablespoon white wine vinegar
1 tablespoon lemon juice
¼ cup (60ml) pouring cream
125g (4 ounces) cold butter, cut into 1cm (½-inch) cubes

1 Trim the sides of each fish fillet into neat rectangular shapes; lightly score the skin at 1cm (½-inch) intervals (to help the skin brown and prevent it curling). Refrigerate until ready to cook.

2 Preheat oven to 220°/425°F; make potato stacks.

3 Meanwhile, make beurre blanc.

4 Reduce oven to 200°C/400°F.

5 Season fish with salt, pepper and juice. Heat oil and butter in large ovenproof frying pan; cook fish, skin-side down, about 3 minutes or until skin is crisp, turn fillets over. Transfer pan to oven; cook, fish, uncovered, about 4 minutes or until cooked to your liking.

6 Slide potato stacks from baking paper rounds onto serving plates; position fish, skin-side up, on plate, drizzle with beurre blanc. Top with chives, if you like.

potato stacks
Finely slice peeled potatoes using a mandoline or V-slicer. Combine potato slices with shallot, garlic and oil in medium bowl; season. Cut out six 8.5cm (3½-inch) rounds of baking paper. Brush paper with a little extra oil, place in base of small shallow baking dish. Layer potato mixture, into stacks on each round of baking paper. Carefully pour stock into dish. Cut butter into six pieces, dot each stack with butter. Bake about 30 minutes or until potato is tender and golden brown.

beurre blanc
Bring wine, vinegar and juice to the boil in small saucepan; boil until reduced by two-thirds. Add cream, return to the boil; reduce heat. Whisk in cold butter, one piece at a time, whisking between additions until sauce is smooth and thickened slightly.

nutritional count per serving
42.4g total fat (22.2g saturated fat); 2625kJ (628 cal); 11.7g carbohydrate; 47.7g protein; 1.7g fibre

for steps, see pages 114 & 115

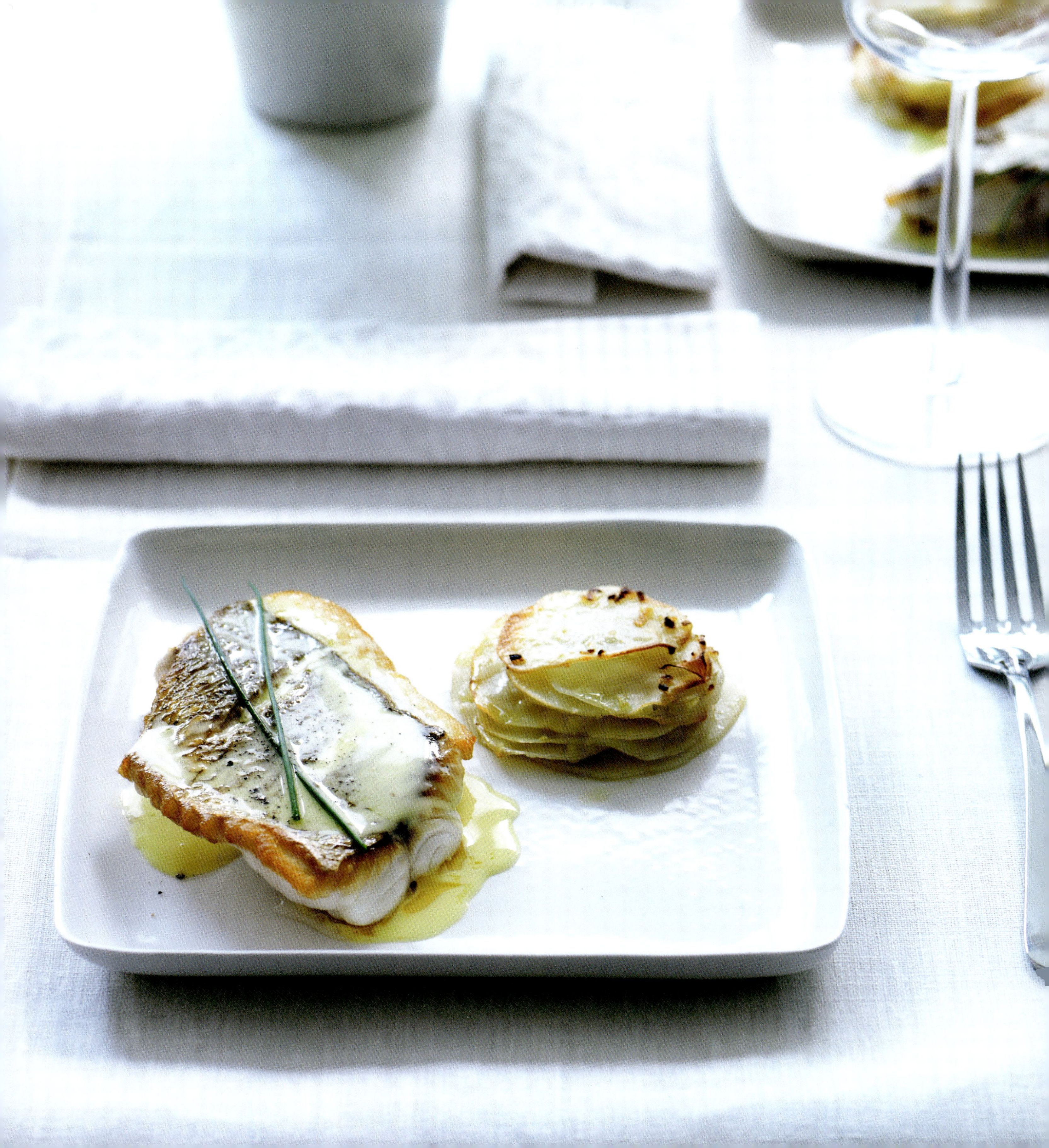

SNAPPER WITH POTATO STACKS AND BEURRE BLANC

Lightly score the fish skin at 1cm (½-inch) intervals, to help the skin brown and prevent it from curling.

Heat the oil and butter in a large ovenproof frying pan; cook the fish, skin-side down, about 3 minutes or until the skin is crisp. Turn the fish over.

Thinly slice the potatoes using a V-slicer or mandoline. These are great for fast, precise slicing. Always use a guard to protect your fingers from the sharp blade.

Cut out six 8.5cm (3½-inch) rounds of baking paper, place on base of baking dish; layer potato slices in stacks on the baking-paper rounds. Carefully pour the fish stock into the baking dish around the potato stacks, not over them.

To make the beurre blanc, whisk the butter, piece by piece, into the wine and cream reduction.

Use an egg slice to lift the potato stacks from the baking dish onto the serving plates.

MOROCCAN FISH KEBABS WITH PRESERVED LEMON COUSCOUS

prep + cook time 35 minutes (+ refrigeration) ~ serves 4

600g (1¼ pounds) skinless firm white fish fillets
½ cup finely chopped fresh coriander (cilantro)
2 cloves garlic, crushed
2 fresh small red thai (serrano) chillies, chopped finely
1 tablespoon olive oil
¼ cup (60ml) lemon juice
1 cup (250ml) salt-reduced chicken stock
½ cup (125ml) water
1½ cups (300g) couscous
½ cup firmly packed fresh coriander (cilantro) leaves, extra
1 tablespoon finely chopped preserved lemon rind
¼ cup (35g) roasted slivered almonds

1 Cut fish into 3cm (1¼-inch) pieces; place in large bowl.

2 Combine coriander, garlic, chilli, oil and juice in small bowl.

3 Add half the coriander mixture to fish in large bowl; toss to coat fish in mixture. Thread fish onto eight skewers; place kebabs on tray. Cover; refrigerate 45 minutes.

4 Cook kebabs on heated oiled grill plate (or grill or barbecue) about 5 minutes or until cooked as desired.

5 Meanwhile, bring stock and the water to the boil in medium saucepan; remove from heat. Add couscous to stock, cover; stand about 5 minutes or until liquid is absorbed, fluffing with fork occasionally. Add remaining coriander mixture, extra coriander leaves, rind and nuts; stir to combine.

6 Serve kebabs with couscous.

nutritional count per serving
12.4g total fat (2g saturated fat); 2220kJ (531 cal); 59.5g carbohydrate; 42.8g protein; 2g fibre

tip You will need to soak eight 25cm (10-inch) bamboo skewers in water for at least an hour before using to prevent them from splintering or scorching during the cooking process.

serving suggestion Serve with a rocket (arugula) leaf or baby spinach leaf salad.

Combine chopped fish with half the coriander mixture until fish is coated in the mixture.

Thread fish pieces onto bamboo skewers.

Off the heat, add the couscous to the hot stock mixture and let stand for 5 minutes or until the liquid has been absorbed, fluffing with a fork occasionally.

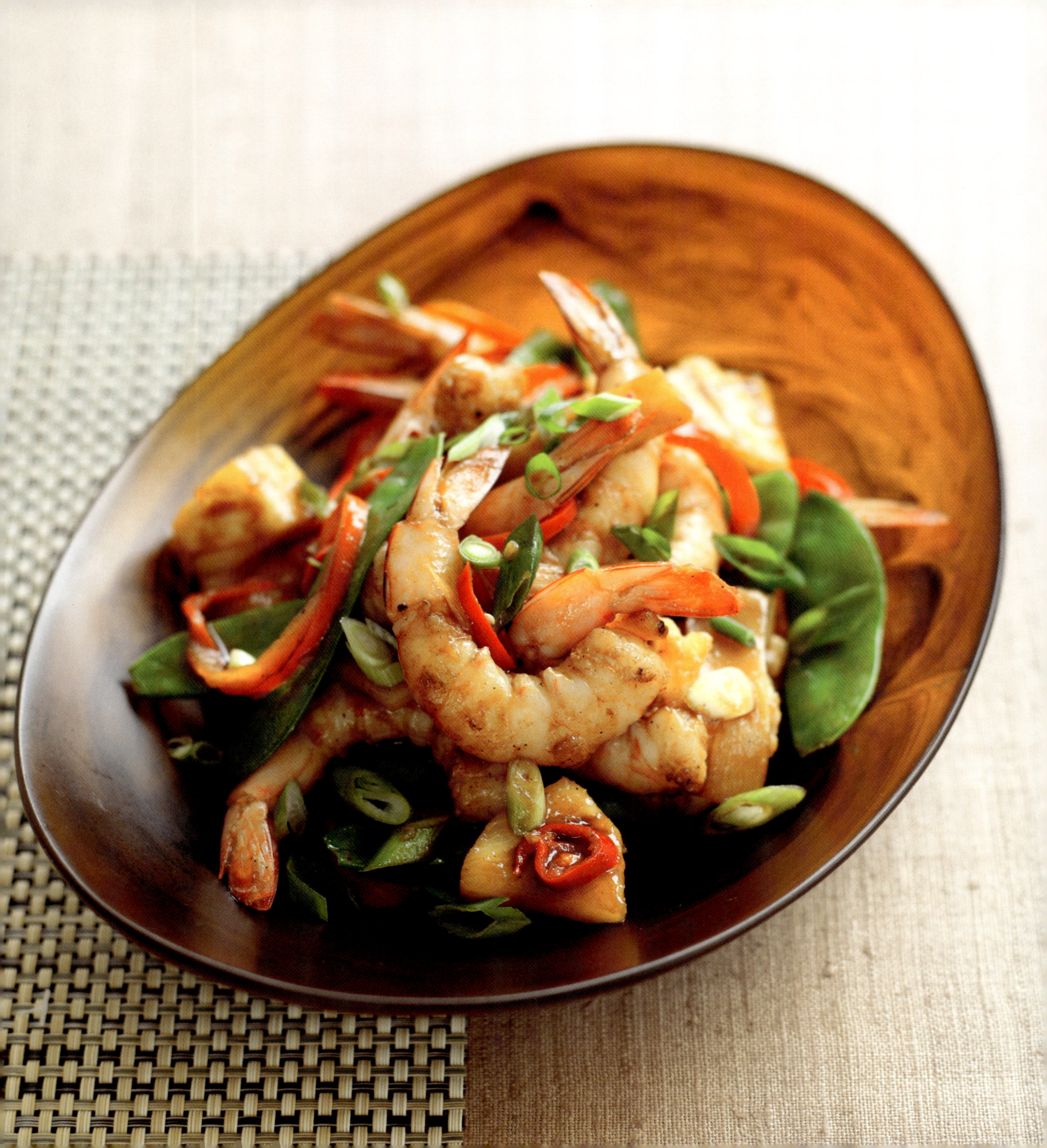

TAMARIND HONEY PRAWNS WITH PINEAPPLE

prep + cook time 35 minutes ~ serves 4

1.2kg (2½ pounds) uncooked medium king prawns (shrimp)
1 tablespoon vegetable oil
3 cloves garlic, crushed
1 fresh long red chilli, sliced thinly
1 medium red capsicum (200g), sliced thinly
150g (4½ ounces) snow peas, trimmed
⅓ cup (100g) tamarind concentrate
2 tablespoons kecap manis
1 tablespoon honey
230g (7 ounces) canned bamboo shoots, rinsed, drained
½ small pineapple (450g), chopped coarsely
4 green onions (scallions), sliced thinly

1 Shell and devein prawns, leaving tails intact.

2 Heat oil in wok; stir-fry prawns, garlic, chilli, capsicum and snow peas until prawns are changed in colour. Add remaining ingredients; stir-fry until hot.

nutritional count per serving
5.8g total fat (0.8g saturated fat); 1141kJ (273 cal); 18.5g carbohydrate; 34.6g protein; 4.3g fibre

Remove and discard the prawn heads. Peel the shell away from the body, keeping the tails intact. Remove and discard the centre vein from the back of each prawn using your fingers or a small knife.

Coarsely chop the fresh pineapple into bite-sized pieces.

Stir-fry prawns, garlic, chilli, capsicum and snow peas, tossing until prawns have changed in colour.

middles ~ 119 ~ middles

RED DUCK CURRY WITH LYCHEES

prep + cook time 50 minutes (+ standing) ~ serves 6

4 boneless duck breast fillets (780g)
1 cup (250ml) canned coconut cream
1 cup (250ml) canned coconut milk
2 tablespoons fish sauce
2 tablespoons finely chopped palm sugar
565g (1¼ pounds) canned lychees in natural juice, drained
4 fresh kaffir lime leaves
1 cup loosely packed fresh thai basil leaves
2 cups (160g) bean sprouts
¼ cup (20g) fried shallots
3 small fresh red thai (serrano) chillies, sliced

red curry paste
12 dried long red chillies
¾ cup (180ml) boiling water
5 white peppercorns
1 teaspoon each ground coriander, cumin and hot paprika
2 shallots (50g), chopped coarsely
4 cloves garlic, chopped coarsely
2cm (¾-inch) piece fresh ginger (10g), chopped coarsely
10cm (4-inch) stick fresh lemon grass (10g), sliced thinly
3 coriander (cilantro) roots, chopped
1 teaspoon shrimp paste
½ teaspoon finely grated fresh lime rind

1   Make red curry paste.

2   Place duck breasts, skin-side down, in large oiled frying pan; cook over low heat, pressing down occasionally, about 15 minutes or until fat has rendered. Turn duck, cook over medium heat about 2 minutes or until browned. Drain on absorbent paper. Cool. Cut duck crossways into thick slices.

3   Open the can of coconut cream and remove about 3 tablespoons of the thick cream. Add to same heated cleaned pan with ⅓ cup of the red curry paste; stir-fry until oil separates and mixture is fragrant. Stir in remaining coconut cream, coconut milk, fish sauce and sugar; bring to the boil. Reduce heat; add duck, lychees and roughly torn lime leaves, simmer 5 minutes. Stir in basil.

4   Serve curry topped with sprouts, fried shallots and chillies.

red curry paste
Place chillies and the water in small heatproof bowl; stand 15 minutes. Dry-fry peppercorns and ground spices in small frying pan, stirring until fragrant. Blend undrained chillies and dry-fried spices with remaining ingredients until mixture forms a paste.

nutritional count per serving
64.9g total fat (29.5g saturated fat); 3106kJ (743 cal); 20.9g carbohydrate; 20.5g protein; 3.3g fibre

tip This recipe needs ⅓ cup of the red curry paste, the remaining paste can be frozen in an airtight container for about a month. This is quite a hot curry paste; if you have a low heat-level tolerance, use less of the curry paste.

serving suggestion Serve with steamed rice.

for steps, see pages 122 & 123

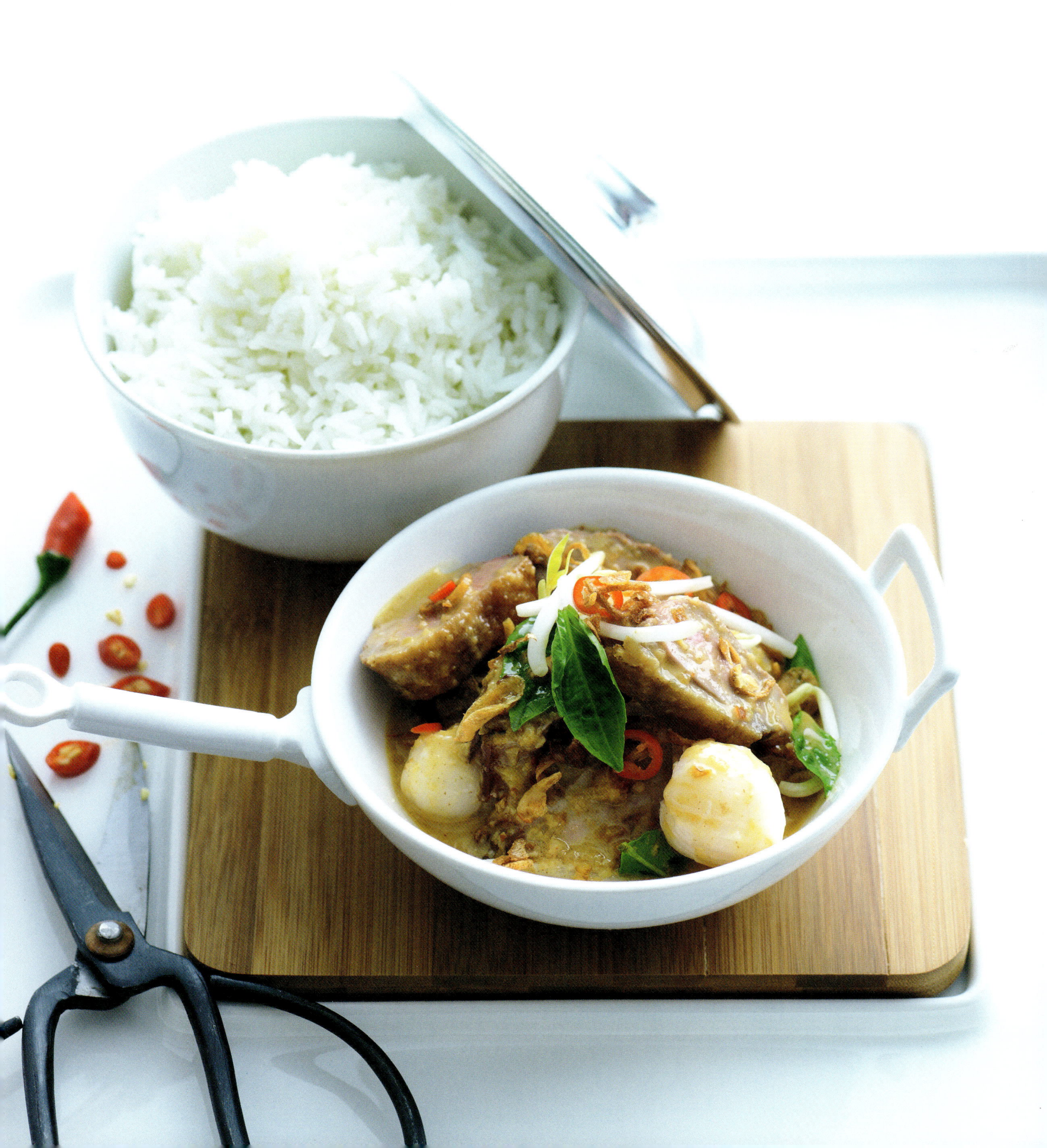

RED DUCK CURRY WITH LYCHEES

Place dried chillies and the boiling water in small heatproof bowl to soak for 15 minutes.

Chop fresh lemon grass starting from the white end, going up 10cm (4 inches) only until you just reach the green part of the stalk. Discard the tough top green section; cut the white part as finely as possible because lemon grass is so fibrous it doesn't soften during in cooking.

Process or blend undrained chillies and dry-fried spices with remaining ingredients until the mixture forms a paste.

Cook the duck, skin-side down, in a large oiled frying pan for about 15 minutes or until the fat has been rendered. Turn duck, cook further 2 minutes or until browned.

Remove 3 tablespoons of the thick cream from the top of the can of coconut cream.

Stir-fry the red curry paste and the thick coconut cream in large frying pan until the oil separates and the mixture is fragrant.

STEAMED BABY SNAPPER WITH CHILLI, GINGER AND PEANUTS

prep + cook time 45 minutes ~ serves 4

4 green onions (scallions), sliced thinly
6cm (2½-inch) piece fresh ginger (30g), cut into matchsticks
2 cloves garlic, sliced thinly
2 fresh long red chillies, sliced thinly, on the diagonal
1½ tablespoons light soy sauce
1 tablespoon chinese cooking wine (shao hsing)
2 teaspoons sesame oil
1 teaspoon light brown sugar
4 x 350g (11-ounce) whole baby snapper, cleaned
⅓ cup (80ml) peanut oil
½ cup (70g) roasted unsalted peanuts
½ cup coriander (cilantro) sprigs

1 Combine onion, ginger, garlic and chilli in small bowl.

2 Combine sauce, cooking wine, sesame oil and sugar in small bowl.

3 Preheat oven to 220°C/425°F.

4 Score each fish through the thickest part of flesh.

5 Place four 60cm (24-inch) square pieces of foil on bench; top each piece of foil with a 30cm (12-inch) square piece of baking paper.

6 Divide half the ginger mixture between pieces of baking-paper-lined foil; top with fish, then top with remaining ginger mixture and drizzle with sauce mixture. Fold foil over to enclose fish tightly. Place fish parcels, slightly apart, on large oven tray; bake about 15 minutes or until fish are cooked through.

7 Heat peanut oil in small saucepan over high heat until almost smoking. Gently open fish parcels; pour about 1 tablespoon hot oil over each fish while still in foil. Lift fish onto heated serving plates. Carefully, pour juices from each foil parcel over fish. Sprinkle with nuts and coriander.

nutritional count per serving
31.8g total fat (6g saturated fat); 2006kJ (480 cal); 3.9g carbohydrate; 42.8g protein; 2.3g fibre

serving suggestion Serve with steamed rice.

Peel the ginger, trimming to flatten out any uneven bits. Cut into long thin slices, then cut into matchsticks.

Use a sharp knife to score the fish through the thickest part of flesh on both sides.

Place half the ginger mixture on the baking-paper-lined foil; top with the fish then sprinkle with the remaining ginger mixture.

Using the heel of your hand, flatten the chicken by pressing on the breast bone.

Turn the chicken over and cut away the breast bones and rib cages.

Place the chicken pieces in a large baking dish and pour over the warm duck fat.

CHICKEN CONFIT WITH SPINACH AND PAN JUS

prep + cook time 2 hours 45 minutes (+ refrigeration) ~ serves 6

Confit means 'to preserve', usually a meat like duck or pork. The meat is salted and cooked slowly in its own fat, packed into a pot and covered with the cooking fat which works as a seal and preservative.

6 x 500g (1 pound) small chickens
½ cup (60g) sea salt flakes
2 shallots (50g), chopped finely
4 cloves garlic, crushed
2 teaspoons fresh thyme leaves
1.2kg (2½ pounds) duck fat
150g (4½ ounces) baby spinach leaves

pan jus
1 tablespoon olive oil
1 stick celery (150g), chopped coarsely
1 small carrot (70g), chopped coarsely
2 sprigs fresh thyme
1 cup (250ml) dry red wine
1 litre (4 cups) chicken stock
2 cups (500ml) water

1 Wash chickens under cold water; pat dry inside and out with absorbent paper. Cut along both sides of backbone with kitchen scissors; reserve bones. Place chickens, breast-side up, on board. Press the breast bone with the heel of your hand to flatten. Cut along breast bones, then cut away rib cages; reserve. Cut wing tips from first joint of wing bone; reserve.

2 Combine chicken halves, salt, shallots, garlic and thyme in large non-metallic dish. Refrigerate 1 hour.

3 Preheat oven to 160°C/325°F.

4 Brush excess salt mixture from chicken; pat dry with absorbent paper. Place chicken in single layer in two large non-metallic casserole dishes. Melt duck fat in medium saucepan over low heat; pour over chicken until completely covered. Cook, uncovered, in the oven, for 1½ hours.

5 Meanwhile, make pan jus.

6 Increase oven to 220°C/425°F.

7 Remove chickens from fat; place, in single layer, on baking-paper-lined oven trays. Roast, uncovered, about 15 minutes or until browned.

8 Serve chickens on spinach with jus.

pan jus
Heat oil in large saucepan; cook reserved chicken bones and wing tips, stirring occasionally, about 10 minutes or until browned. Drain fat from pan. Add celery, carrot and thyme; cook until browned lightly. Add wine; bring to the boil. Reduce heat; simmer, uncovered, until mixture is reduced by about two-thirds. Add stock and the water; bring to the boil. Reduce heat; simmer, uncovered, 1 hour, skimming regularly. Strain jus through muslin-lined colander over large heatproof bowl; discard solids. Return jus to same pan; bring to the boil. Reduce heat; simmer, uncovered, about 10 minutes or until reduced to about 1 cup.

nutritional count per serving
53.6g total fat (17g saturated fat); 3060kJ (732 cal); 3.7g carbohydrate; 52.8g protein; 1.6g fibre

tips Rendered duck fat is available from gourmet food stores and some supermarkets and gourmet butcher shops.

You can use trimmed watercress instead of baby spinach leaves.

CHICKEN AND LEEK STRUDEL

prep + cook time 1 hour (+ cooling) ~ serves 8

1 medium leek (350g), trimmed
1 tablespoon olive oil
1 medium brown onion (150g), chopped finely
2 cloves garlic, crushed
1 large carrot (180g), chopped finely
500g (1 pound) chicken thigh fillets, chopped finely
2 tablespoons plain (all-purpose) flour
1¼ cups (310ml) pouring cream
½ cup (60g) frozen peas
8 sheets fillo pastry
80g (2½ ounces) butter, melted
⅓ cup (40g) ground almonds

1 Cut the white part of leek in half lengthways; rinse well under cold running water to remove any dirt between the layers. Slice thinly.

2 Heat oil in large frying pan; cook leek, onion, garlic and carrot, stirring, until carrot softens.

3 Add chicken; cook, stirring, until browned. Add flour; cook, stirring, 1 minute. Gradually stir in cream; cook, stirring, until mixture boils and thickens. Remove from heat; stir in peas. Season to taste. Cool.

4 Preheat oven to 200°C/400°F. Line large oven tray with baking paper.

5 Brush one pastry sheet with butter, then sprinkle with a little of the ground almonds. Layer with remaining pastry, butter and ground almonds, ending with a pastry sheet.

6 Spoon chicken mixture along one long side of pastry, leaving a 5cm (2-inch) border on each side. Roll to enclose filling, fold in sides, roll up. Transfer roll to tray; brush with butter.

7 Bake strudel about 25 minutes or until browned. Stand on tray 5 minutes before serving.

nutritional count per serving
35g total fat (18.4g saturated fat); 1812kJ (434 cal); 14.6g carbohydrate; 16.5g protein; 3.1g fibre

tip You can use just one 300ml carton of cream for this recipe.

Cut the trimmed leek in half lengthways, then rinse well to remove any dirt between the layers. Cut each half into thin slices.

Brush one pastry sheet with butter, then sprinkle with a little of the ground almonds. Continue layering with remaining pastry, butter and ground almonds, ending with a pastry sheet.

Spoon the chicken mixture along one long side of the pastry, leaving a 5cm border around the sides. Roll the pastry over the filling, fold in the sides, then roll up to completely enclose.

Tie the legs of the chicken together with kitchen string to secure the stuffing.

To test if the chicken is cooked, insert a skewer into the thickest part of the chicken (the thigh); the juices should run clear.

Gradually whisk the oil into the mayonnaise in a thin stream, until the mayonnaise is thick and creamy. Place a tea towel under the bowl to keep it from moving.

ROASTED CHICKEN FOR TWO

prep + cook time 1 hour 30 minutes (+ standing) ~ serves 2

1kg (2-pound) whole chicken
1 medium leek (350g), trimmed
1 small brown onion (80g), quartered
2 garlic cloves, bruised
2 sprigs fresh tarragon
¼ medium lemon
50g (1½ ounces) butter, melted

tarragon mayonnaise
1 egg yolk
2 teaspoons white wine vinegar
1 teaspoon dijon mustard
½ cup (125ml) grape seed oil
1 green onion (scallion), chopped finely
1½ tablespoons Greek-style yogurt
2 teaspoons drained baby capers, rinsed
2 teaspoons lemon juice
2 teaspoons finely chopped fresh tarragon
1 teaspoon horseradish relish

watercress and radish salad
3 teaspoons red wine vinegar
2 tablespoons olive oil
¼ teaspoon caster (superfine) sugar
3 red radishes (105g), cut into matchsticks
2 cups lightly packed watercress sprigs

1 Preheat oven to 200°C/400°F.

2 Wash chicken under cold water; pat dry inside and out with absorbent paper. Cut the white part of the leek into quarters. Place leek, onion, garlic, tarragon and lemon in cavity of chicken. Tie legs together with kitchen string. Brush butter all over chicken; season. Place chicken on a wire rack inside a baking dish.

3 Roast chicken, uncovered, about 1 hour or until juices run clear. Cover loosely with foil; stand 15 minutes before carving.

4 Meanwhile, make tarragon mayonnaise. Make watercress and radish salad.

5 Serve roast chicken with mayonnaise and salad.

tarragon mayonnaise
Whisk yolk, vinegar and mustard in small bowl. Gradually whisk in oil, in a thin, steady stream, until mayonnaise is thick and creamy. Stir in remaining ingredients. Season to taste.

watercress and radish salad
Whisk vinegar, oil and sugar in medium bowl; season to taste. Add radish and watercress; toss gently to combine.

nutritional count per serving
131.5g total fat (33.2g saturated fat); 6094kJ (1458 cal); 10.1g carbohydrate; 59.6g protein; 5.9g fibre

tip Major supermarkets sell 1kg chickens in packs of two. Freeze the unused chicken to cook at a later date.

CHICKEN, TOMATO AND FETTA PATTIES WITH SPINACH SALAD

prep + cook time 30 minutes ~ serves 4

750g (1½ pounds) minced (ground) chicken
⅓ cup (50g) drained semi-dried tomatoes, chopped coarsely
½ cup (35g) stale breadcrumbs
200g (6½ ounces) fetta cheese, crumbled
1 egg, beaten lightly
1 small white onion (80g), sliced thinly
100g (3 ounces) baby spinach leaves
1 tablespoon olive oil
1 tablespoon balsamic vinegar

1 Combine chicken, tomato, breadcrumbs, half the cheese and the egg in large bowl; shape mixture into 12 patties.

2 Cook patties in heated oiled large frying pan, in batches, until cooked through. Drain on absorbent paper.

3 Meanwhile, place onion, spinach, oil, vinegar and remaining cheese in medium bowl; toss gently to combine.

4 Serve patties with spinach salad.

nutritional count per serving
33.7g total fat (13.3g saturated fat); 2320kJ (555 cal); 11.8g carbohydrate; 50.1g protein; 3.2g fibre

tip If you have time, refrigerate patties for 30 minutes before cooking, this stops them from falling apart while cooking. You could easily turn these patties into burgers if you wanted to. When you shape them into patties just make them a little wider and flatter than if you were serving them on their own.

Combine chicken, semi-dried tomato, breadcrumbs, half the cheese and the egg.

Form the chicken mixture into 12 patties. (If you have the time, refrigerate the patties for 30 minutes before cooking.)

Cook the patties in a heated oiled frying pan, in batches, until browned both sides and cooked through.

To bruise the cardamom pods, place pods on chopping coard then press down with the flat blade of a knife to break them open.

Process ingredients for coriander and chilli paste until mixture forms a smooth paste.

Combine chicken and paste in large bowl, rubbing paste into the cuts.

GRILLED CHICKEN WITH CORIANDER AND CHILLI

prep + cook time 35 minutes (+ refrigeration) ~ serves 4

8 chicken thigh cutlets (1.6kg)
1 lime, cut into wedges

coriander and chilli paste
2 teaspoons coriander seeds
4 fresh small red thai (serrano) chillies, chopped coarsely
1 teaspoon ground cumin
2 whole cloves
3 cardamom pods, bruised
¼ teaspoon ground turmeric
10cm (4-inch) stick fresh lemon grass (20g), chopped coarsely
2 medium brown onions (300g), chopped coarsely
4 cloves garlic
⅓ cup (80ml) lime juice
2 teaspoons coarse cooking salt (kosher salt)
2 tablespoons peanut oil

1 Make coriander and chilli paste.

2 Pierce chicken all over with sharp knife. Combine chicken and paste in large bowl, rubbing paste into cuts. Cover; refrigerate overnight.

3 Cook chicken, covered, on heated oiled grill plate (or grill or barbecue), 5 minutes. Uncover; cook, turning occasionally, about 20 minutes or until cooked. Serve with lime wedges.

coriander and chilli paste
Blend or process ingredients until mixture forms a smooth paste.

nutritional count per serving
29.5g total fat (7.8g saturated fat); 2094kJ (501 cal); 5.2g carbohydrate; 53.5g protein; 1.7g fibre

tip To get more juice from a lime, place the lime in a microwave oven for about 30 seconds or until warm.

PAD THAI

prep + cook time 40 minutes (+ standing) ~ serves 4

Preserved turnip is also called hua chai po or cu cai muoi, or dried radish because of its similarity to daikon. Sold packaged whole or sliced, it is very salty and must be rinsed and dried before use.

40g (1½ ounces) tamarind pulp
½ cup (125ml) boiling water
2 tablespoons grated palm sugar
⅓ cup (80ml) sweet chilli sauce
⅓ cup (80ml) fish sauce
375g (12 ounces) rice stick noodles
12 uncooked medium prawns (shrimp) (500g)
2 cloves garlic, crushed
2 fresh small red thai (serrano) chillies, chopped coarsely
2 tablespoons finely chopped preserved turnip
2 tablespoons dried shrimp
1 tablespoon grated fresh ginger
1 tablespoon peanut oil
250g (8 ounces) minced (ground) pork
3 eggs, beaten lightly
2 cups (160g) bean sprouts
4 green onions (scallions), sliced thinly
⅓ cup coarsely chopped fresh coriander (cilantro)
¼ cup (35g) coarsely chopped roasted unsalted peanuts
1 lime, cut into wedges

1 Soak tamarind pulp in the boiling water 30 minutes. Pour tamarind into fine strainer over small bowl; push as much tamarind pulp through strainer as possible, scraping underside of strainer occasionally. Discard any tamarind solids left in strainer; reserve pulp liquid in bowl. Stir sugar and sauces into bowl of pulp liquid.

2 Meanwhile, place noodles in large heatproof bowl; cover with boiling water. Stand until just tender; drain.

3 Shell and devein prawns, leaving tails intact.

4 Blend or process garlic, chilli, turnip, shrimp and ginger until mixture forms a paste.

5 Heat oil in wok; stir-fry garlic paste until fragrant. Add pork; stir-fry until just cooked through. Add prawns; stir-fry 1 minute. Add egg; stir-fry until egg just sets. Add noodles, tamarind mixture, sprouts and half the onion; stir-fry, tossing gently until combined. Remove from heat, add remaining onion with coriander and nuts; toss gently until combined. Serve with lime wedges.

nutritional count per serving
19.7g total fat (4.5g saturated fat); 2608kJ (624 cal); 65.6g carbohydrate; 42.6g protein; 5.4g fibre

Place soaked tamarind pulp in a fine strainer over a bowl and push as much pulp as possible through the strainer by pressing down with the back of a spoon.

Place preserved turnip, flat-side down, on a clean chopping board and, using a sharp knife, cut into slices. Chop slices into very small pieces.

Place turnip, garlic, dried shrimp and chilli in a mortar (bowl), grinding each ingredient with a pestle before adding the next one, to make a paste. Or process the ingredients using a hand blender or food processor.

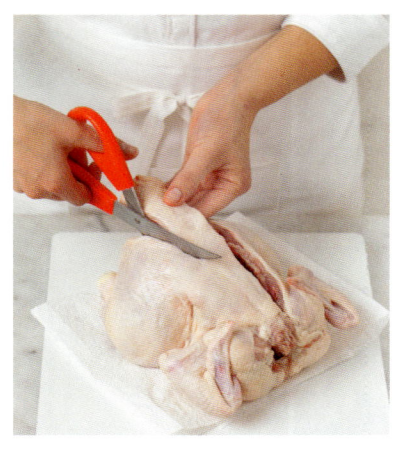

Using kitchen scissors, cut along both sides of the chicken backbone, then discard the backbone.

Turn chicken over, then flatten out by pressing down on the breastbone. Sprinkle half the spice mixture over the chicken, rubbing all over the skin.

Add turmeric, saffron and remaining spice mixture into the softened onion mixture.

CHICKEN TAGINE WITH OLIVES AND LEMON

prep + cook time 2 hours ~ serves 6

2kg (4-pound) whole chicken
2 teaspoons each ground coriander, ginger and cumin
1 tablespoon olive oil
1 large brown onion (200g), sliced thickly
3 cloves garlic, crushed
¼ teaspoon ground turmeric
pinch saffron threads
1 cup (250ml) water
1 cup (250ml) chicken stock
625g (1¼ pounds) baby new potatoes, halved
375g (12 ounces) jap pumpkin, cut into wedges
1 cup (120g) seeded green olives
2 tablespoons thinly sliced preserved lemon rind
2 tablespoons lemon juice
½ cup coarsely chopped fresh flat-leaf parsley
¼ cup coarsely chopped fresh coriander (cilantro)

1 Rinse chicken under cold water; pat dry inside and out with absorbent paper. Using kitchen scissors, cut along both sides of backbone; discard backbone. Press down on breastbone to flatten out chicken. Combine ground coriander, ginger and cumin in small bowl; rub half the spice mixture all over chicken.

2 Preheat oven to 220°C/425°F.

3 Heat oil in tagine or flameproof casserole dish on stove top; cook chicken until browned all over. Remove from tagine. Reserve 1 tablespoon pan drippings; discard remainder.

4 Heat reserved pan drippings in same tagine; cook onion and garlic, stirring, until soft. Add turmeric, saffron and remaining spice mixture; cook, stirring, about 1 minute or until fragrant.

5 Halve potatoes; cut unpeeled pumpkin into wedges. Add the water, stock, potatoes and pumpkin; top with chicken. Bring to the boil.

6 Cover tagine, transfer to oven; cook about 1¼ hours or until chicken is cooked.

7 Stir olives, preserved lemon and juice into sauce; season to taste. Serve tagine sprinkled with herbs.

nutritional count per serving
34.5g total fat (9.6g saturated fat); 2316kJ (554 cal); 20.1g carbohydrate; 38.4g protein; 4.4g fibre

tip You can soak the saffron in 1 tablespoon boiling water before adding to the tagine. This helps to release the flavour.

serving suggestion Serve tagine with couscous.

CRISP-SKINNED PORK BELLY WITH BRAISED GREEN LENTILS

prep + cook time 3 hours ~ serves 6

2kg (4-pound) pork belly, rind on, bones in
1 tablespoon olive oil
1 tablespoon fine table salt
2 bulbs garlic, halved horizontally
2 large brown onions (600g), unpeeled, sliced thickly
2 large carrots (360g), quartered
2 sprigs fresh thyme
2 fresh bay leaves
1 cup (250ml) dry white wine
⅓ cup (80ml) sherry vinegar
2 cups (500ml) salt-reduced chicken stock, approximately
1 teaspoon finely chopped fresh tarragon

braised green lentils
2 tablespoons olive oil
1 medium brown onion (150g), chopped finely
2 cloves garlic, crushed
2 cups (400g) french-style green lentils
1 teaspoon fresh thyme leaves
1 litre (4 cups) salt-reduced chicken stock
¼ cup coarsely chopped fresh flat-leaf parsley

1 Preheat oven to 220°C/425°F.

2 Using a sharp knife, score pork rind at 2cm (¾-inch) intervals. Place pork on wire rack over large shallow baking dish, rind side-up; rub oil and salt over rind. Roast, uncovered, about 35 minutes or until rind begins to blister.

3 Reduce oven to 180°C/350°F.

4 Remove pork and rack from dish; discard fat from dish. Add garlic, onion, carrot, thyme and bay leaves to dish; pour in wine and vinegar. Place pork, rind-side up, on top of vegetables. Pour enough stock into the dish to come halfway up side of pork (do not allow liquid to touch pork rind). Cover dish tightly with foil; roast about 1½ hours or until pork is cooked through.

5 Meanwhile, make braised green lentils.

6 Remove dish from oven; increase oven to 220°C/425°F. Remove pork from dish. Strain pan juices through muslin-lined sieve into heatproof jug; discard solids. Pour strained juices into medium saucepan. Return pork to dish; roast, uncovered, about 15 minutes or until rind is crisp.

7 Meanwhile, bring pan juices to the boil. Reduce heat; simmer, uncovered, skimming fat from surface, until juices are reduced by half. Stir in tarragon.

8 Cut pork into six pieces; serve with lentils and pan juices.

braised green lentils
Heat oil in large frying pan; cook onion and garlic, stirring, until onion softens. Add lentils, thyme and stock; bring to the boil. Reduce heat; simmer, uncovered, about 25 minutes or until lentils are tender. Stir in parsley; season to taste. Cover to keep warm.

nutritional count per serving
27.2g total fat (7.3g saturated fat); 3202kJ (1766 cal); 37.1g carbohydrate; 81.5g protein; 13.9g fibre

for steps, see pages 142 & 143

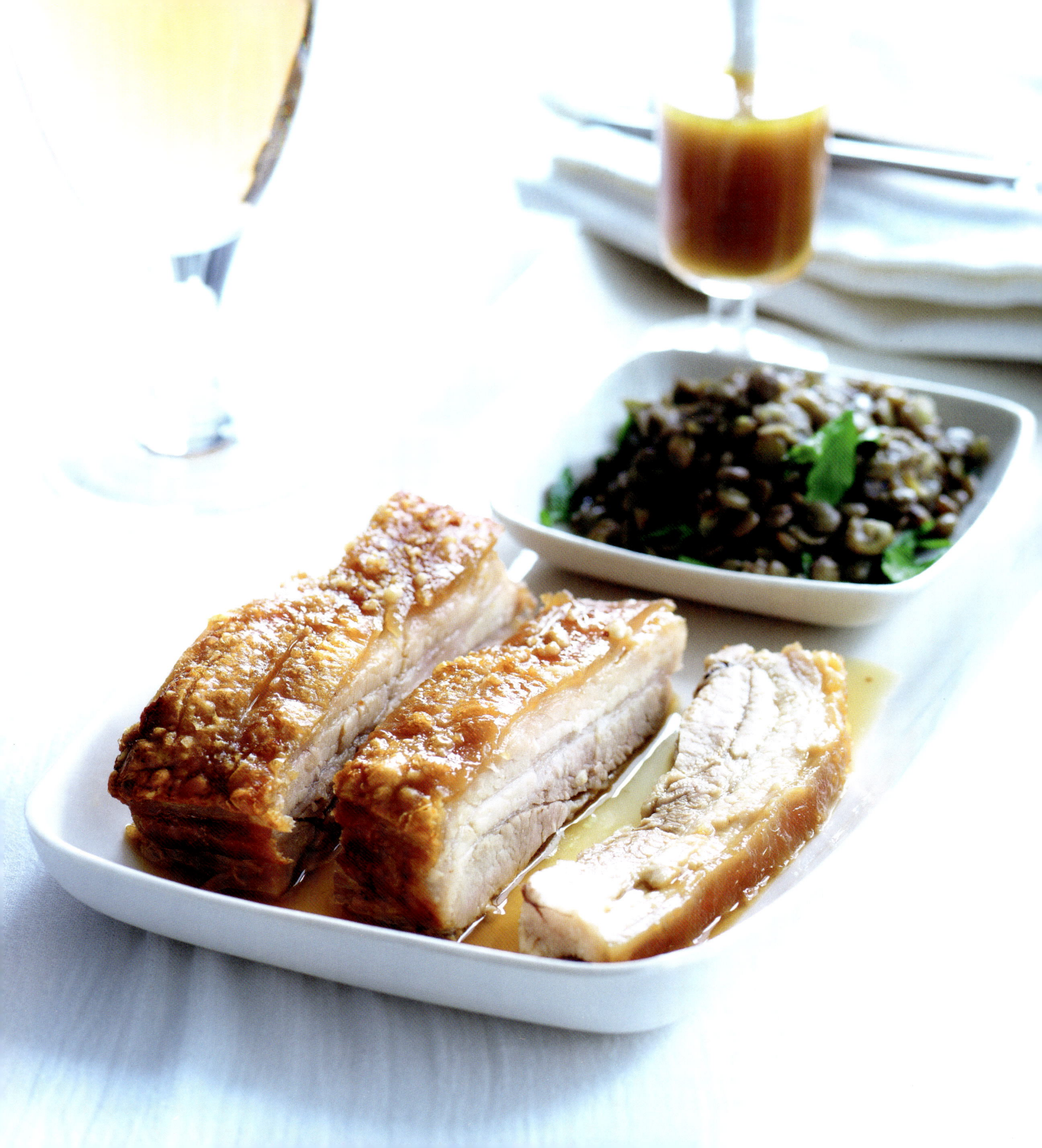

CRISP-SKINNED PORK BELLY WITH BRAISED GREEN LENTILS

Using a sharp knife, score the pork rind, without cutting all the way through, at 2cm (¾-inch) intervals.

Roast the pork, uncovered, until the rind is starting to blister. Remove the pork from the baking dish.

Place the garlic, onion, carrot, thyme and bay leaves in the same baking dish. Place the pork on top of the vegetables; pour stock into the dish to come halfway up the side of the pork (don't let the liquid touch the rind – it will stop the rind from crackling).

Strain the pan juices through a muslin-lined sieve into a heatproof jug; discard the solids. Pour the strained juices into a medium saucepan.

Bring pan juices to the boil, then reduce the heat and simmer, skimming the fat off the surface.

Return the pork to the oven and roast until the rind is crackled.

Cut the pork fillets into thin slices.

Stir-fry the pork, in batches, until browned all over. Remove pork from the wok.

Add peaches to cooked capsicum and pork mixture, tossing gently until peaches are heated through.

PORK WITH SWEET AND SOUR PEACHES

prep + cook time 30 minutes ~ serves 4

Sweet and sour are two flavours considered essential by the Chinese for a well-balanced meal. You can marry sweet and sour sauce with anything from beef to seafood.

800g (1½ pounds) pork fillets, sliced thinly
2 tablespoons cornflour (cornstarch)
2 tablespoons peanut oil
1 medium red onion (170g), chopped coarsely
1 medium red capsicum (bell pepper) (200g), cut into thin strips
1 medium yellow capsicum (bell pepper) (200g), cut into thin strips
⅓ cup (80ml) water
2 cloves garlic, crushed
2 tablespoons white (granulated) sugar
2 tablespoons white wine vinegar
2 tablespoons tomato sauce
2 tablespoons light soy sauce
2 large peaches (440g), cut into wedges
⅓ cup coarsely chopped fresh coriander (cilantro)

1 Combine pork and cornflour in medium bowl.

2 Heat half the oil in wok; stir-fry pork, in batches, until browned. Remove from wok.

3 Heat remaining oil in same wok; stir-fry onion and capsicums until tender.

4 Return pork to wok with the water, garlic, sugar, vinegar and sauces; stir-fry until pork is cooked. Add peach; stir-fry until hot. Remove from heat; add coriander, toss to combine.

nutritional count per serving
25.4g total fat (7.1g saturated fat); 2203kJ (527 cal); 26.9g carbohydrate; 45.9g protein; 3g fibre

CURRIED FRIED RICE WITH PORK AND PRAWNS

prep + cook time 45 minutes ~ serves 4

800g (1½ pounds) pork leg steaks, sliced thinly
1 tablespoon white (granulated) sugar
2 tablespoons light soy sauce
125g (4 ounces) uncooked small prawns (shrimp)
2 tablespoons peanut oil
2 eggs, beaten lightly
1 teaspoon curry powder
2 cloves garlic, crushed
2 cups cold cooked white long-grain rice
4 green onions (scallions), sliced thinly
2 cups (240g) frozen peas and corn

1 Combine pork, sugar and half the sauce in medium bowl.

2 Shell and devein prawns, leaving tails intact.

3 Heat 1 teaspoon of the oil in wok; cook egg, over medium heat, tilting wok, until almost set. Remove omelette from wok; roll tightly, slice thinly.

4 Heat 2 teaspoons of the remaining oil in wok; stir-fry pork mixture, in batches, until cooked as desired. Remove from wok.

5 Heat 1 teaspoon of remaining oil in wok; stir-fry prawns until just changed in colour. Remove from wok.

6 Heat remaining oil in wok; cook curry powder and garlic, stirring, until fragrant. Add rice, onion, peas and corn, and remaining sauce; stir-fry until vegetables are just tender.

7 Return pork, prawns and half the omelette to wok; stir-fry until heated through. Serve sprinkled with remaining omelette.

nutritional count per serving
18.1g total fat (4.3g saturated fat); 2337kJ (559 cal); 38g carbohydrate; 57.5g protein; 4.9g fibre

tips Packages of mixed frozen peas and corn are found in most supermarkets.

You need to cook approximately ⅔ cup of rice for this recipe.

Pour the egg into a heated oiled wok, tilting the wok until the omelette is almost set. Remove from wok; roll tightly, then slice thinly.

Stir-fry the cooked rice, onion, peas and corn, and remaining sauce into the curry powder mixture until vegetables are just tender.

Return pork to wok with prawns and half the omelette, then stir-fry until heated through.

Place the pork, fat-side down, on a chopping board. Slice through the thickest part of the pork horizontally, without cutting all the way through to the other side.

Open out the pork to form one large piece, then press the stuffing mixture against the loin along the width of the pork.

Roll the pork to completely enclose the stuffing, then secure the roll with kitchen string at 2cm intervals.

PORK LOIN WITH SPINACH AND PANCETTA STUFFING

prep + cook time 2 hours ~ serves 8

4 slices white bread (120g)
2 tablespoons olive oil
1 medium brown onion (150g), chopped coarsely
1 clove garlic, crushed
6 slices pancetta (90g), chopped coarsely
100g (3 ounces) baby spinach leaves
¼ cup (35g) roasted macadamias, chopped coarsely
½ cup (125ml) chicken stock
2kg (4-pound) boneless loin of pork, rind on

plum and red wine sauce
1½ cups (480g) plum jam
2 tablespoons dry red wine
⅔ cup (160ml) chicken stock

1 Preheat oven to 200°C/400°F.

2 Discard bread crusts; cut bread into 1cm (½-inch) cubes. Heat half the oil in large frying pan; cook bread, stirring, until browned. Drain croûtons on absorbent paper.

3 Heat remaining oil in same pan; cook onion, garlic and pancetta until onion browns lightly. Stir in spinach; remove from heat. Stir in nuts, stock and croûtons.

4 Place pork on board, fat-side down; slice through thickest part of pork horizontally, without cutting through other side. Open out pork to form one large piece; press stuffing mixture against loin along width of pork. Roll pork to enclose stuffing, securing with kitchen string at 2cm (¾-inch) intervals.

5 Place pork on wire rack in large shallow baking dish. Roast, uncovered, 1¼ hours or until cooked through.

6 Meanwhile, make plum and red wine sauce.

7 Serve sliced pork with sauce.

plum and red wine sauce
Bring ingredients in small saucepan to the boil. Reduce heat; simmer, uncovered, about 10 minutes or until sauce thickens slightly.

nutritional count per serving
30g total fat (8.6g saturated fat); 2934kJ (702 cal); 47.9g carbohydrate; 57.9g protein; 2.1g fibre

tip When you order the pork loin, ask the butcher to leave a flap measuring about 20cm (8 inches) in length with rind removed, to help make rolling the stuffed loin easier.

serving suggestion Serve with steamed asparagus spears.

BEEF RIB EYE FOR TWO

prep + cook time 1 hour (+ refrigeration & standing) ~ serves 2

2 x 500g (1-pound) rib-eye beef steaks, bone-in
1 tablespoon olive oil

anchovy butter
75g (2½ ounces) softened butter
2 anchovy fillets, drained
½ garlic clove, crushed
1 tablespoon each finely chopped fresh chives and fresh flat-leaf parsley

sautéed mushrooms
2 tablespoons vegetable oil
1 large flat brown mushroom (100g), sliced thinly, lengthways
100g (3 ounces) swiss brown mushrooms, sliced thinly
100g (3 ounces) shiitake mushrooms, sliced thickly
100g (3 ounces) oyster mushrooms, torn in half
1 tablespoon olive oil
2 shallots (50g), sliced thinly
1 clove garlic, sliced thinly
1 tablespoon red wine vinegar
2 tablespoons coarsely chopped fresh flat-leaf parsley

1 Preheat oven to 200°C/400°F.

2 Make anchovy butter.

3 Rub beef with oil, season. Heat oiled medium ovenproof frying pan over high heat; cook beef until browned both sides. Transfer to oven; roast, uncovered, 15 minutes. Reduce oven to 180°C/350°F; roast a further 15 minutes. Cover beef, bone-side down, loosely with foil; stand 15 minutes.

4 Meanwhile, make sautéed mushrooms.

5 Serve beef with sautéed mushrooms and slices of anchovy butter.

anchovy butter
Combine ingredients in medium bowl. Shape butter mixture into a log on large piece of plastic wrap. Roll to enclose; twist ends to secure. Refrigerate 30 minutes.

sautéed mushrooms
Heat vegetable oil in large frying pan; cook mushrooms, in two batches, over high heat until softened. Remove from pan. Heat olive oil in same pan; cook shallots and garlic until shallots are soft. Return mushrooms to pan, stirring, until heated. Remove from heat, stir in vinegar and parsley. Season to taste.

nutritional count per serving
90.8g total fat (35.1g saturated fat); 4891kJ (1170 cal); 3.6g carbohydrate; 83.1g protein; 8.1g fibre

tip If your pan doesn't have an ovenproof handle, cover the handle well with several layers of foil.

serving suggestion Serve with steamed green beans.

for steps, see pages 152 & 153

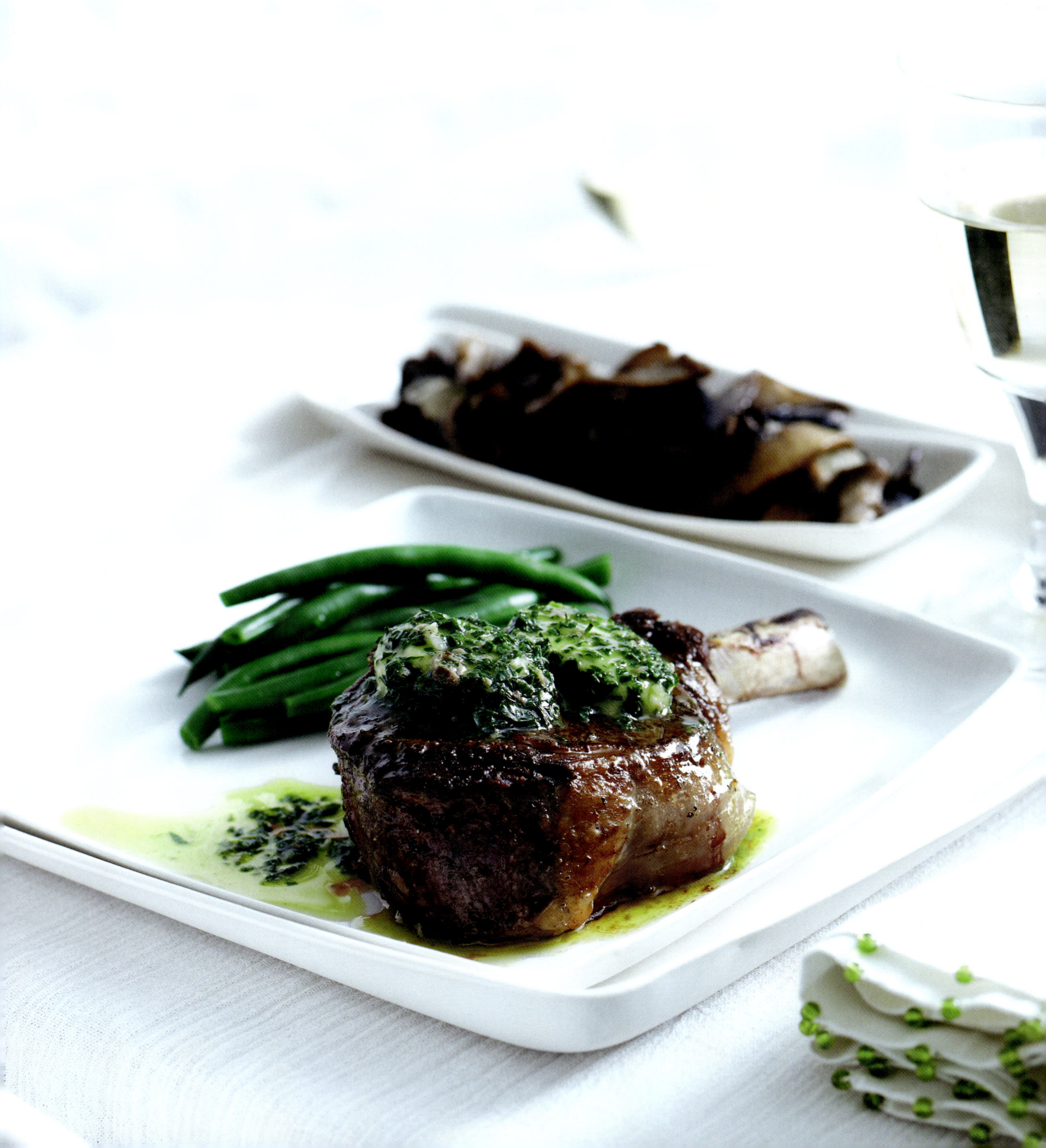

BEEF RIB EYE FOR TWO

Mould the anchovy butter mixture into a log shape on a large piece of plastic wrap. Roll up the butter log to enclose, then twist both ends to secure.

Rub rib-eye steaks with the olive oil, then season with salt and freshly ground black pepper.

Cook beef in a heated oiled ovenproof frying pan until browned both sides.

Place flat mushrooms, stem-side down, on a chopping board, then slice thinly.

Thinly slice the swiss brown mushrooms and thickly slice the shiitake mushrooms. Roughly tear the oyster mushrooms in half.

Cook all the mushrooms in a large heated oiled frying pan, in two batches, over high heat until softened. Remove mushrooms from pan.

Line the base and sides of the loaf pan with prosciutto, overlapping the slices and allowing them to overhang the sides of the pan.

Spoon two-thirds of the beef mixture into the prosciutto-lined pan, pressing the mixture into the sides and corners. Spread the onion mixture over the beef mixture.

Cover onion mixture with the remaining beef mixture, pressing down and smoothing the surface. Fold prosciutto slices over to completely cover the beef mixture.

CARAMELISED ONION AND PROSCIUTTO GLAZED MEATLOAF

prep + cook time 2 hours (+ cooling) ~ serves 6

1 tablespoon olive oil
2 large brown onions (400g), sliced thinly
¼ cup (55g) light brown sugar
¼ cup (60ml) cider vinegar
12 slices prosciutto (180g)
1kg (2 pounds) minced (ground) beef
1 clove garlic, crushed
1 cup (70g) stale breadcrumbs
1 egg, beaten lightly
2 tablespoons tomato paste
2 tablespoons tomato sauce
2 tablespoons barbecue sauce
1 tablespoon wholegrain mustard
1 tablespoon light brown sugar, extra

1 Heat oil in large frying pan; cook onion, stirring, about 5 minutes or until softened and browned lightly. Add sugar and vinegar; cook, stirring, about 15 minutes or until onion is caramelised. Cool.

2 Preheat oven to 200°C/400°F. Oil 14cm x 21cm (5½-inch x 8½-inch) loaf pan; line base and long sides of pan with prosciutto slices, extending 7cm (2¾ inches) over long sides of pan.

3 Combine beef, garlic, breadcrumbs, egg and paste in large bowl. Press two-thirds of the beef mixture into pan; top with onion mixture, cover with remaining beef mixture. Fold prosciutto slices over to cover beef mixture.

4 Bake meatloaf, covered, 40 minutes; remove from oven. Drain excess juices from pan. Turn pan upside-down onto foil-lined oven tray; remove pan.

5 Combine sauces, mustard and extra sugar in small bowl. Brush loaf with sauce mixture; bake, uncovered, basting occasionally with sauce mixture, for further 20 minutes or until cooked through. Stand meatloaf 10 minutes; slice thickly to serve.

nutritional count per serving
17.8g total fat (6.2g saturated fat); 1898kJ (454 cal); 28.6g carbohydrate; 43.5g protein; 2.1g fibre

ROAST BEEF WITH YORKSHIRE PUDDINGS

prep + cook time 2 hours 35 minutes (+ refrigeration & standing) ~ serves 8

This dish is the most traditional British roast and probably the most famous of all British food. While the beef is resting, make the yorkshire puddings and gravy.

2kg (4-pound) corner piece beef topside roast
1 medium brown onion (150g), chopped coarsely
2 cups (500ml) dry red wine
¼ cup (70g) wholegrain mustard
4 cloves garlic, sliced
6 black peppercorns
2 bay leaves
4 sprigs fresh thyme
2 medium carrots (240g), chopped coarsely
1 large leek (500g), chopped coarsely
2 sticks celery (300g), chopped coarsely
2 tablespoons olive oil

yorkshire puddings
1 cup (150g) plain (all-purpose) flour
2 eggs
½ cup (125ml) milk
½ cup (125ml) water

gravy
2 tablespoons plain (all-purpose) flour
1½ cups (375ml) beef stock, approximately

1 Place beef in large shallow dish with onion, wine, mustard, garlic, peppercorns, bay leaves and thyme. Cover; refrigerate 3 hours or overnight.

2 Preheat oven to 180°C/350°F.

3 Drain beef over medium bowl; reserve 1 cup marinade. Combine carrot, leek and celery in large baking dish, top with beef; brush beef with oil.

4 Roast beef, uncovered, about 1½ hours. Remove beef from dish, wrap in foil; stand 20 minutes before serving.

5 Increase oven to 220°C/425°F.

6 Remove vegetables from dish with slotted spoon; discard vegetables. Pour pan juices into jug; stand 2 minutes. Reserve ⅓ cup (80ml) of the oil from the surface for yorkshire puddings and the gravy. Spoon out and discard remaining oil. Reserve pan juices for the gravy.

7 Make yorkshire puddings then gravy.

8 Serve beef with puddings and gravy.

yorkshire puddings
Sift flour into medium bowl; whisk in combined eggs, milk and water at once until smooth. Stand batter 30 minutes. Spoon half the reserved oil into eight holes of 12-hole (⅓-cup/80ml) muffin pan; heat in oven 2 minutes. Divide batter into pan holes. Bake 20 minutes or until puffed and golden.

gravy
Add remaining reserved oil to baking dish. Stir in flour until smooth; cook, over medium heat, stirring constantly until mixture bubbles. Gradually pour in reserved marinade, pan juices and half the stock, stirring constantly over heat until gravy boils and thickens. Add more stock for the consistency you like.

nutritional count per serving
15.4g total fat (4.8g saturated fat); 2169kJ (519 cal); 21.1g carbohydrate; 61.2g protein; 4g fibre

tip For light fluffy puddings the batter must be well rested and cold, and the oven and reserved oil are both very hot.

serving suggestion Serve with baked potatoes and vegetables.

for steps, see pages 158 & 159

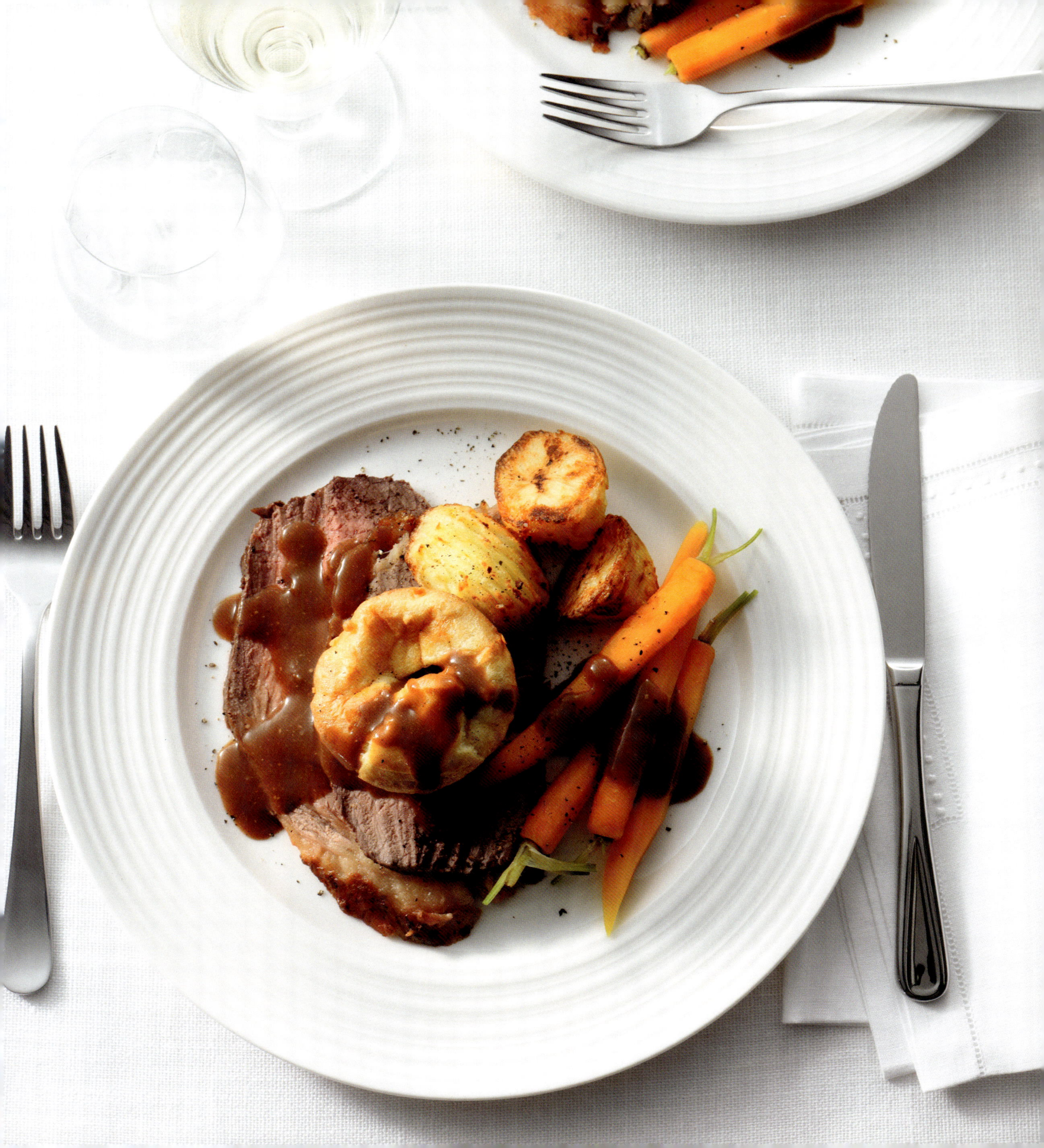

ROAST BEEF WITH YORKSHIRE PUDDINGS

Place the beef in a large baking dish with the onion, wine, mustard, garlic, peppercorns, bay leaves and thyme. Cover and refrigerate 3 hours or overnight.

Drain the beef and discard the herb mixture. Reserve 1 cup of the marinade to use in the gravy. Place the beef on a bed of vegetables and roast for about 1½ hours.

Pour the pan juices into a jug – the oil will rise to the surface. Remove 2 tablespoons of this oil for cooking the yorkshire puddings and another 2 tablespoons for making the gravy. Spoon out and discard the remaining oil. Remove pan juices for the gravy.

While the roast is cooking, mix the batter for the yorkshire puddings and leave to stand for 30 minutes.

Divide one batch of the reserved oil between the muffin pan holes; heat the pan in the oven until the oil is hot. Carefully remove the pan from the oven, then pour in the yorkshire pudding batter. Return the pan to the hot oven quickly so the puddings will start to cook right away.

To make the gravy, add the remaining reserved oil to the baking dish. Stir in the flour until smooth; cook over medium heat, stirring constantly until the mixture bubbles. Gradually pour in the reserved marinade, pan juices and half the stock; stir constantly over the heat until the gravy boils and thickens. Add more stock to make the gravy the consistency you like.

middles ~ 159 ~ middles

ROAST BEEF WITH MUSTARD BEARNAISE

prep + cook time 1 hour 45 minutes (+ standing) ~ serves 6

2kg (4-pound) standing rib of beef (bone in rib or baron of beef)
1 tablespoon olive oil
sea salt flakes

mustard béarnaise
1 small shallot (25g), chopped finely
1 tablespoon coarsely chopped fresh tarragon
1 teaspoon whole black peppercorns
1½ tablespoons white wine vinegar
2 egg yolks
200g (6½ ounces) unsalted butter, melted
1 tablespoon wholegrain mustard
1 tablespoon finely chopped fresh tarragon, extra

1 Preheat oven to 220°C/425°F.

2 Tie beef with kitchen string at 2cm (¾-inch) intervals. Place beef in large roasting dish, brush beef with oil; sprinkle with salt.

3 Roast beef 15 minutes; reduce oven to 180°C/350°F. Roast, uncovered, about 1 hour for medium rare or until beef is cooked as desired. Cover beef with foil; stand 20 minutes.

4 Meanwhile, make mustard béarnaise.

5 Serve beef with béarnaise.

mustard béarnaise
Bring shallot, tarragon, peppercorns and vinegar to the boil in small saucepan. Reduce heat; simmer, uncovered, until reduced by half. Strain into medium heatproof bowl; discard solids. Place the bowl over medium saucepan of simmering water (ensuring base of the bowl does not touch the water), add egg yolks; whisk vigorously until egg yolks are frothy. Slowly whisk in melted butter until mixture thickens. Stir in mustard and extra tarragon.

nutritional count per serving
48.6g total fat (26g saturated fat); 2450kJ (586 cal); 0.6g carbohydrate; 37.8g protein; 0.2g fibre

tip If the sauce is too thick or starts to separate, whisk in 1-2 tablespoons hot water until smooth and creamy.

serving suggestion Serve with roasted potatoes.

Tie beef with kitchen string at 2cm intervals.

Pour the vinegar mixture for the mustard béarnaise through a strainer into a medium heatproof bowl; discard the solids.

Place the bowl of strained vinegar mixture over a medium saucepan of simmering water; vigorously whisk in the egg yolks until frothy. Slowly pour in the melted butter, whisking constantly, until the mixture thickens.

Cook beef cheeks in flameproof dish over heat, in batches, until browned all over. Remove from dish.

Place beef cheeks on top of onion, carrot, tomato, fennel and herb mixture. Cook, covered, in oven for 2 hours.

Gradually pour the polenta into boiling milk mixture, stirring constantly. Reduce heat; simmer, stirring, about 10 minutes or until polenta thickens.

BRAISED BEEF CHEEKS IN RED WINE

prep + cook time 3 hours 30 minutes ~ serves 6

1.8kg (3½ pounds) beef cheeks
2 tablespoons olive oil
1 large brown onion (250g), chopped coarsely
2 medium carrot (240g), chopped coarsely
3 cups (750ml) dry red wine
¼ cup (60ml) red wine vinegar
2 x 400g (12½ ounces) canned whole tomatoes
1 tablespoon light brown sugar
1 large fennel bulb (550g), trimmed, cut into thin wedges
6 black peppercorns
2 sprigs fresh rosemary
2 tablespoons fresh oregano leaves
400g (12½ ounces) spring onions, halved
250g (8 ounces) swiss brown mushrooms

cheesy polenta
2½ cups (625ml) water
2½ cups (625ml) milk
1¼ cup (210g) polenta
½ cup (50g) finely grated parmesan cheese
40g (1½ ounces) butter

1 Preheat oven to 160°C/325°F.

2 Trim beef. Heat half the oil in large flameproof casserole dish; cook beef, over heat, in batches, until browned all over. Remove from dish.

3 Heat remaining oil in same dish; cook brown onion and carrot, stirring, until onion softens. Add wine, vinegar, undrained tomatoes, sugar, fennel, peppercorns, rosemary and oregano, then return beef; bring to the boil. Cover; cook in oven 2 hours.

4 Stir in spring onion and mushrooms; cook 45 minutes or until beef is tender.

5 Meanwhile, make cheesy polenta.

6 Serve beef with cheesy polenta and, if you like, sprinkle with extra rosemary leaves.

cheesy polenta
Bring the water and milk to the boil in large saucepan. Gradually add polenta, stirring constantly. Reduce heat; simmer, stirring, about 10 minutes or until polenta thickens. Stir in cheese and butter.

nutritional count per serving
43.3g total fat (19.2g saturated fat); 4041kJ (996 cal); 46.4g carbohydrate; 76.8g protein; 7.6g fibre

tip Polenta tends to thicken on standing, so serve immediately after cooking.

PEPPERED FILLET STEAKS WITH CREAMY BOURBON SAUCE

prep + cook time 20 minutes ~ serves 4

This bistro-style meal is robust, simple and perfect for casual dining.

4 x 125g (4 ounces) beef fillet steaks
2 teaspoons cracked black pepper
2 tablespoons olive oil
6 shallots (150g), sliced thinly
1 clove garlic, crushed
⅓ cup (80ml) bourbon
¼ cup (60ml) beef stock
2 teaspoons dijon mustard
1¼ cups (310ml) pouring cream

1 Rub beef both sides with pepper. Heat half the oil in large frying pan; cook beef, both sides, until cooked as desired. Remove from pan; cover to keep warm.

2 Heat remaining oil in same pan; cook shallot and garlic, stirring, until shallot softens. Add bourbon; stir until mixture simmers and starts to thicken. Stir in remaining ingredients; bring to the boil. Reduce heat; simmer, uncovered, about 5 minutes or until sauce thickens slightly.

3 Place beef on serving plates, drizzle with sauce.

nutritional count per serving
49.3g total fat (25.9g saturated fat); 2742kJ (656 cal); 13.2g carbohydrate; 28.7g protein; 0.7g fibre

tip You can use just one 300ml carton cream for this recipe.

serving suggestion Serve with fried potatoes and steamed green beans.

Cook peppered beef in heated oiled frying pan, in batches, on both sides, until cooked to your liking.

Pour bourbon into softened shallot mixture, stirring, until the mixture simmers and starts to thicken.

Stir in stock, mustard and cream and bring to the boil; reduce heat and simmer until sauce thickens slightly.

Cook veal pieces, in batches, until browned all over. Remove from pan.

Add flour, seeds and paprika to cooked onion and capsicum mixture; cook, stirring, 2 minutes.

Spoon mash potato all over top of goulash; sprinkle top with cheese, then place under hot grill until browned.

VEAL GOULASH AND POTATO PIES

prep + cook time 2 hours 25 minutes ~ serves 6

1kg (2 pounds) boneless veal shoulder
¼ cup (60ml) olive oil
1 large brown onion (200g), chopped coarsely
1 clove garlic, crushed
1 large red capsicum (bell pepper) (350g), chopped coarsely
1 tablespoon plain (all-purpose) flour
2 teaspoons hot paprika
2 teaspoons sweet paprika
2 teaspoons caraway seeds
2 cups (500ml) beef stock
400g (12½ ounces) canned diced tomatoes
1 tablespoon tomato paste
4 medium potatoes (800g), chopped coarsely
1 cup (120g) coarsely grated cheddar cheese

1 Cut veal into 2cm (¾-inch) pieces. Heat 1 tablespoon of the oil in large saucepan; cook veal, in batches, until browned. Remove from pan.

2 Heat remaining oil in same pan; cook onion, garlic and capsicum, stirring, until onion softens. Add flour, paprika and seeds; cook, stirring, 2 minutes.

3 Return veal to pan with stock, undrained tomatoes and paste; bring to the boil. Reduce heat; simmer, covered, 1 hour. Uncover; simmer about 30 minutes or until veal is tender and sauce thickens slightly.

4 Meanwhile, boil, steam or microwave potato until tender; drain. Mash potato in medium bowl until smooth.

5 Preheat grill (broiler).

6 Divide veal goulash among six oiled 1¼-cup (310ml) ovenproof dishes; top with potato, sprinkle with cheese. Place under grill until browned.

nutritional count per serving
20.6g total fat (6.8g saturated fat); 2011kJ (481 cal); 23g carbohydrate; 48.8g protein; 3.9g fibre

serving suggestion Serve with a green leaf salad.

OSSO BUCO

prep + cook time 2 hours 45 minutes ~ serves 6

Veal osso buco, Italian for "bone with a hole", is another name that butchers use for veal shin, usually cut into 3cm (1¼-inch) to 5cm (2-inch) thick slices.

2kg (4 pounds) veal osso buco
½ cup (75g) plain (all-purpose) flour
2 tablespoons olive oil
100g (3-ounce) piece pancetta, chopped finely
1 medium brown onion (150g), chopped finely
2 cloves garlic, crushed
2 sticks celery (300g), chopped finely
2 medium carrots (240g), chopped finely
2 tablespoons tomato paste
700g (1½ pounds) bottled tomato pasta sauce
1½ cups (375ml) chicken stock
½ cup (125ml) dry white wine
4 sprigs fresh lemon thyme
2 bay leaves
2 tablespoons coarsely chopped fresh basil

1 Coat veal in flour; shake off excess. Heat oil in large deep saucepan; cook veal, in batches, until browned. Remove from pan.

2 Add pancetta, onion, garlic, celery and carrot to same pan; cook, stirring, until onion softens.

3 Add paste; cook, stirring, 1 minute. Add pasta sauce, stock, wine, thyme and bay leaves; cook, stirring 1 minute.

4 Return veal to pan, standing pieces upright and pushing into sauce mixture; bring to the boil. Reduce heat; simmer, covered, 1½ hours. Uncover; simmer about 30 minutes or until veal is almost falling off the bone.

5 Discard thyme and bay leaves. Serve osso buco sprinkled with basil.

nutritional count per serving
8.6g total fat (1.6g saturated fat); 1701kJ (407 cal); 21.2g carbohydrate; 54.5g protein; 5.4g fibre

Coat each piece of veal in flour, then shake off the excess.

Pour tomato pasta sauce into the onion and pancetta mixture, then add the stock, wine, thyme and bay leaves; cook for 1 minute.

Return veal to the pan, standing the pieces upright and pushing them gently into the sauce mixture.

Cover noodles with boiling water in heatproof bowl, separating with a fork. Drain noodles.

Stir-fry the beef in hot wok until browned, breaking up the lumps with a wooden spoon.

Cut the tomatoes in half; scoop the seeds out with a spoon.

UDON NOODLES WITH BEEF AND TOMATO

prep + cook time 25 minutes ~ serves 4

800g (1½ pounds) fresh udon noodles
2 tablespoons peanut oil
600g (1¼ pounds) minced (ground) beef
2 tablespoons chinese cooking wine (shao hsing)
4cm (1½-inch) piece fresh ginger (20g), grated finely
2 cloves garlic, crushed
4 green onions (scallions), sliced thinly
⅓ cup (80ml) hoisin sauce
1 tablespoon japanese soy sauce
1 tablespoon tomato paste
1½ cups (325ml) chicken stock
2 large tomatoes (440g)
½ cup loosely packed fresh coriander leaves (cilantro)

1 Place noodles in large heatproof bowl, cover with boiling water; separate with fork, drain.

2 Heat half the oil in wok; stir-fry beef until browned. Add cooking wine; stir-fry until liquid has evaporated. Remove from wok.

3 Heat remaining oil in wok; stir-fry ginger, garlic and onion until fragrant. Return beef to wok with sauces, paste and stock; bring to the boil. Simmer, stirring occasionally, until sauce thickens slightly.

4 Meanwhile, cut tomatoes in half; remove seeds and thinly slice flesh.

5 Add noodles and tomato to wok; stir-fry until hot, season to taste. Serve noodles sprinkled with coriander.

nutritional count per serving
21.7g total fat (6.3g saturated fat); 2583kJ (618 cal); 59.9g carbohydrate; 40.8g protein; 6.9g fibre

tip Place coriander leaves in a bowl of iced water, this will stop them from wilting.

VEAL AND FENNEL ROLLS WITH HORSERADISH MASH

prep + cook time 1 hour 10 minutes ~ serves 4

2 teaspoons olive oil
2 small fennel bulbs (400g), sliced thinly
2 cloves garlic, crushed
3 flat mushrooms (240g), sliced thickly
½ cup (125ml) dry white wine
1 cup (250ml) water
6 veal steaks (600g)
2 tablespoons wholemeal plain (all-purpose) flour
½ cup (125ml) salt-reduced chicken stock
1 tablespoon finely chopped fresh flat-leaf parsley

horseradish mash
600g (1¼ pounds) potatoes, chopped coarsely
1 tablespoon horseradish cream
¾ cup (180ml) hot low-fat milk
2 tablespoons finely chopped fresh flat-leaf parsley

1 Heat half the oil in large frying pan; cook fennel and garlic, stirring, until fennel softens. Add mushrooms, half the wine and ½ cup of the water; bring to the boil. Reduce heat; simmer, uncovered, about 15 minutes or until liquid has evaporated. Cool 10 minutes.

2 Meanwhile, using meat mallet, gently pound veal steaks, one at a time, between pieces of plastic wrap until about 5mm (¼ inch) thick; cut each piece in half crossways. Divide fennel mixture among veal pieces; roll to enclose filling, securing each roll with a toothpick.

3 Make horseradish mash.

4 Toss veal rolls in flour; shake off excess. Heat remaining oil in same cleaned frying pan; cook rolls, in batches, until browned all over and cooked as desired. Remove from pan, cover to keep warm.

5 Add remaining wine and remaining water to same pan with stock; bring to the boil, stirring. Boil, uncovered, 5 minutes.

6 Serve veal with mash and sauce, sprinkle with parsley.

horseradish mash
Boil, steam or microwave potato; drain. Mash potato in large bowl; stir in horseradish and milk, then parsley.

nutritional count per serving
7g total fat (1.8g saturated fat); 1492kJ (357 cal); 23.7g carbohydrate; 40.9g protein; 6.1g fibre

tip Mash potato as soon as it is cooked, otherwise it will not be as soft and creamy.

serving suggestion Serve with steamed beans or a green salad.

Using a meat mallet, gently pound the veal steaks, one at a time, between pieces of plastic wrap until 5mm thick.

Spoon a little of the fennel mixture onto each piece of veal, then roll up to enclose the filling. Secure the roll with a toothpick.

Toss the veal rolls in flour to coat, then shake off the excess.

Using a sharp knife, cut small slits into the top of each lamb backstrap; gently push a slice of garlic into each cut.

Wrap the prosciutto slices around each backstrap.

Cut the top and bottom off each grapefruit; cut down the side of the fruit following the curve, to remove the rind and white pith. Segment grapefruit over a bowl, cutting between the membrane.

PROSCIUTTO-WRAPPED LAMB WITH ROASTED KIPFLERS

prep + cook time 55 minutes ~ serves 8

2kg (4 pounds) kipfler (fingerling) potatoes
1.2kg (2½ pounds) lamb backstrap
4 cloves garlic, sliced thinly
12 slices prosciutto (180g)
400g (12½ ounces) green beans
3 ruby red grapefruits (1kg)
150g (4½ ounces) fetta cheese, crumbled
1 cup coarsely chopped fresh flat-leaf parsley
¼ cup (60ml) olive oil

1 Preheat oven to 220°C/425°F.

2 Cut potatoes in half, lengthways; place in large ovenproof dish. Roast, uncovered, 15 minutes.

3 Meanwhile, cut small slits in lamb; fill each slit with a garlic slice. Wrap prosciutto around lamb. Cook lamb in heated large frying pan, in batches, 1 minute each side. Remove from pan; place on top of potato.

4 Roast lamb and potato, uncovered, about 10 minutes.

5 Meanwhile, boil, steam or microwave beans until tender.

6 Peel grapefruits; cut into segments. Place beans and grapefruit in large bowl with remaining ingredients; toss gently to combine.

7 Serve lamb, sliced, with potatoes and salad.

nutritional count per serving
20.6g total fat (7.6g saturated fat); 2156kJ (515 cal); 33.9g carbohydrate; 47.3g protein; 6.3g fibre

tip Segment grapefruit over a bowl to catch the juices. Squeeze excess juice from the grapefruit and add to the salad.

ROSEMARY LAMB SKEWERS

prep + cook time 35 minutes ~ serves 4

These flavourful skewers, made smaller, are also perfect as party nibbles. You can make them ahead of time and gently reheat them in the oven before serving.

8 sprigs fresh rosemary
600g (1¼ pounds) minced (ground) lamb
1 egg yolk
2 cloves garlic, crushed
1 tablespoon tomato paste
⅓ cup (25g) stale breadcrumbs
¼ cup (60ml) olive oil
1 large brown onion (200g), sliced thinly
1 tablespoon plain (all-purpose) flour
1 cup (250ml) beef stock
2 medium tomatoes (300g), chopped coarsely

1 Remove two-thirds of the leaves from the bottom part of each rosemary sprig to make skewers. Finely chop 2 teaspoons of the leaves; reserve.

2 Combine lamb, egg yolk, garlic, paste, breadcrumbs and reserved rosemary in medium bowl. Shape lamb mixture into sausage shapes; mould onto rosemary skewers.

3 Heat 1 tablespoon of the oil in large frying pan; cook skewers until browned and cooked through. Remove from pan; cover to keep warm.

4 Heat remaining oil in same pan; cook onion, stirring, until soft. Add flour; cook, stirring, until mixture bubbles and thickens. Gradually add stock, stirring until smooth. Add tomato; cook, stirring, until gravy boils and thickens.

5 Serve rosemary lamb skewers with gravy.

nutritional count per serving
26g total fat (7.1g saturated fat); 1781kJ (426 cal); 11.9g carbohydrate; 35.1g protein; 2.5g fibre

serving suggestion Serve with mashed potato or a green salad.

To make the rosemary skewers, remove at least two-thirds of the leaves from the bottom part of the sprig. Finely chop 2 teaspoons of the leaves and reserve.

Combine lamb, egg yolk, garlic, paste, breadcrumbs and reserved rosemary. Shape lamb mixture into sausage shapes.

Mould the lamb mixture around the rosemary skewers or push the skewer through.

Cut the onions in half, then slice into thin wedges. Place onion in large baking dish.

Combine sage, garlic and oil; press sage mixture onto lamb.

Carefully position lamb on onion mixture.

GARLIC AND SAGE LAMB RACKS

prep + cook time 35 minutes ~ serves 4

3 large red onions (900g)
12 fresh sage leaves
⅓ cup (80ml) olive oil
2 tablespoons coarsely chopped fresh sage, extra
4 cloves garlic, chopped coarsely
4 x 4 french-trimmed lamb cutlet racks (600g)

1 Preheat oven to 220°C/425°F.

2 Cut onions in half then slice into thin wedges; place in large baking dish with sage leaves and half the oil.

3 Combine chopped sage, garlic and remaining oil in small bowl. Press sage mixture onto lamb; place on onion in dish.

4 Roast lamb, uncovered, about 25 minutes or until lamb is browned all over and cooked as desired. Cover lamb; stand 10 minutes before serving.

nutritional count per serving
31.3g total fat (8.5g saturated fat); 1676kJ (401 cal); 12.4g carbohydrate; 18.4g protein; 3.4g fibre

serving suggestion Serve with steamed vegetables.

SLOW-ROASTED SPICED LAMB SHOULDER

prep + cook time 3 hours 30 minutes ~ serves 4

2 teaspoons fennel seeds
1 teaspoon each ground cinnamon, ginger and cumin
¼ teaspoon chilli powder
2 tablespoons olive oil
1.2kg (2½ pound) lamb shoulder, shank intact
2 cloves garlic, sliced thinly
6 baby brown onions (150g)
375g (12 ounces) baby carrots, trimmed
1 cup (250ml) water

1 Preheat oven to 180°C/350°F.

2 Dry-fry spices in small frying pan until fragrant. Combine spices and half the oil in small bowl.

3 Using sharp knife, cut slits in lamb at 2.5cm (1-inch) intervals; push garlic into cuts. Rub lamb all over with spice mixture, season.

4 Heat remaining oil in large flameproof dish; cook lamb, turning, until browned all over. Remove lamb from dish.

5 Meanwhile, peel onions, leaving root ends intact. Add onions to dish; cook, stirring, until browned.

6 Add carrots and the water to dish; bring to the boil. Place lamb on vegetables, cover loosely with foil. Transfer to oven; roast 1½ hours.

7 Reduce oven to 160°C/325°F.

8 Remove foil from lamb; roast a further 1½ hours or until lamb is tender. Cover lamb; stand 10 minutes, then slice thinly. Strain pan juices into small heatproof jug.

9 Serve lamb with onions, carrots and pan juices.

nutritional count per serving
21.9g total fat (7.3g saturated fat); 1722kJ (412 cal); 6.5g carbohydrate; 45.7g protein; 3.1g fibre

serving suggestion Serve with steamed green beans.

Stir the seeds, ground spices and chilli powder in small dry frying pan until mixture is fragrant.

Using a sharp knife, cut slits into the lamb at 2.5cm intervals, then gently push the garlic slices into the cuts.

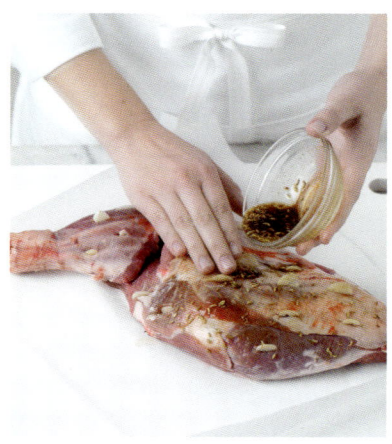

Rub the spice mixture all over the lamb, then season with salt and freshly ground black pepper.

Stir five-spice, chilli flakes, cinnamon stick and star anise in small dry frying pan until mixture is fragrant.

Position lamb in large baking dish, then pour over the spice mixture. Roast 2 hours.

Cut the choy sum into 10cm lengths, trim the sugar snap peas.

LAMB SHANKS IN FIVE-SPICE, TAMARIND AND GINGER

prep + cook time 2 hours 30 minutes ~ serves 4

Small, fresh and plump sugar snap peas, also known as honey snap peas, are eaten whole, pod and all, like snow peas.

2 teaspoons five-spice powder
1 teaspoon dried chilli flakes
1 cinnamon stick
2 star anise
¼ cup (60ml) soy sauce
½ cup (125ml) chinese rice wine
2 tablespoons tamarind concentrate
2 tablespoons light brown sugar
8cm (3¼-inch) piece fresh ginger (40g), grated
2 cloves garlic, chopped coarsely
1¼ cups (310ml) water
8 french-trimmed lamb shanks (1.6kg)
500g (1 pound) choy sum, cut into 10cm (4-inch) lengths
150g (4½ ounces) sugar snap peas

1 Preheat oven to 180°C/350°F.

2 Dry-fry five-spice, chilli, cinnamon and star anise in small frying pan, stirring, until fragrant. Combine spices with soy, wine, tamarind, sugar, ginger, garlic and the water in medium jug.

3 Place lamb, in single layer, in large shallow baking dish; pour over spice mixture. Roast lamb, uncovered, turning occasionally, about 2 hours or until meat is almost falling off the shanks. Remove lamb from dish; cover to keep warm. Skim away excess fat; strain sauce into small saucepan.

4 Meanwhile, boil, steam or microwave choy sum and peas, separately, until tender; drain.

5 Divide vegetables among serving plates; serve with lamb, drizzled with reheated sauce.

nutritional count per serving
20g total fat (9g saturated fat); 1885kJ (451 cal); 12.5g carbohydrate; 48.3g protein; 3.1g fibre

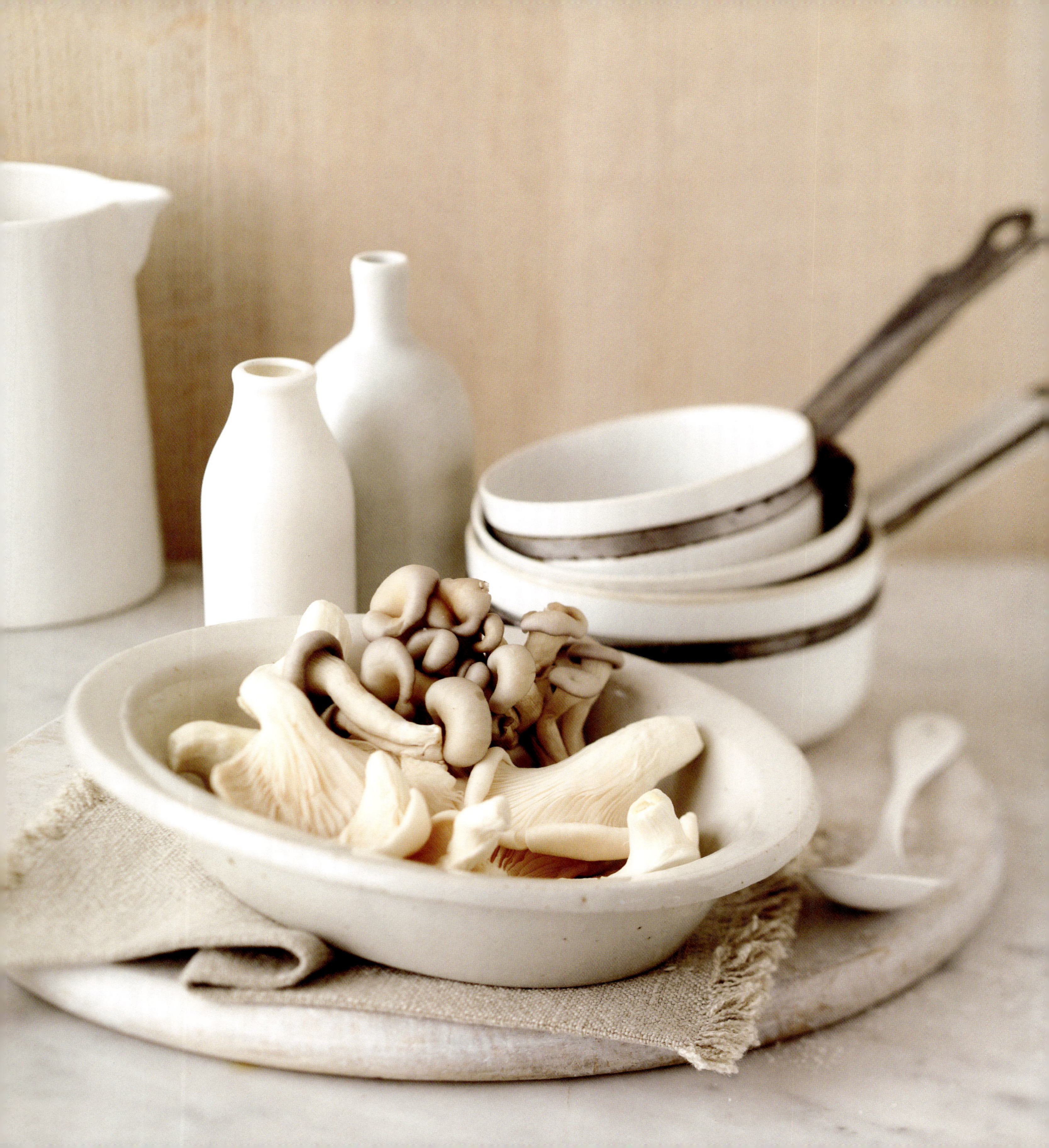

SIDES

HASSELBACK POTATOES

prep + cook time 1 hour 30 minutes ~ serves 4

This Swedish version of roasted potatoes produces a wonderfully crisp crust and makes an excellent accompaniment to roast beef or lamb. You could also use ruby lou potatoes for this recipe.

4 medium desiree potatoes (800g)
20g (¾ ounce) butter
1 tablespoon olive oil
¼ cup (25g) packaged breadcrumbs
½ cup (60g) finely grated cheddar cheese

1 Preheat oven to 180°C/350°F.

2 Peel potatoes; halve horizontally. Place one potato half, cut-side down, on chopping board; place a chopstick on board along each side of potato. Slice potato thinly, cutting through to chopsticks to prevent cutting all the way through. Repeat with remaining potato halves.

3 Melt butter. Coat potatoes in combined butter and oil in medium baking dish; place, rounded-side up, in single layer. Roast 1 hour, brushing frequently with oil mixture.

4 Sprinkle combined breadcrumbs and cheese over potatoes; roast about 10 minutes or until browned.

nutritional count per serving
14.1g total fat (6.6g saturated fat); 1225kJ (293 cal); 30.4g carbohydrate; 9.5g protein; 3.5g fibre

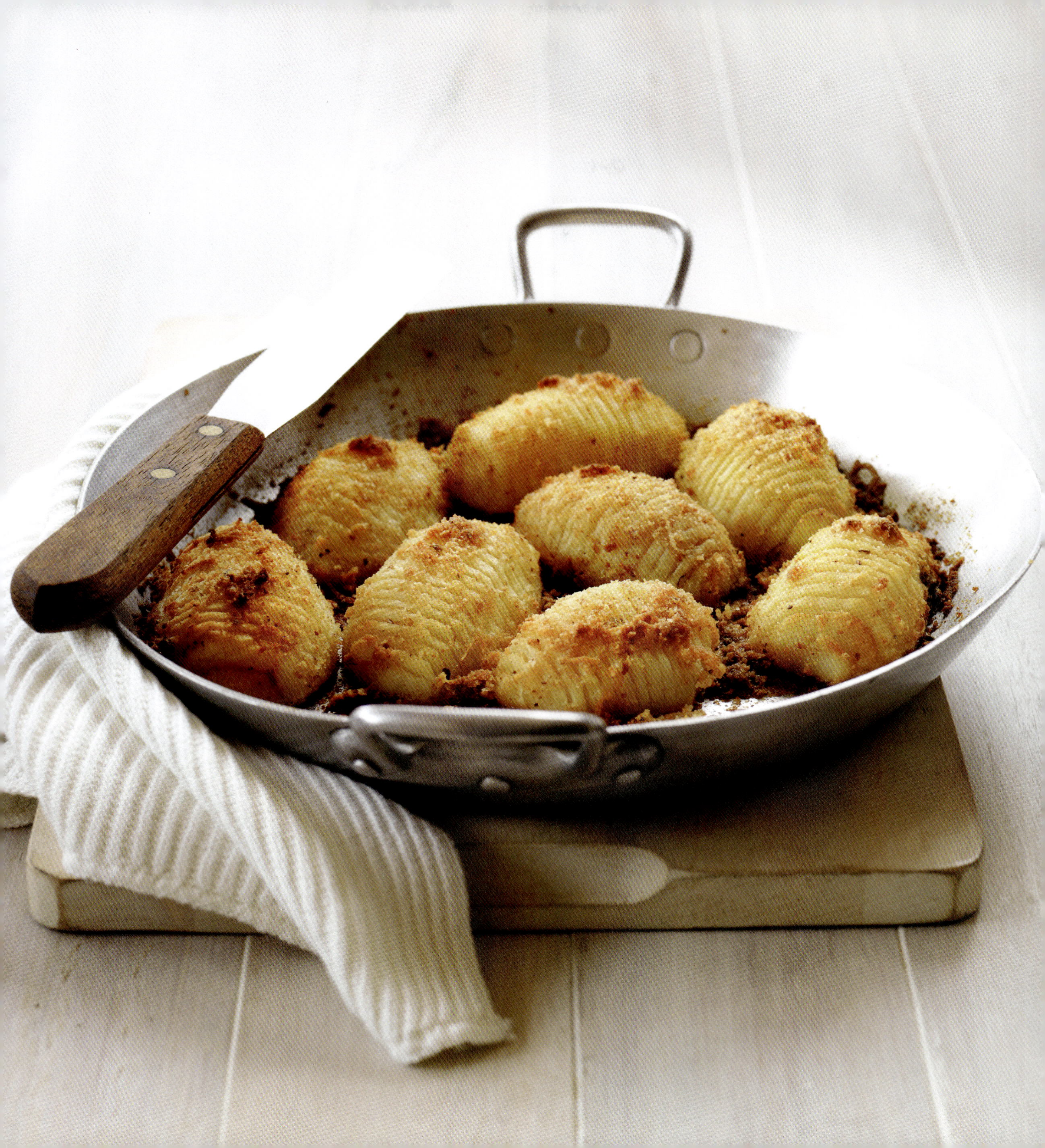

SAUTEED POTATOES

prep + cook time 25 minutes ~ serves 4

Cut 1kg (2 pounds) unpeeled desiree potatoes into 1cm (½-inch) slices. Heat 2 tablespoons olive oil and 50g (1½ ounces) chopped butter in large frying pan; cook potato, covered, over medium heat, turning occasionally, until browned lightly. Reduce heat; cook, tossing pan to turn potato slices, about 10 minutes or until tender.

nutritional count per serving
19.6g total fat (8g saturated fat); 1419kJ (339 cal); 32.8g carbohydrate; 6.1g protein; 4g fibre

tip You can also use bintje or russet burbank potatoes for this recipe.

POTATO WEDGES WITH SUN-DRIED TOMATO

prep + cook time 50 minutes ~ serves 4

Preheat oven to 220°C/425°F. Cut 1kg (2 pounds) unpeeled kipfler (fingerling) potatoes into wedges; toss wedges in large bowl with 2 tablespoons olive oil. Place wedges, in single layer, on oiled oven trays. Combine 1 tablespoon sun-dried tomato pesto, 2 teaspoons tomato sauce and 1 teaspoon sambal oelek in small bowl; brush mixture on wedges. Roast, uncovered, turning occasionally, about 40 minutes or until crisp and cooked through.

nutritional count per serving
10g total fat (1.4g saturated fat); 1087kJ (260 cal); 33.7g carbohydrate; 6.2g protein; 5g fibre

tip You could also use coliban or sebago potatoes for this recipe.

POTATO CHIPS

prep + cook time 30 minutes (+ standing) ~ serves 4

Cut 1kg (2 pounds) russet burbank potatoes lengthways into 1cm (½-inch) slices; cut each slice lengthways into 1cm (½-inch) wide pieces. Stand pieces in large bowl of cold water 30 minutes to avoid discolouration. Drain; pat dry with absorbent paper. Heat peanut oil in deep-fryer, wok or large saucepan; cook chips, in three batches, about 4 minutes each batch or until just tender but not browned. Drain on absorbent paper; stand 10 minutes. Reheat oil; cook chips again, in three batches, separating any that stick together by shaking deep-fryer basket or with a slotted spoon, until crisp and golden brown. Drain on absorbent paper.

nutritional count per serving
12.8g total fat (2.3g saturated fat); 1162kJ (278 cal); 32.8g carbohydrate; 6g protein; 4g fibre

PERFECT MASHED POTATO

prep + cook time 30 minutes ~ serves 4

Boil, steam or microwave 1kg (2 pounds) coarsely chopped spunta potatoes until tender; drain. Using the back of a wooden spoon, push potato through a fine sieve into a large bowl; stir in 40g (1½ ounces) butter and ¾ cup hot milk.

nutritional count per serving
10.2g total fat (6.6g saturated fat); 1028kJ (246 cal); 30.1g carbohydrate; 6.7g protein; 3.4g fibre

tip Using hot milk instead of cold gives a creamier mash.

BROAD BEANS AND THYME
prep + cook time 40 minutes ~ serves 4

Broad beans have a musky, fresh flavour, and they combine beautifully with mint and fetta in a salad, or slip easily into a spring vegetable soup. Early in the season they are sweet; later in the season, when they become mealy, they should be pureed.

600g (1¼ ounces) frozen broad beans (fava beans), thawed
10g (½ ounce) butter
2 shallots (50g), chopped finely
150g (4½ ounces) speck, chopped finely
1 tablespoon fresh thyme leaves
1 tablespoon lemon juice

1 Drop beans into medium saucepan of boiling water, return to the boil; drain. When beans are cool enough to handle, peel away grey-coloured outer shells.

2 Heat butter in large frying pan; cook shallot and speck, stirring, until speck is browned lightly. Add beans and thyme; cook, stirring, until beans are heated through. Stir in juice.

nutritional count per serving
7.7g total fat (3.5g saturated fat); 589kJ (141 cal); 2g carbohydrate; 13.9g protein; 4.8g fibre

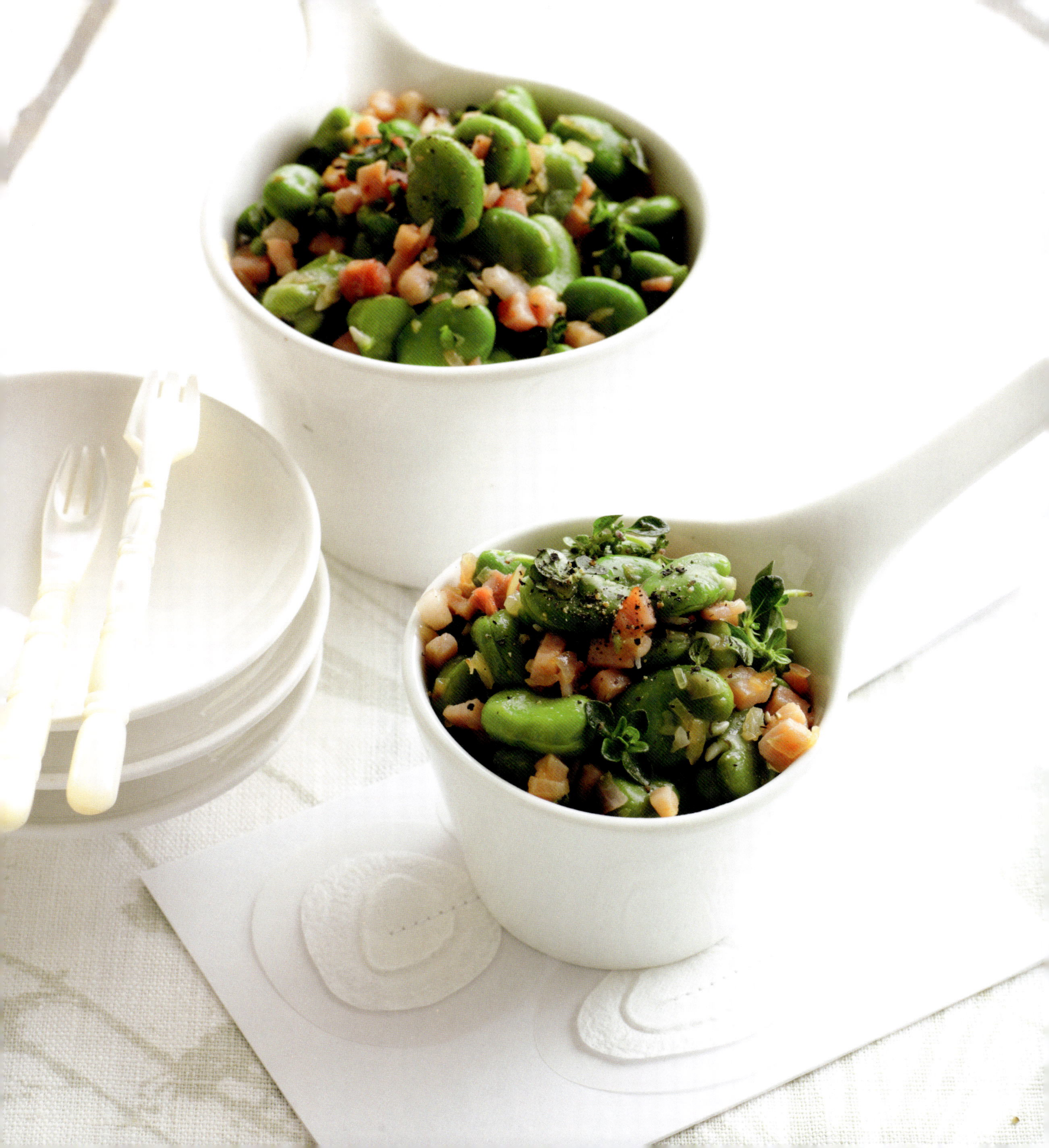

FENNEL MASH

prep + cook time 30 minutes ~ serves 4

Thinly slice 1 large fennel bulb. Melt 60g (2 ounces) butter in large frying pan; cook fennel, covered, over low heat, about 10 minutes or until fennel is very soft. Blend or process fennel mixture until smooth. Meanwhile, boil, steam or microwave 1kg (2 pounds) coarsely chopped potatoes until tender; drain. Mash potato in large bowl; stir in fennel mixture and ½ cup hot pouring cream. Season to taste.

nutritional count per serving
13.8g total fat (8.9g saturated fat); 1296kJ (310 cal); 36g carbohydrate; 7.3g protein; 6.1g fibre

CAPSICUM MASH

prep + cook time 30 minutes ~ serves 4

Quarter 2 red capsicums (bell peppers); discard seeds and membranes. Roast under hot grill (broiler), skin-side up, until skin blisters and blackens. Cover capsicum with plastic or paper for 5 minutes, then peel away skin; chop capsicum coarsely. Blend capsicum until smooth. Meanwhile, boil, steam or microwave 1kg (2 pounds) peeled and coarsely chopped potatoes until tender; drain. Mash potato in large bowl; stir in ½ cup hot pouring cream and 20g (¾ ounce) softened butter. Add capsicum to mash; stir until combined. Season to taste.

nutritional count per serving
18g total fat (11.6g saturated fat); 1446kJ (346 cal); 36.2g carbohydrate; 7.7g protein; 4.7g fibre

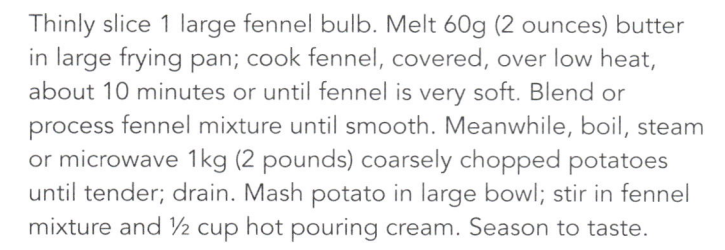

PEA MASH

prep + cook time 30 minutes ~ serves 4

Boil, steam or microwave 1kg (2 pounds) coarsely chopped potatoes and 1½ cups frozen peas, separately, until tender; drain. Mash potato in large bowl; stir in ¾ cup hot milk and 50g (1½ ounces) softened butter. Using fork, mash peas in small bowl; stir into potato mixture. Season to taste.

nutritional count per serving
12.6g total fat (8g saturated fat); 1392kJ (333 cal); 39.8g carbohydrate; 11.1g protein; 7.5g fibre

SPINACH MASH

prep + cook time 30 minutes ~ serves 4

Boil, steam or microwave 1kg (2 pounds) coarsely chopped potatoes until tender; drain. Meanwhile, boil, steam or microwave 220g (7 ounces) trimmed spinach leaves until wilted; drain. When cool enough to handle, squeeze out excess liquid. Blend or process spinach with 40g (1½ ounces) softened butter until almost smooth. Mash potato in large bowl; stir in ½ cup hot pouring cream and spinach mixture. Season to taste.

nutritional count per serving
22.1g total fat (14.3g saturated fat); 1576kJ (377 cal); 34g carbohydrate; 8g protein; 5.5g fibre

POTATO AND GREEN BEAN SALAD

prep + cook time 1 hour 15 minutes ~ serves 8

6 medium potatoes (650g), unpeeled, quartered lengthways
1 tablespoon olive oil
1 cup (180g) baby black olives, seeded
250g (8 ounces) green beans, halved

thyme vinaigrette
¼ cup (60ml) olive oil
2 tablespoons white wine vinegar
pinch caster (superfine) sugar
1 clove garlic, crushed
2 teaspoons fresh lemon thyme leaves

1   Preheat oven to 200°C/400°F.

2   Combine potatoes and oil in large baking dish; roast, uncovered, about 1 hour or until tender.

3   Make thyme vinaigrette.

4   Add hot potatoes and olives to vinaigrette; cool.

5   Meanwhile, boil, steam or microwave beans until tender; drain. Refresh under cold water; drain.

6   Add beans to potato mixture; toss gently to combine.

thyme vinaigrette
Whisk ingredients in large bowl.

nutritional count per serving
10g total fat (1.4g saturated fat); 711kJ (170 cal); 15.7g carbohydrate; 2.8g protein; 2.7g fibre

tip We used desiree potatoes in this salad but you could also use kipfler (fingerling) potatoes.

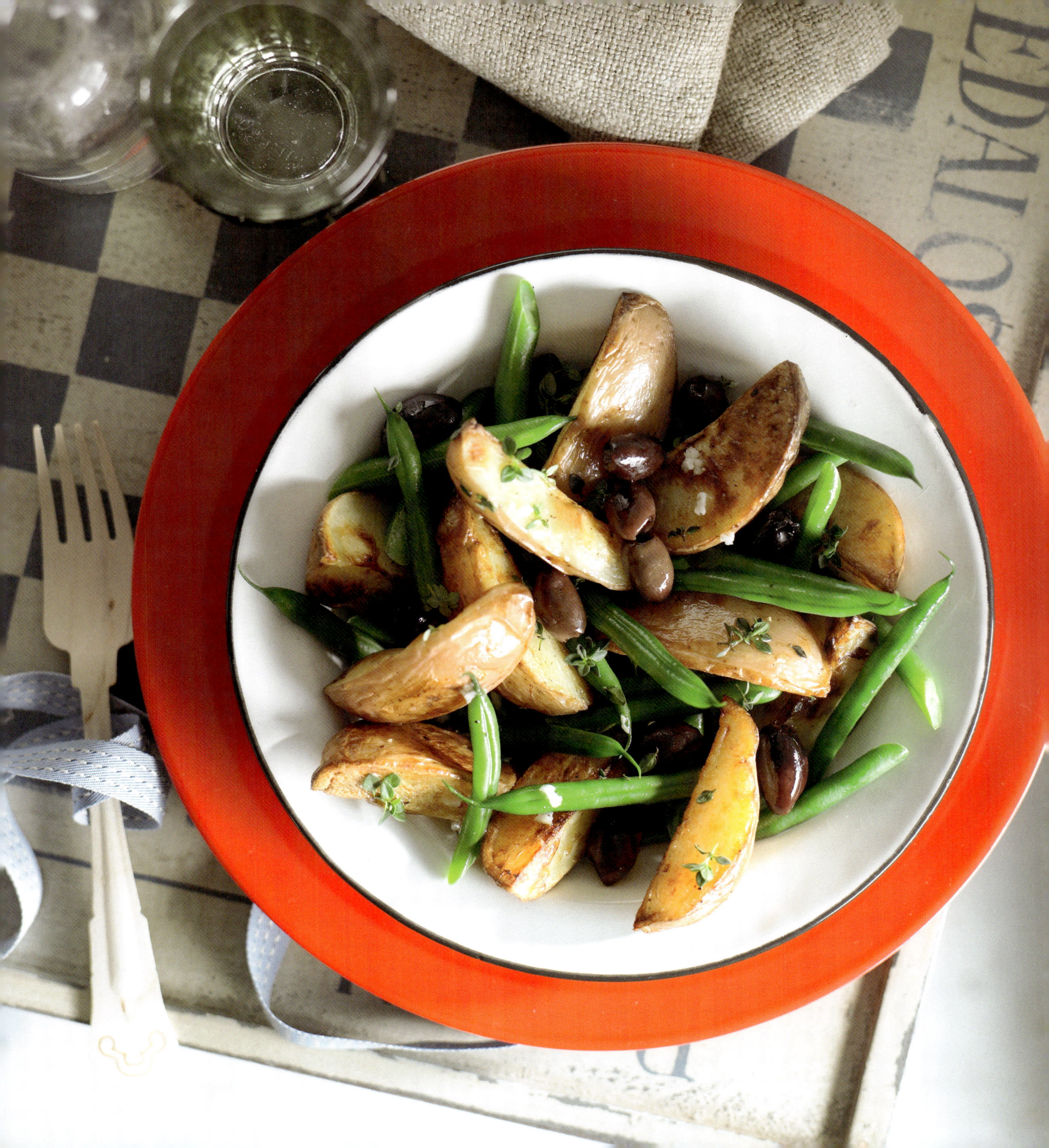

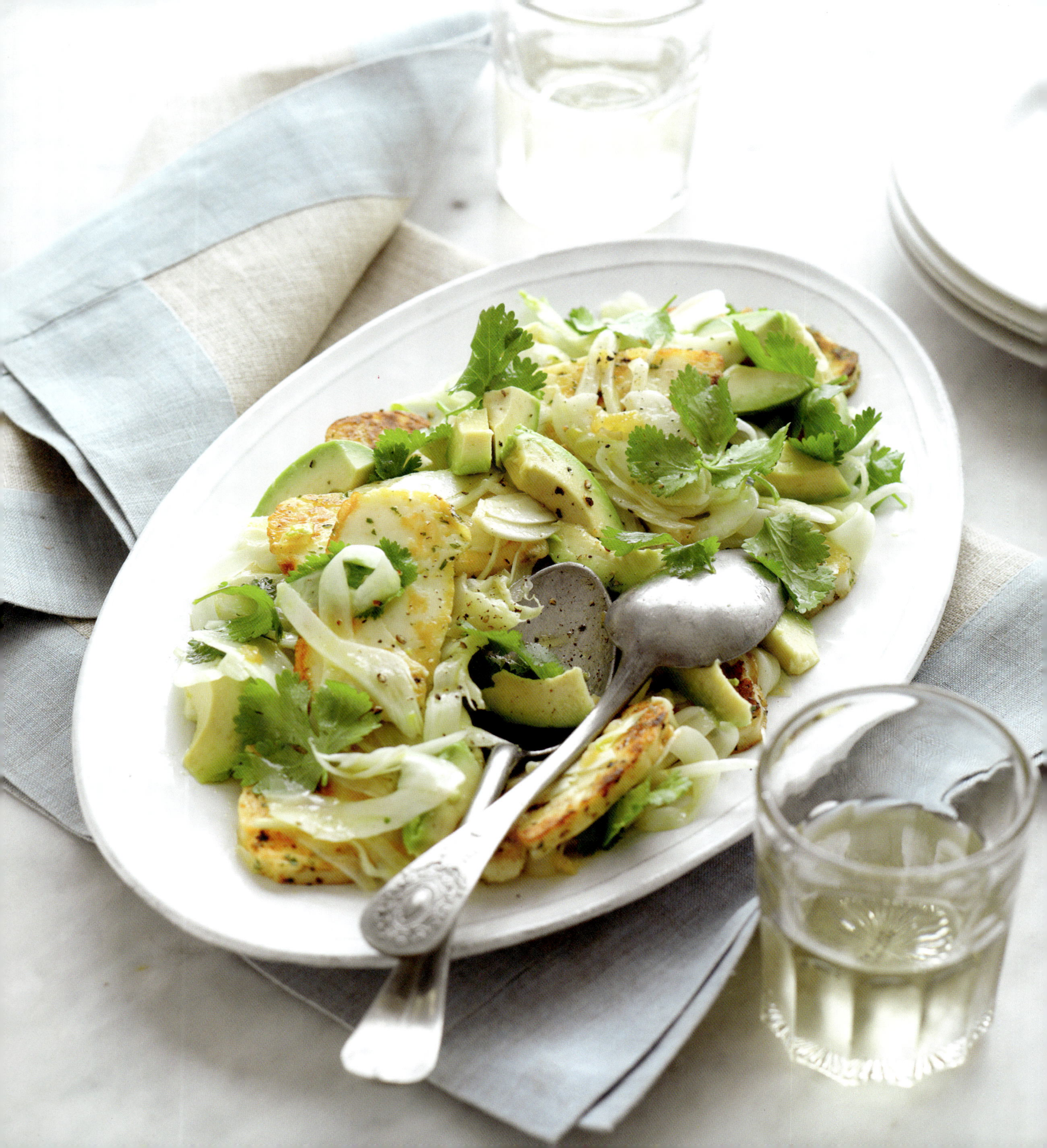

FENNEL AND PRESERVED LEMON SALAD WITH HALOUMI

prep + cook time 25 minutes ~ serves 8

250g (8 ounces) haloumi cheese, sliced thinly
1 tablespoon finely chopped fresh coriander (cilantro)
1 tablespoon olive oil
1 tablespoon lemon juice

fennel and preserved lemon salad
2 medium fennel bulbs (600g), sliced thinly
1 medium avocado (250g), halved, chopped coarsely
2 pieces preserved lemon rind (80g), rinsed, chopped finely
1 tablespoon lemon juice
2 tablespoons olive oil
½ cup firmly packed fresh coriander (cilantro) leaves

1 Make fennel and preserved lemon salad.

2 Combine cheese, coriander, oil and juice in small bowl. Heat large frying pan; cook cheese over medium heat until browned both sides.

3 Serve cheese immediately, topped with salad.

fennel and preserved lemon salad
Combine ingredients in medium bowl; toss gently to combine.

nutritional count per serving
17.2g total fat (5.5g saturated fat); 811kJ (194 cal); 2.1g carbohydrate; 7.5g protein; 1.5g fibre

tip Fried haloumi needs to be eaten as soon as possible after cooking as it becomes tough and rubbery as it cools. It takes a minute or so to fry, so it is best to cook the cheese just before serving.

PROSCIUTTO-WRAPPED BEAN BUNDLES

prep + cook time 30 minutes ~ serves 8

Cook 200g (6½ ounces) trimmed green beans and 200g (6½ ounces) trimmed yellow beans in medium saucepan of boiling water until just tender. Rinse under cold water; drain. Divide beans into eight equal bundles then wrap 1 slice prosciutto around each bundle. Cook bean bundles in heated oiled frying pan until prosciutto is crisp. Remove from pan; cover to keep warm. Melt 60g (2 ounces) butter in same frying pan; cook 1 tablespoon drained and rinsed baby capers, stirring, 1 minute. Stir in 1 tablespoon lemon juice. Serve bean bundles drizzled with caper mixture and topped with ⅓ cup coarsely chopped fresh flat-leaf parsley.

nutritional count per serving
6.9g total fat (4.3g saturated fat); 347kJ (83 cal); 1.5g carbohydrate; 3.3g protein; 1.5g fibre

BRUSSELS SPROUTS WITH CREAM AND ALMONDS

prep + cook time 10 minutes ~ serves 4

Melt 10g (½ ounce) butter in large frying pan; cook ⅓ cup (25g) flaked almonds, stirring, until browned lightly. Remove nuts from pan. Melt 40g (1½ ounces) butter in same pan; cook 1kg (2 pounds) trimmed and halved brussels sprouts and 2 cloves crushed garlic until sprouts are browned lightly. Add 1¼ cups pouring cream; bring to the boil. Reduce heat; simmer, uncovered, until sprouts are tender and sauce thickens slightly. Serve sprinkled with nuts.

nutritional count per serving
46.7g total fat (28.4g saturated fat); 2061kJ (493 cal); 6.6g carbohydrate; 9.5g protein; 7.3g fibre

tip You can use just one 300ml carton cream for this recipe.

BRAISED BABY LEEKS
prep + cook time 40 minutes ~ serves 4

ORANGE AND MAPLE-GLAZED BABY CARROTS
prep + cook time 25 minutes ~ serves 4

Carefully trim root end from 16 baby pencil leeks (1.3kg), leaving each leek in one piece. Trim leeks into 15cm (6-inch) lengths, then halve lengthways. Rinse under cold water; drain. Melt 30g (1 ounce) butter in large frying pan; cook leeks 1 minute. Stir in ⅔ cup chicken stock, 2 tablespoons dry white wine, 1 teaspoon finely grated lemon rind and 2 tablespoons lemon juice; bring to the boil. Reduce heat; simmer, covered, 15 minutes or until leeks are tender. Uncover, simmer 5 minutes or until liquid has reduced by half. Serve leeks drizzled with cooking liquid and sprinkled with ¼ cup (20g) flaked parmesan cheese and ¼ cup coarsely chopped fresh flat-leaf parsley.

nutritional count per serving
8.7g total fat (5.2g saturated fat); 644kJ (154 cal); 8.3g carbohydrate; 6.5g protein; 6g fibre

Melt 30g (1 ounce) butter in large frying pan; cook 800g (1½ pounds) baby carrots, turning occasionally, until almost tender. Add 2 teaspoons finely grated orange rind, ¼ cup orange juice, 2 tablespoons dry white wine and 2 tablespoons maple syrup; bring to the boil. Reduce heat; simmer, uncovered, until liquid has almost evaporated and carrots are tender and caramelised. Serve carrots topped with ½ cup (70g) coarsely chopped roasted hazelnuts.

nutritional count per serving
17.2g total fat (4.5g saturated fat); 1145kJ (274 cal); 20.8g carbohydrate; 4.1g protein; 7.7g fibre

ROASTED CAPSICUM AND BEETROOT SALAD

prep + cook time 50 minutes ~ serves 4

500g (1 pound) baby beetroot (beets)
1 small red capsicum (bell pepper) (150g)
1 small orange capsicum (bell pepper) (150g)
1 small yellow capsicum (bell pepper) (150g)
cooking-oil spray
½ small red onion (50g), chopped finely
1 tablespoon finely chopped fresh flat-leaf parsley
1 tablespoon thinly sliced preserved lemon rind
1 tablespoon lemon juice

1 Preheat oven to 220°C/425°F.

2 Trim leaves from beetroot; wrap each beetroot in foil, place on oven tray. Place capsicums on baking-paper-lined oven tray; spray with oil. Roast beetroot and capsicums about 30 minutes or until beetroot are tender and capsicums have blistered and blackened.

3 Cool beetroot 10 minutes then peel and quarter. Cover capsicums with plastic or paper for 5 minutes. Quarter capsicums; discard seeds and membranes. Peel away skin, then halve each quarter lengthways.

4 Arrange beetroot and capsicum on large serving platter. Sprinkle with onion, parsley and preserved lemon; drizzle with juice.

nutritional count per serving
1.6g total fat (0.2g saturated fat); 397kJ (95 cal); 13.9g carbohydrate; 3.9g protein; 4.8g fibre

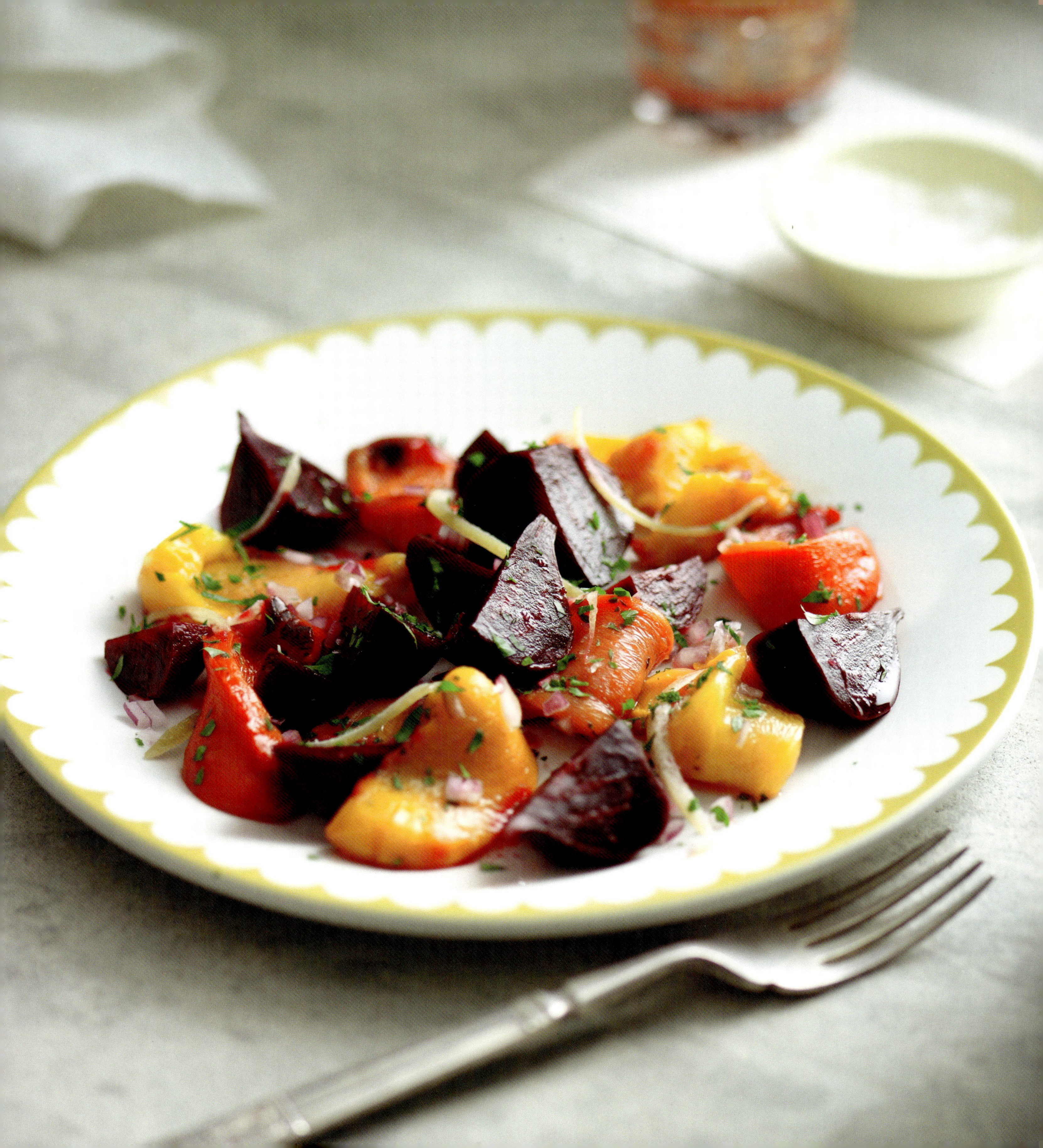

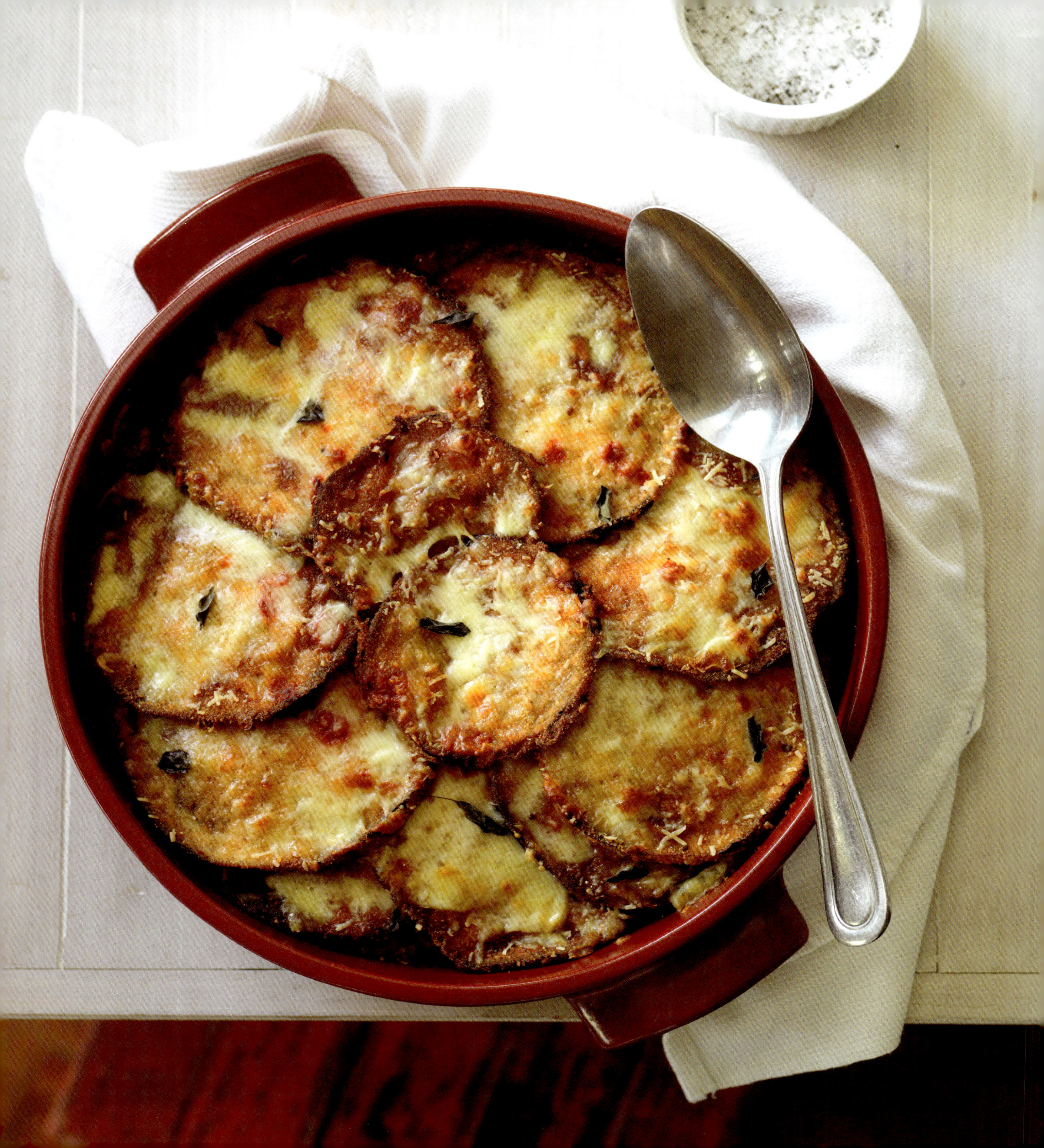

EGGPLANT PARMIGIANA

prep + cook time 1 hour ~ serves 6

2 large eggplants (1kg)
vegetable oil, for shallow-frying
½ cup (75g) plain (all-purpose) flour
4 eggs, beaten lightly
2 cups (200g) packaged breadcrumbs
3 cups (750ml) bottled tomato pasta sauce
1 cup (100g) coarsely grated mozzarella cheese
¼ cup (20g) finely grated parmesan cheese
⅓ cup loosely packed fresh oregano leaves

1 Using vegetable peeler, peel random strips of skin from eggplants; discard skins. Slice eggplants thinly.

2 Heat oil in large frying pan. Coat eggplant in flour; shake off excess. Dip in egg, then in breadcrumbs. Shallow-fry eggplant, in batches, until browned lightly. Drain on absorbent paper.

3 Preheat oven to 200°C/400°F.

4 Spread about one-third of the pasta sauce over base of greased 2.5-litre (10-cup) ovenproof dish. Top with about one-third of the eggplant, one-third of the cheeses and one-third of the oregano. Repeat layering.

5 Bake eggplant, covered, 20 minutes. Uncover; bake about 10 minutes or until browned lightly.

nutritional count per serving
27.7g total fat (6.6g saturated fat); 2266kJ (542 cal); 49.4g carbohydrate; 19.9g protein; 8.3g fibre

tip If the eggplants are old and large with dark seeds you can sprinkle them with salt, this releases the bitter flavour. There is no need to salt fresh smaller eggplants.

EGGPLANT AND TOMATO SALAD

prep + cook time 35 minutes ~ serves 6

6 baby eggplants (360g)
¼ cup (60ml) olive oil
½ teaspoon each ground coriander, cumin and smoked paprika
1 medium tomato (150g), halved, seeded, chopped finely
1 small red onion (100g), chopped finely
2 tablespoons (20g) seeded black olives, chopped finely
1 tablespoon finely chopped fresh flat-leaf parsley
2 teaspoons finely chopped fresh mint
1 teaspoon finely grated lemon rind
2 teaspoons lemon juice

1 Cut each eggplant lengthways into four slices, leaving tops intact. Combine eggplants and half the oil in medium bowl; season.

2 Cook eggplants on heated oiled grill plate (or grill or barbecue), flattening and fanning with the back of a spatula, until eggplants are tender.

3 Meanwhile, dry-fry spices in small frying pan until fragrant; cool.

4 Combine spices, remaining oil, tomato, onion and remaining ingredients in small bowl; season.

5 Serve eggplant topped with tomato mixture.

nutritional count per serving
9.3g total fat (1.3g saturated fat); 435kJ (104 cal); 3.3g carbohydrate; 1.1g protein; 1.8g fibre

tip Vine-ripened tomatoes are ideal to use in this salad.

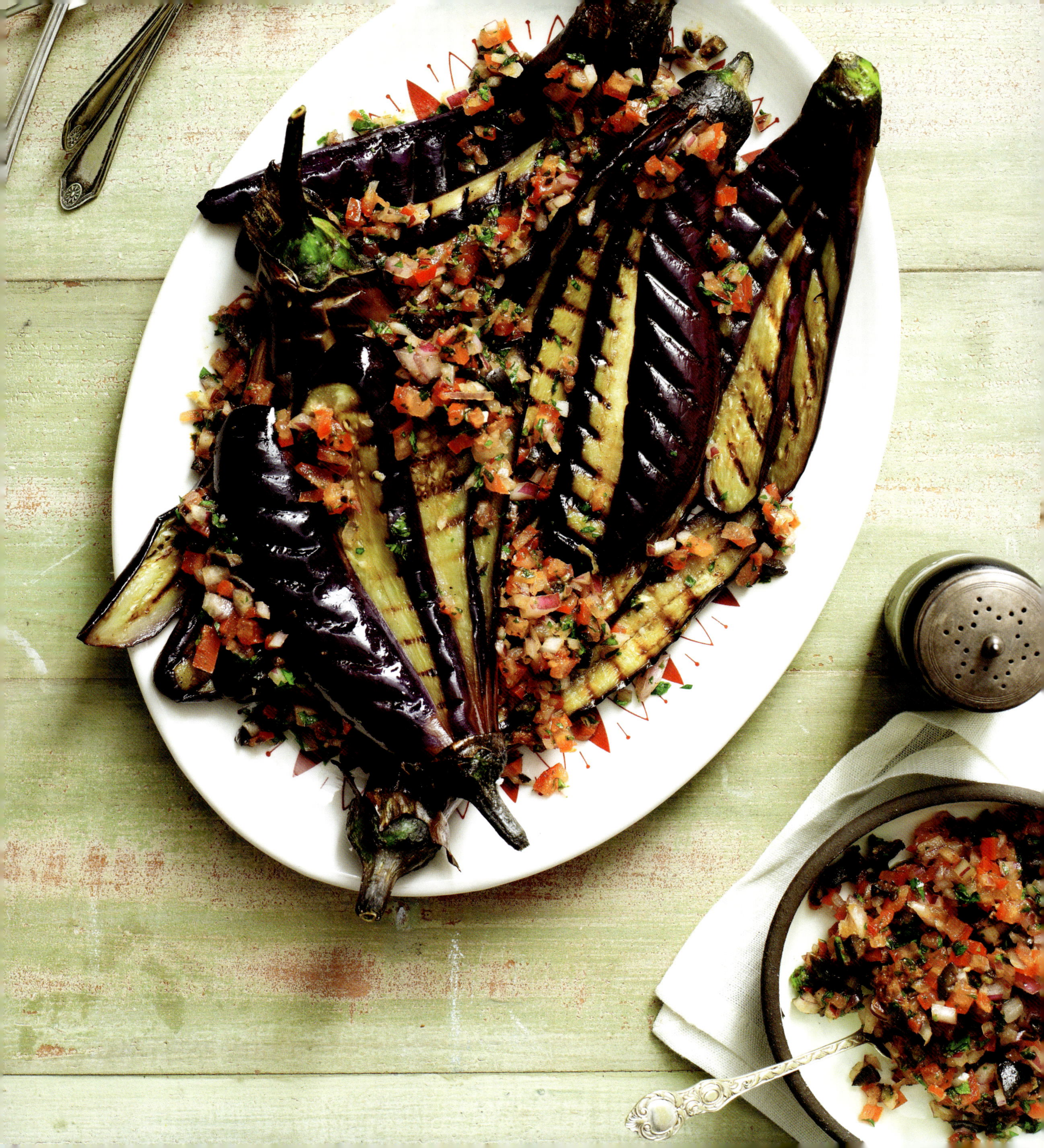

CAPRESE SALAD
prep time 15 minutes ~ serves 4

Thinly slice 3 large (270g) roma (plum) tomatoes and 300g (9½ ounces) bocconcini cheese; overlap slices on serving platter. Drizzle with 2 tablespoons olive oil and sprinkle with ¼ cup firmly packed fresh torn basil leaves.

nutritional count per serving
20.6g total fat (8.8g saturated fat); 1028kJ (246 cal); 1.6g carbohydrate; 13.6g protein; 1.1g fibre

BABY ROCKET AND PARMESAN SALAD
prep time 20 minutes ~ serves 8

Using a vegetable peeler, shave 60g (2-ounce) piece parmesan cheese into long pieces. Place cheese in large bowl with ½ cup (75g) drained and halved semi-dried tomatoes, 200g (6½ ounces) baby rocket (arugula) leaves, ¼ cup (40g) roasted pine nuts, ¼ cup balsamic vinegar and ¼ cup olive oil; toss gently to combine.

nutritional count per serving
13.4g total fat (2.8g saturated); 673kJ (161 cal); 4.1g carbohydrate; 5.2g protein; 2g fibre

GOAT'S CHEESE, FIG AND PROSCIUTTO SALAD

prep + cook time 15 minutes ~ serves 4

Preheat grill (broiler). Place ¼ cup cider vinegar, 2 tablespoons olive oil, 1 tablespoon wholegrain mustard and 1 tablespoon honey in screw-top jar; shake well. Cook 6 slices prosciutto (90g) under hot grill until crisp; drain, then chop coarsely. Place 120g (4 ounces) trimmed baby rocket (arugula) leaves, 4 large (320g) quartered fresh figs, 150g (4½ ounces) crumbled soft goat's cheese and dressing in large bowl; toss gently to combine.

nutritional count per serving
16.9g total fat (5.7g saturated fat); 1062kJ (254 cal); 13.7g carbohydrate; 11.1g protein; 2.6g fibre

GREEN BEAN AND TOMATO SALAD

prep + cook time 20 minutes ~ serves 4

Place ½ cup (70g) skinned, coarsely chopped roasted hazelnuts, 2 tablespoons hazelnut oil, 2 tablespoons cider vinegar and 1 teaspoon wholegrain mustard in screw-top jar; shake well. Boil, steam or microwave 200g (6½ ounces) green beans; drain. Rinse under cold water; drain. Place beans and dressing in medium bowl with 250g (8 ounces) halved cherry tomatoes; toss gently until combined.

nutritional count per serving
20.2g total fat (1.8g saturated fat); 920kJ (220 cal); 3.6g carbohydrate; 4.2g protein; 4.3g fibre

TOMATO AND KUMARA BROWN RICE SALAD

prep + cook time 40 minutes ~ serves 4

1 cup (200g) brown long-grain rice
1 small kumara (orange sweet potato) (250g), chopped coarsely
250g (8 ounces) red grape tomatoes, halved
2 green onions (scallions), sliced thinly
⅓ cup firmly packed fresh small basil leaves
40g (1½ ounces) trimmed rocket (arugula) leaves

balsamic dressing
2 tablespoons orange juice
1 tablespoon balsamic vinegar
1 teaspoon olive oil
1 clove garlic, crushed

1 Cook rice in large saucepan of boiling water, uncovered, about 30 minutes or until tender; drain. Rinse under cold water; drain.

2 Meanwhile, boil, steam or microwave kumara until tender; drain.

3 Make balsamic dressing.

4 Place rice, kumara and dressing in large bowl with tomatoes, onion, basil and rocket; toss gently to combine.

balsamic dressing
Place ingredients in screw-top jar; shake well.

nutritional count per serving
3g total fat (0.5g saturated fat); 1287kJ (308 cal); 60.3g carbohydrate; 6.9g protein; 5g fibre

tip To keep basil leaves fresh, wrap them in wet absorbent paper until ready to use.

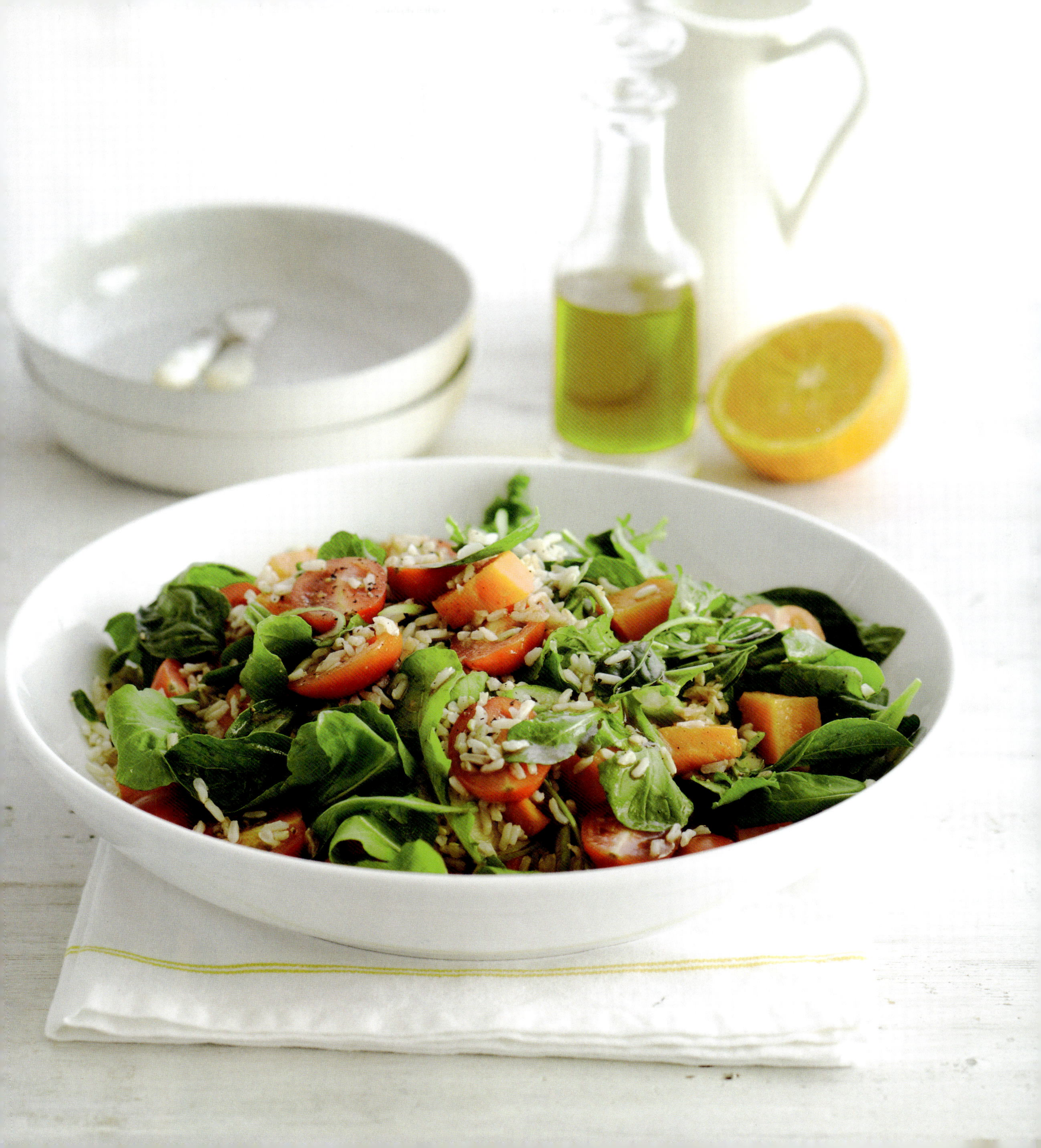

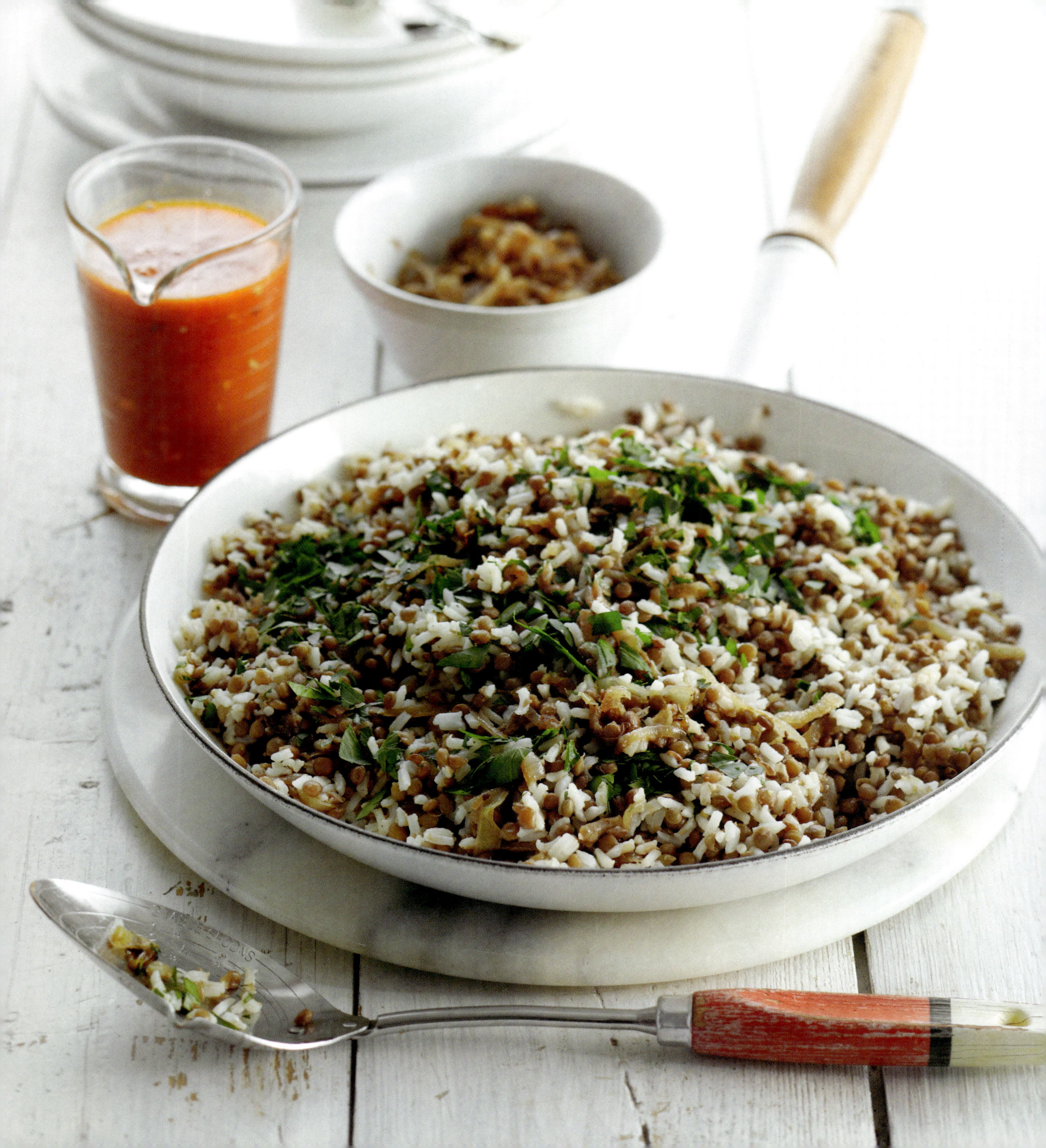

KOSHARI

prep + cook time 1 hour ~ serves 4

Various combinations of rice and lentils are eaten throughout the Middle East and India, with perhaps the two most well-known versions being Lebanese mujadara and Indian kitcheree. Our Egyptian take on this homely dish, however, adds delicious "oomph" to the rice-lentil theme with its fragrantly spicy caramelised onion and piquant chilli sauce.

1½ cups (300g) brown lentils
¾ cup (150g) doongara rice
1 cup coarsely chopped fresh flat-leaf parsley

caramelised onion
1 tablespoon olive oil
5 large brown onions (1kg), sliced thinly
1½ teaspoons ground allspice
1 teaspoon ground coriander
2 teaspoons white (granulated) sugar

tomato chilli sauce
2 teaspoons olive oil
3 cloves garlic, crushed
½ teaspoon ground cumin
½ teaspoon dried chilli flakes
⅓ cup (80ml) white vinegar
1⅔ cups (410ml) canned tomato juice

1 Make caramelised onion and tomato chilli sauce.

2 Meanwhile, cook lentils and rice, separately, in medium saucepans of boiling water, until both are tender; drain.

3 Remove half the caramelised onion from pan; reserve. Add lentils and rice to remaining onion in pan; stir until hot. Remove from heat; stir in half the parsley.

4 Divide koshari among serving bowls; top with reserved caramelised onion, remaining parsley and tomato sauce.

caramelised onion
Heat oil in large frying pan; cook onion, allspice and coriander, stirring, until onion softens. Add sugar; cook, stirring occasionally, about 30 minutes or until onion caramelises.

tomato chilli sauce
Heat oil in small saucepan; cook garlic, cumin and chilli, stirring, until fragrant. Add vinegar and juice; bring to the boil. Boil, uncovered, 2 minutes.

nutritional count per serving
8.8g total fat (1.2g saturated fat); 2157kJ (516 cal); 77.5g carbohydrate; 25g protein; 15.2g fibre

tip Always rinse rice under cold water until water runs clear, it removes excess starch so the cooked rice is not gluggy.

serving suggestion Serve with steamed green vegetables.

SOFT POLENTA
prep + cook time 20 minutes ~ serves 6

Boil 3 cups water and 2 cups vegetable stock in large saucepan. Gradually add 2 cups polenta, stirring constantly. Reduce heat; simmer, stirring, about 10 minutes or until polenta thickens. Stir in 1 cup milk and ¼ cup finely grated parmesan cheese until cheese melts. Season to taste.

nutritional count per serving
4.2g total fat (2.1g saturated fat); 1016kJ (243 cal); 41.7g carbohydrate; 8.2g protein; 1.6g fibre

SPANISH RICE AND PEAS
prep + cook time 30 minutes ~ serves 6

Combine 3 cups water and ¼ cup olive oil in medium saucepan; bring to the boil. Stir in 2 cups white medium-grain rice; cook, uncovered, without stirring, about 10 minutes or until liquid has almost evaporated. Reduce heat; simmer, covered, 5 minutes. Gently stir in 1 cup frozen peas; simmer, covered, about 5 minutes or until rice and peas are tender. Season to taste.

nutritional count per serving
9.5g total fat (1.4g saturated fat); 1379kJ (330 cal); 54.3g carbohydrate; 5.6g protein; 1.7g fibre

CLASSIC PULAO

prep + cook time 30 minutes (+ standing) ~ serves 4

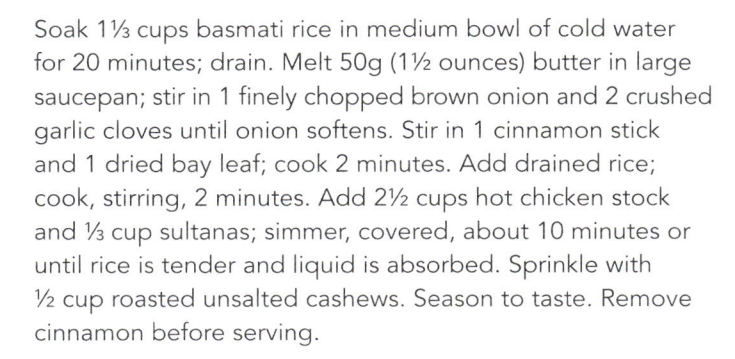

Soak 1⅓ cups basmati rice in medium bowl of cold water for 20 minutes; drain. Melt 50g (1½ ounces) butter in large saucepan; stir in 1 finely chopped brown onion and 2 crushed garlic cloves until onion softens. Stir in 1 cinnamon stick and 1 dried bay leaf; cook 2 minutes. Add drained rice; cook, stirring, 2 minutes. Add 2½ cups hot chicken stock and ⅓ cup sultanas; simmer, covered, about 10 minutes or until rice is tender and liquid is absorbed. Sprinkle with ½ cup roasted unsalted cashews. Season to taste. Remove cinnamon before serving.

nutritional count per serving
20.6g total fat (8.8g saturated fat); 2128kJ (509 cal); 68.7g carbohydrate; 10.5g protein; 3g fibre

OLIVE AND PARSLEY COUSCOUS

prep + cook time 15 minutes ~ serves 6

Bring 1½ cups vegetable stock to the boil in medium saucepan. Remove from heat; stir in 1½ cups couscous and 30g (1 ounce) butter. Cover; stand about 5 minutes or until liquid is absorbed, fluffing with fork occasionally. Stir in 1 cup seeded kalamata olives and ½ cup chopped fresh flat-leaf parsley. Season to taste.

nutritional count per serving
4.9g total fat (2.9g saturated fat); 1074kJ (257 cal); 45.5g carbohydrate; 6.8g protein; 1g fibre

ASPARAGUS AND ZUCCHINI RICE

prep + cook time 25 minutes ~ serves 4

185g (6 ounces) asparagus
1 large zucchini (150g)
¾ cup (180ml) chicken consommé
500g (1 pound) cooked brown medium-grain rice
2 tablespoons finely chopped fresh flat-leaf parsley
1 cup (80g) finely grated parmesan cheese

1 Trim asparagus; coarsely chop asparagus and zucchini. Combine consommé, zucchini and asparagus in deep frying pan; bring to the boil, simmer, uncovered, until liquid is reduced by half.

2 Add rice and parsley; cook,stirring, until hot. Stir in cheese; season to taste. Serve topped with extra parmesan.

nutritional count per serving
5.4g total fat (3g saturated fat); 840kJ (201 cal); 27.6g carbohydrate; 9.2g protein; 2.2g fibre

tips You can use vegetable stock instead of the chicken consommé.

Stir a little chopped preserved lemon rind and fresh tarragon into the rice, if you like.

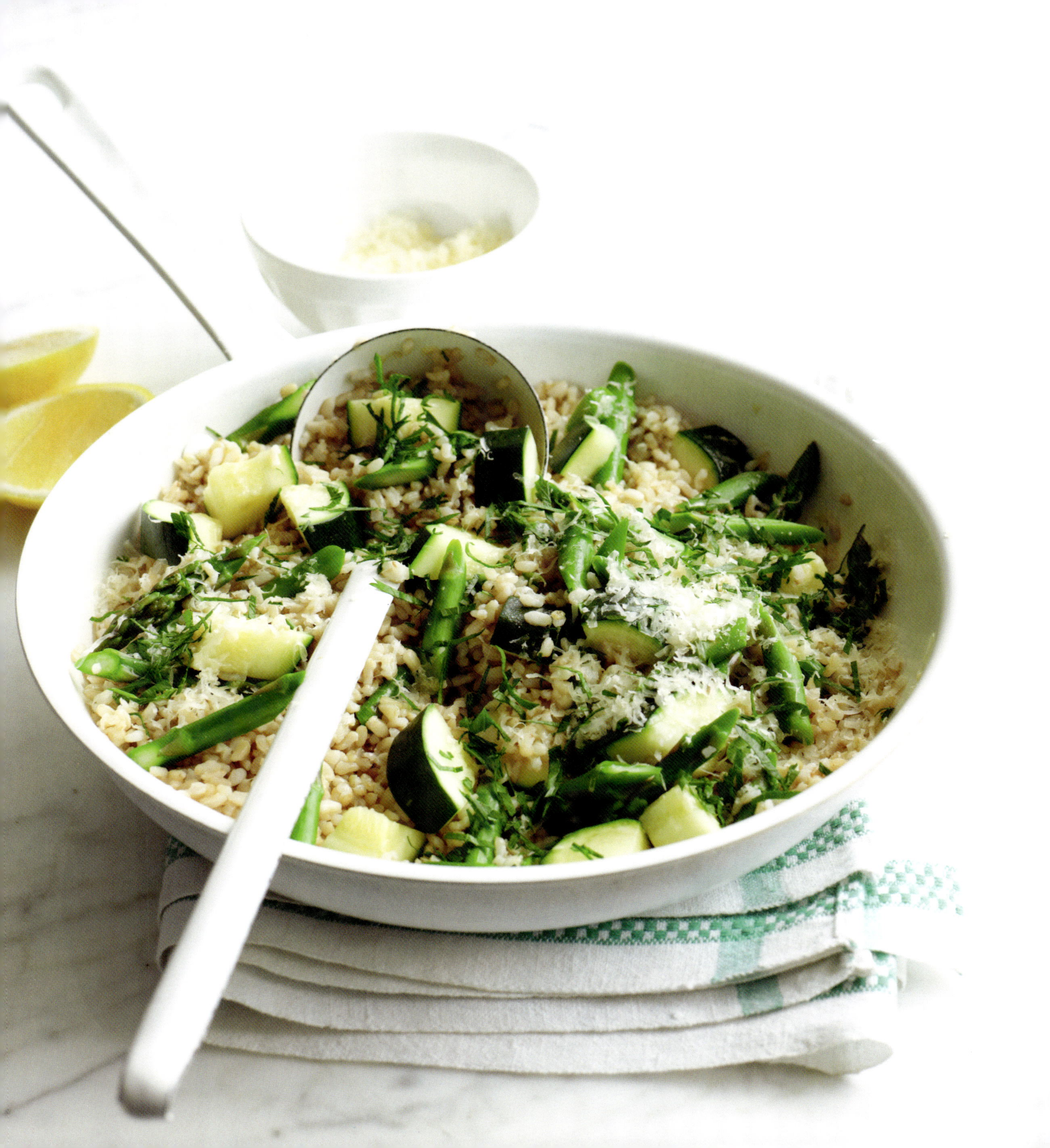

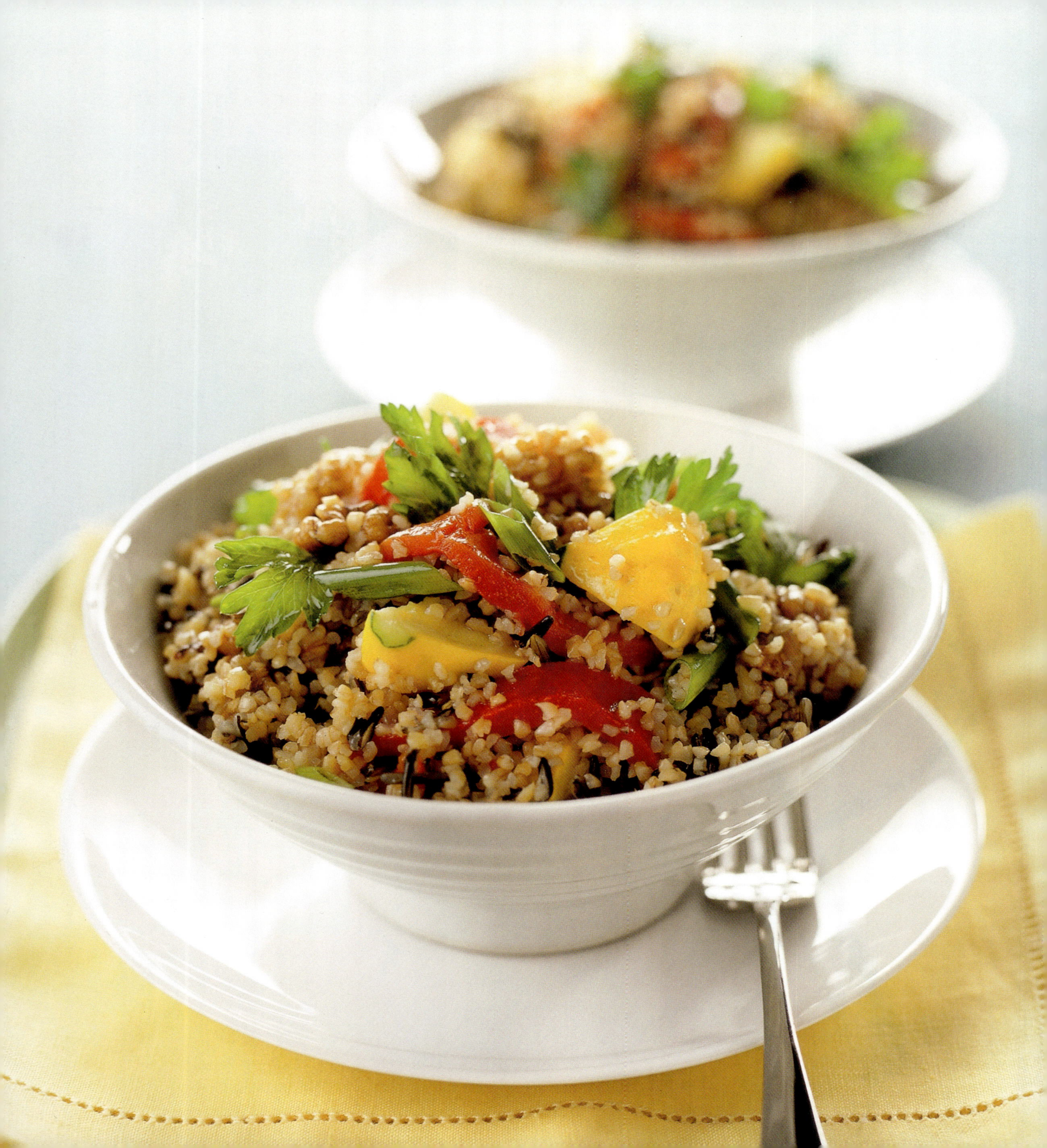

BURGHUL AND WILD RICE SALAD

prep + cook time 1 hour 35 minutes (+ standing) ~ serves 4

This is a good salad for a barbecue as it keeps well and is not fussy about the temperature at which it is served.

2 cups (320g) burghul
⅔ cup (130g) wild rice
2 medium red capsicums (bell peppers) (400g)
200g (6½ ounces) yellow patty-pan squash, quartered
4 green onions (scallions), chopped finely
⅔ cup (70g) walnuts
2 tablespoons finely chopped fresh flat-leaf parsley

dressing
1 clove garlic, crushed
⅔ cup (160ml) olive oil
2 tablespoons lemon juice

1 Place burghul in medium heatproof bowl; cover with boiling water. Stand 15 minutes; drain. Rinse under cold water; drain on absorbent paper.

2 Cook rice in large saucepan of boiling water, uncovered, about 35 minutes or until rice is tender; drain. Rinse under cold water; drain.

3 Quarter capsicums; discard seeds and membranes. Roast under grill or in very hot oven, skin-side up, until skin blisters and blackens. Cover capsicum pieces with plastic or paper for 5 minutes; peel away skin, then slice capsicum thickly.

4 Boil, steam or microwave squash until tender; drain. Rinse under cold water; drain.

5 Meanwhile, make dressing.

6 Place burghul, rice, capsicum and squash in large bowl with dressing and onion, nuts, parsley and dressing in large bowl.

dressing
Place ingredients in screw-top jar; shake well.

nutritional count per serving
50.3g total fat (6g saturated); 3277kJ (784 cal); 60.2g carbohydrate; 15.2g protein; 17.2g fibre

GREEK SALAD
prep time 20 minutes ~ serves 4

Whisk ¼ cup olive oil, 1 tablespoon lemon juice, 1 tablespoon white wine vinegar, 1 tablespoon finely chopped fresh oregano and 1 clove crushed garlic in a large bowl. Add 3 medium (450g) tomatoes, cut into wedges, 2 coarsely chopped lebanese cucumbers (260g), 200g (6½ ounces) chopped fetta cheese, 1 small (150g) thinly sliced red capsicum (bell pepper), 1 small (100g) thinly sliced red onion and ½ cup (75g) seeded black olives; toss gently to combine.

nutritional count per serving
25.8g total fat (9.6g saturated fat); 1359kJ (325 cal); 10.8g carbohydrate; 11.5g protein; 3.2g fibre

BURGHUL, TOMATO AND HERB SALAD
prep + cook time 15 minutes (+ standing) ~ serves 8

Stand 1½ cups (240g) burghul (cracked wheat) in medium bowl in enough boiling water to cover for about 30 minutes or until tender. Meanwhile, combine ⅓ cup lemon juice, 2 tablespoons olive oil and 2 teaspoons finely grated lemon rind in small jug. Drain burghul in sieve, pressing out as much water as possible; place in large bowl. Add 300g (9½ ounces) halved mixed cherry tomatoes, 1 cup coarsely chopped fresh flat-leaf parsley, ½ cup coarsely chopped fresh mint and 6 thinly sliced red radishes (200g) to bowl with dressing; toss gently to combine. Season to taste.

nutritional count per serving
5.2g total fat (0.8g saturated fat); 627kJ (150 cal); 20.2g carbohydrate; 3.6g protein; 5.2g fibre

WHITE BEAN SALAD

prep time 15 minutes (+ standing) ~ serves 6

Place 800g (1½ pounds) drained and rinsed canned white beans, 1 medium (200g) thinly sliced red capsicum (bell pepper), 1 small (80g) thinly sliced white onion, 1 cup finely shredded fresh flat-parsley leaves, ½ cup (90g) thinly sliced cornichons, 1 tablespoon drained and rinsed baby capers, 2 tablespoons olive oil and ¼ cup red wine vinegar in medium bowl; toss gently to combine. Season to taste. Stand at room temperature at least 1 hour before serving.

nutritional count per serving
6.7g total fat (1.2g saturated fat); 616kJ (147 cal); 16.1g carbohydrate; 6.6g protein; 7.4g fibre

tip You can use any cooked white beans such as cannellini, butter and haricot for this recipe.

CAPSICUM, ZUCCHINI AND ORZO SALAD

prep + cook time 40 minutes ~ serves 4

Quarter 1 medium (200g) red capsicum (bell pepper) and 1 medium (200g) yellow capsicum (bell pepper); discard seeds and membranes. Roast capsicums, skin-side up, under hot grill or in very hot oven, until skin blisters and blackens. Cover capsicum with plastic or paper 5 minutes; peel away skin then slice thinly. Meanwhile, cook 1 cup (220g) orzo pasta in large saucepan boiling salted water until tender; drain. Place capsicum and orzo in large bowl with 2 large (300g) grated zucchini, ½ cup fresh oregano leaves, ¼ cup coarsely chopped fresh flat-parsley leaves, ½ cup (75g) seeded and quartered kalamata olives, 2 tablespoons olive oil and 2 tablespoons red wine vinegar; toss to combine. Season.

nutritional count per serving
14.3g total fat (2.1g saturated fat); 1418kJ (339 cal); 43.2g carbohydrate; 8.6g protein; 5.2g fibre

BARBECUED FENNEL, ORANGE AND RED ONION WITH QUINOA

prep + cook time 40 minutes ~ serves 4

Quinoa, pronounced keen-wa, is a gluten-free grain. It has a delicate, slightly nutty taste and chewy texture, partnering rich or spicy foods perfectly. Quinoa makes a nice change from rice or couscous.

- 5 small fennel bulbs (1kg), quartered lengthways
- 1 large red onion (300g), cut into thick wedges
- ¼ cup (60ml) olive oil
- 2 cups (500ml) water
- 1 cup (100g) quinoa
- 1 medium orange (240g)
- ½ cup (125ml) white wine vinegar
- ¼ cup coarsely chopped fresh dill
- 1 cup firmly packed fresh flat-leaf parsley leaves

1 Cook fennel and onion on heated oiled grill plate (or grill or barbecue) until vegetables are just tender, brushing occasionally with 1 tablespoon of the oil.

2 Meanwhile, bring the water to the boil in small saucepan. Add quinoa, reduce heat; simmer, covered, about 10 minutes or until water is absorbed, drain.

3 Peel orange; cut into segments. Place orange, fennel, onion and quinoa in large bowl with remaining oil and remaining ingredients; toss gently to combine.

nutritional count per serving
14.4g total fat (2g saturated fat); 1170kJ (280 cal); 26.9g carbohydrate; 5.8g protein; 10.6g fibre

tip *Cooking quinoa in stock boosts its flavour.*

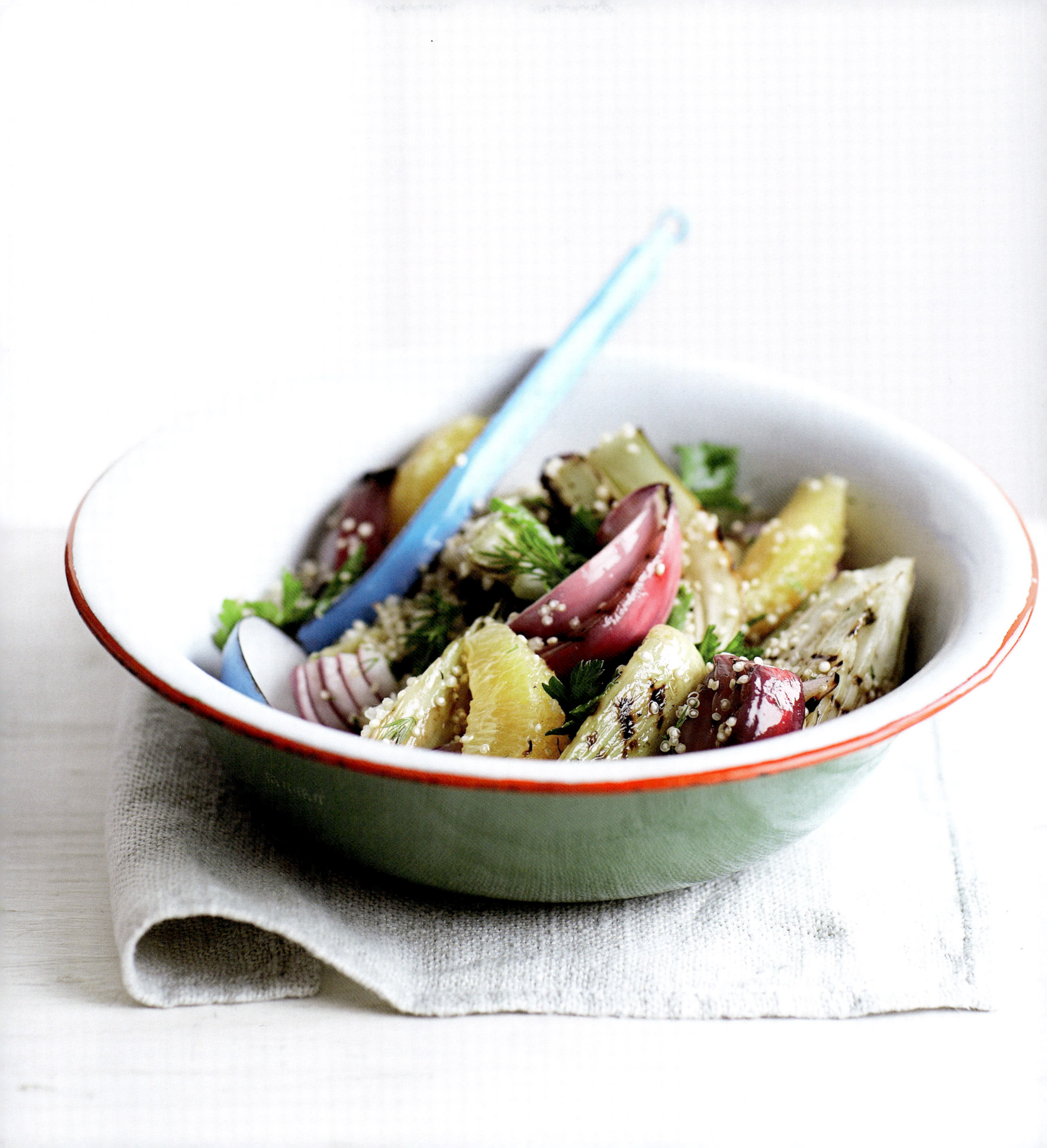

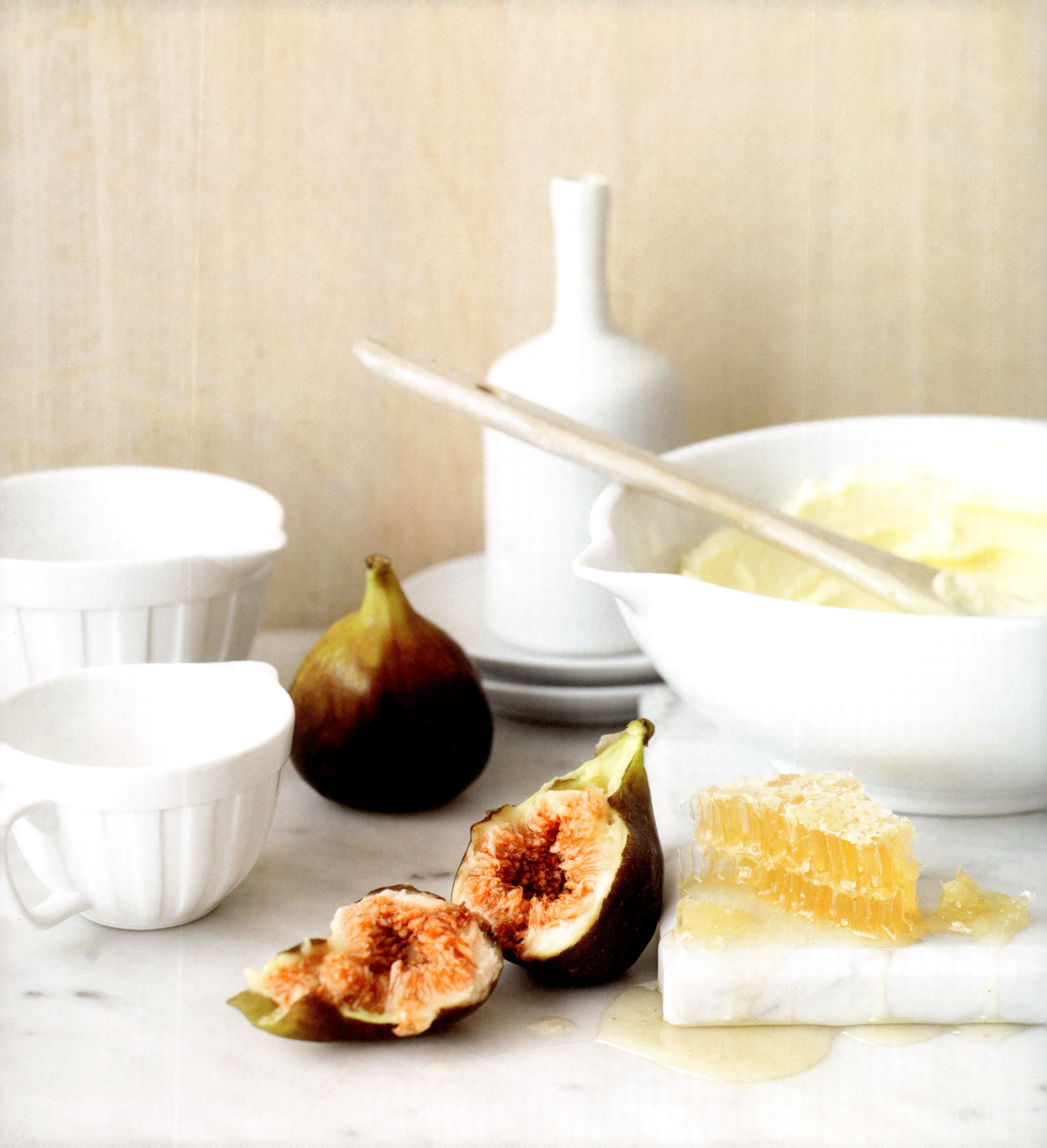

ENDS

COCONUT PANNA COTTA WITH COCONUT WAFERS AND CARAMELISED MANGO

prep + cook time 45 minutes (+ cooling & refrigeration) ~ serves 8

1¼ cups (310ml) pouring cream
½ cup (110g) caster (superfine) sugar
2 tablespoons powdered gelatine
⅓ cup (80ml) boiling water
375g (12 ounces) Greek-style vanilla yogurt
1 teaspoon coconut extract

coconut wafers
1 sheet puff pastry
1 egg white
½ cup (40g) desiccated coconut

caramelised mango
2 medium mangoes (860g)
⅓ cup (75g) caster (superfine) sugar

1 Stir cream and sugar in medium saucepan over high heat, without boiling, until sugar dissolves.

2 Sprinkle gelatine over the boiling water in small heatproof jug, stand jug in small saucepan of simmering water; stir until gelatine dissolves. Stir gelatine mixture into hot cream mixture. Transfer to medium bowl; cool.

3 Stir yogurt and extract into cooled cream mixture.

4 Rinse eight ¾-cup (180ml) moulds with cold water; drain, do not wipe dry. Pour yogurt mixture into moulds, cover loosely with plastic wrap; refrigerate 4 hours or until set.

5 Make coconut wafers then caramelised mango.

6 Carefully turn each panna cotta onto a serving plate. Serve with wafers and mango pieces.

coconut wafers
Preheat oven to 200°C/400°F. Grease and line oven tray with baking paper. Cut pastry in half, cut each half into four triangles; place on oven tray. Bake about 10 minutes. Remove from oven, brush with egg white, sprinkle with coconut. Bake a further 5 minutes or until coconut is golden.

caramelised mango
Remove cheeks from mangoes; using large metal spoon, scoop flesh from skin. Sprinkle cut surfaces of mango cheeks with sugar. Heat large frying pan; cook mango, cut-side down, about 2 minutes or until caramelised. Remove from pan; cool, then slice thinly.

nutritional count per serving
24.4g total fat (16.2g saturated fat); 1839kJ (440 cal); 48g carbohydrate; 8.2g protein; 1.8g fibre

tip You can use just one 300ml carton of cream for this recipe.

Stir dissolved gelatine mixture into hot cream mixture. Transfer to a medium heatproof bowl and cool.

Brush each partially baked pastry triangle with a little egg white, then sprinkle with desiccated coconut.

Using a sharp knife, cut the cheeks from the mangoes.

Stir butter and chocolate in a medium saucepan over low heat until smooth.

Fold the egg mixture and sifted flour into the chocolate mixture.

Cook the anglaise mixture over medium heat, without boiling, until the mixture thickens and coats the back of a wooden spoon.

CHOCOLATE FONDANTS WITH ESPRESSO ANGLAISE

prep + cook time 1 hour 15 minutes (+ refrigeration) ~ makes 6

200g (6½ ounces) butter, chopped coarsely
150g (4½ ounces) dark eating (semi-sweet) chocolate 70% cocoa, chopped coarsely
3 egg yolks
3 eggs
⅓ cup (75g) caster (superfine) sugar
⅔ cup (100g) plain (all-purpose) flour

espresso anglaise
2 cups (500ml) milk
½ vanilla bean
4 egg yolks
2 tablespoons caster (superfine) sugar
2 tablespoons strong espresso coffee

1 Grease 6-hole (¾-cup/180ml) texas muffin pan with 50g (1½ ounces) of the butter; line pan hole bases with a round of baking paper.

2 Stir butter and chocolate in medium saucepan over low heat until smooth. Transfer mixture to large bowl.

3 Beat egg yolks, eggs and sugar in small bowl with electric mixer until thick and creamy. Fold egg mixture and sifted flour into chocolate mixture. Spoon mixture into pan holes, place on oven tray; refrigerate 3 hours.

4 Make espresso anglaise.

5 Preheat oven to 180°C/350°F.

6 Bake fondants 14 minutes. Stand fondants 3 minutes. Use a small metal spatula to lever the fondants out of pan onto serving plates. Serve fondants immediately with anglaise.

espresso anglaise
Bring milk to the boil in small saucepan. Meanwhile, scrape seeds from vanilla bean into medium bowl; add egg yolks and sugar, whisk until combined. Gradually whisk hot milk mixture into egg mixture; stir in coffee. Strain mixture into same pan; cook, stirring, over medium heat, without boiling until mixture thickens and coats the back of a wooden spoon. Strain mixture into medium bowl; stand bowl inside a larger bowl filled with ice, stirring occasionally, until mixture is cold.

nutritional count per serving
47.6g total fat (30.2g saturated fat); 2579kJ (617 cal); 48.7g carbohydrate; 12.8g protein; 1.8g fibre

WHITE CHOCOLATE MERINGUE TORTE WITH LIQUEUR PEACHES

prep + cook time 1 hour 30 minutes (+ cooling & standing) ~ serves 8

6 egg whites
1½ cups (330g) caster (superfine) sugar
¼ teaspoon cream of tartar
½ teaspoon vanilla extract
1 teaspoon white vinegar
2 teaspoons cornflour (cornstarch)

white chocolate cream
180g (5½ ounces) white eating chocolate, chopped coarsely
2 cups (500ml) thickened (heavy) cream
1 tablespoon orange-flavoured liqueur
2 tablespoons icing (confectioners') sugar

liqueur peaches
4 large white peaches (880g)
¼ cup (60ml) orange-flavoured liqueur
¼ cup (55g) caster (superfine) sugar

1   Preheat oven to 100°C/210°F. Line three large oven trays with baking paper. Mark a 12cm x 30cm (5-inch x 12-inch) rectangle on each piece of paper; turn paper, marked-side down, on trays.

2   Beat egg whites, sugar and cream of tartar in medium bowl with electric mixer about 8 minutes or until sugar is dissolved and firm peaks form. Beat in extract, vinegar and cornflour.

3   Divide meringue evenly between marked rectangles; spread meringue to just inside marked lines.

4   Bake meringues about 40 minutes or until dry to touch. Cool in oven with door ajar.

5   Make white chocolate cream then liqueur peaches.

6   Place one meringue on serving plate. Spread with half the white chocolate cream. Repeat layering, finishing with meringue.

7   Serve meringue torte with liqueur peaches.

white chocolate cream
Stir chocolate and ¼ cup of the cream in small heatproof bowl over a small saucepan of simmering water until smooth. Transfer to large bowl, cool. Beat remaining cream, liqueur and sifted icing sugar in small bowl with electric mixer until soft peaks form. Fold into chocolate mixture, in two batches.

liqueur peaches
Make a small cross in skin of peaches at stem end. Place peaches in large heatproof bowl; cover with boiling water. Stand 30 seconds; drain. Peel away skins. Halve peaches; remove stones. Slice peaches into wedges. Place peach slices in large bowl with liqueur and sugar; toss gently. Stand about 20 minutes or until sugar is dissolved, stirring occasionally.

nutritional count per serving
24.7g total fat (16g saturated fat); 2019kJ (483 cal); 58.6g carbohydrate; 5.2g protein; 1g fibre

Beat egg whites, sugar and cream of tartar in medium bowl with electric mixer until sugar is dissolved and firm peaks form.

Divide the meringue between the baking-paper-lined oven trays, spreading the mixture just inside the marked rectangles.

Stir the white chocolate and ¼ cup of the thickened cream in a small heatproof bowl, over a small saucepan of simmering water, until smooth.

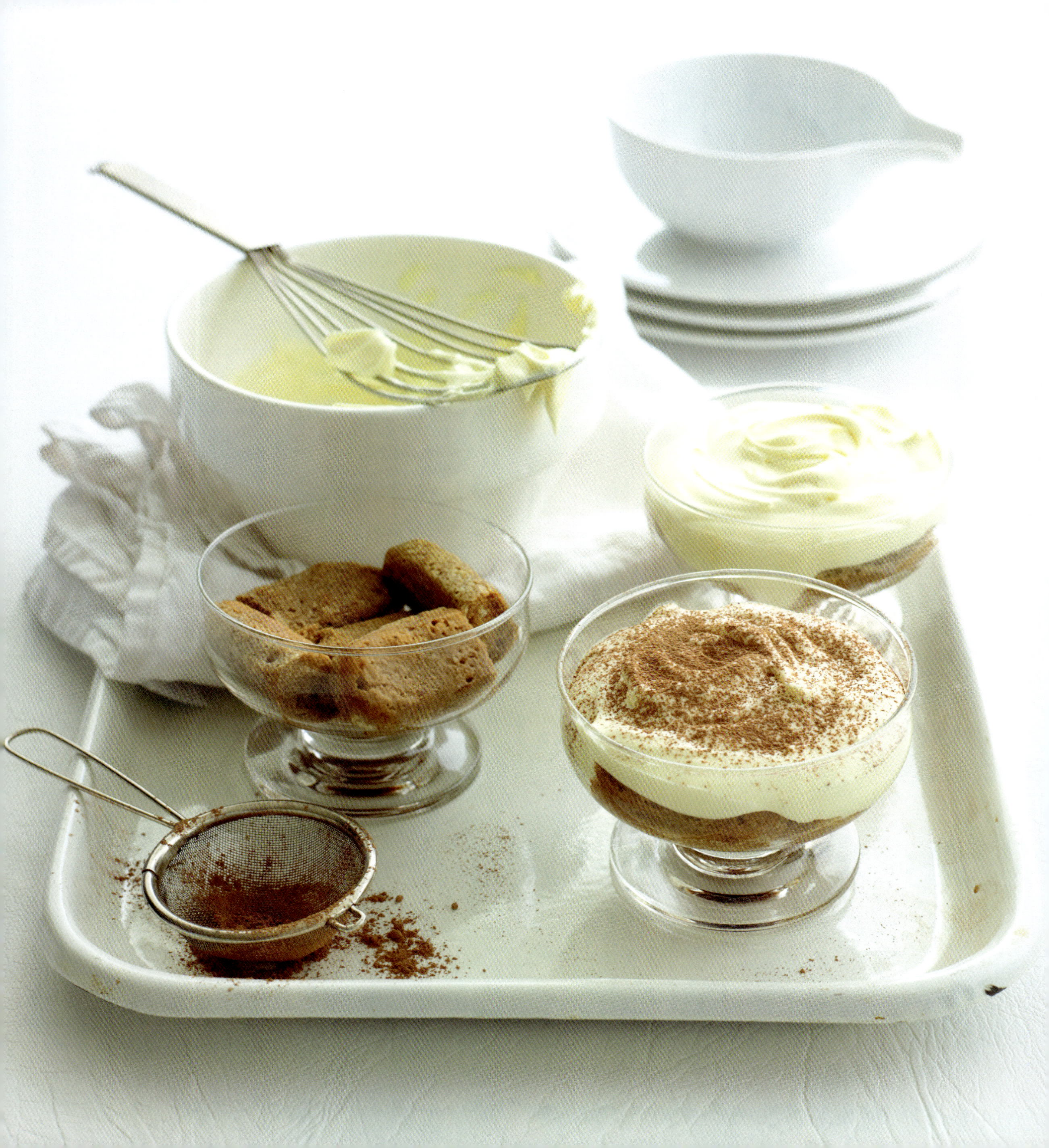

FREE-FORM TIRAMISU

prep time 10 minutes ~ serves 4

1 cup (250ml) strong espresso coffee, cooled
½ cup (125ml) coffee-flavoured liqueur
10 sponge finger biscuits, halved crossways
⅔ cup (160ml) thickened (heavy) cream
¼ cup (40g) icing (confectioners') sugar
250g (8 ounces) mascarpone cheese

1 Combine coffee and ⅓ cup of the liqueur in small bowl. Dip biscuits, one at a time, into coffee mixture. Line four 1 cup (250ml) serving glasses with biscuits; drizzle with any remaining coffee mixture.

2 Beat cream and sifted icing sugar in small bowl with electric mixer until soft peaks form; beat in mascarpone and remaining liqueur.

3 Spoon cream mixture into glasses; serve, dusted with a little sifted cocoa, if you like.

nutritional count per serving
37g total fat (23.5g saturated fat); 2550kJ (610 cal); 47.4g carbohydrate; 8.6g protein; 0.4g fibre

tip To make a strong espresso coffee, combine 4 tablespoons instant espresso coffee and 1 cup boiling water.

Dip sponge finger biscuit halves, one at a time, into the coffee mixture. Be careful not to soak them for too long or they will become soggy and fall apart.

Place the coffee-soaked biscuits into four serving glasses.

Pour the remaining liqueur into the whipped cream mixture, then add the mascarpone and beat until combined. Spoon the mixture onto the coffee-soaked biscuits.

MASCARPONE BERRY PILLOWS

prep + cook time 15 minutes ~ serves 4

300g (10 ounces) frozen mixed berries
2 tablespoons citrus-flavoured liqueur
⅓ cup (55g) icing (confectioners') sugar
1 sheet butter puff pastry
200g (6½ ounces) mascarpone cheese
½ cup (125ml) thickened (heavy) cream

1 Place berries in medium bowl; sprinkle with liqueur and 1 tablespoon of the sifted icing sugar.

2 Preheat oven to 220°C/425°F. Line oven tray with baking paper.

3 Cut pastry sheet into eight rectangles. Place on oven tray. Dust pastry with 2 teaspoons of the sifted icing sugar. Bake about 10 minutes. Cool.

4 Beat mascarpone, cream and 2 tablespoons of the remaining sifted icing sugar in small bowl with electric mixer until soft peaks form.

5 Sandwich mascarpone mixture, berries and any berry juices between pastry pieces. Just before serving, dust with remaining sifted icing sugar.

nutritional count per serving
37.8g total fat (23.3g saturated fat); 2391kJ (572 cal); 42.8g carbohydrate; 8g protein; 3.5g fibre

tip Be careful not to over-beat mascarpone as it could curdle.

Cut the sheet of pastry into eight equal-sized rectangles. Place on a baking-paper-lined oven tray.

Dust the pastry rectangles with 2 teaspoons of the icing sugar.

Spoon the mascarpone mixture then berry mixture onto four pastry rectangles; top with the remaining pastry.

Grease the soufflé dishes with butter, sprinkle inside the dish with caster sugar to coat the base and side. Shake out any excess sugar.

Stir the chocolate in a large heatproof bowl over a large saucepan of simmering water until melted.

Fold the beaten egg white mixture into the chocolate mixture, in two batches.

HOT CHOCOLATE SOUFFLES WITH POACHED CHERRIES

prep + cook time 50 minutes (+ cooling) ~ serves 6

2 tablespoons caster (superfine) sugar
200g (6½ ounces) dark eating (semi-sweet) chocolate, chopped coarsely
4 eggs, separated
2 egg whites
¼ cup (55g) caster (superfine) sugar, extra
1 teaspoon icing (confectioners') sugar
3 cups (750ml) vanilla ice-cream

poached cherries
¼ cup (55g) caster (superfine) sugar
5cm (2-inch) strip orange rind
½ cup (125ml) orange juice
½ cup (125ml) water
500g (1 pound) fresh cherries, seeded
2 tablespoons orange-flavoured liqueur

1 Make poached cherries.

2 Preheat oven to 200°C/400°F. Grease six ½-cup (125ml) soufflé dishes with butter, sprinkle with caster sugar; shake out excess sugar.

3 Place chocolate in large heatproof bowl over large saucepan of simmering water (don't let water touch base of bowl); stir until chocolate is melted. Cool 5 minutes; stir in egg yolks.

4 Beat all six egg whites and extra caster sugar in medium bowl with electric mixer until soft peaks form. Fold into chocolate mixture, in two batches. Spoon mixture into dishes; smooth tops. Place dishes on oven tray.

5 Bake soufflés about 10 minutes. Serve immediately, dusted with sifted icing sugar, poached cherries and ice-cream.

poached cherries
Stir sugar, rind, juice and the water in medium saucepan over high heat, without boiling, until sugar dissolves. Bring to the boil, reduce heat; simmer, uncovered, 2 minutes. Add cherries, return to the boil. Reduce heat; simmer, covered, 2 minutes. Remove from heat; stir in liqueur. Cool.

nutritional count per serving
20.5g total fat (16.7g saturated fat); 2094kJ (501 cal); 68.7g carbohydrate; 10.1g protein; 3g fibre

CHOCOLATE MOUSSE

prep + cook time 35 minutes (+ refrigeration) ~ serves 6

200g (6½ ounces) dark eating (semi-sweet) chocolate, chopped coarsely
30g (1 ounce) unsalted butter
3 eggs, separated
1¼ cups (310ml) thickened (heavy) cream

1 Melt chocolate and butter in large heatproof bowl over large saucepan of simmering water (don't let water touch base of bowl). Cool 5 minutes; stir in egg yolks. Cool.

2 Beat egg whites in small bowl with electric mixer until soft peaks form. Beat cream in another small bowl with electric mixer until soft peaks form.

3 Fold cream into chocolate mixture; fold in egg whites, in two batches.

4 Spoon mousse mixture into ¾ cup (180ml) serving dishes; refrigerate 3 hours or overnight.

nutritional count per serving
34.8g total fat (21.4g saturated fat); 1777kJ (425 cal); 22.5g carbohydrate; 6.1g protein; 0.4g fibre

tips The eggs must be at room temperature for success with this recipe.

You can use just one 300ml carton of cream for this recipe.

serving suggestion Serve with whipped cream, chocolate curls and fresh raspberries.

Stir the chocolate and butter in a large heatproof bowl over a large saucepan of simmering water until melted.

Fold the egg white mixture into the chocolate mixture, in two batches.

To make the chocolate curls for decorating, use a vegetable peeler to scrape along the side of a long piece of room-temperature chocolate. Clean the peeler often so the chocolate doesn't clog up the blade.

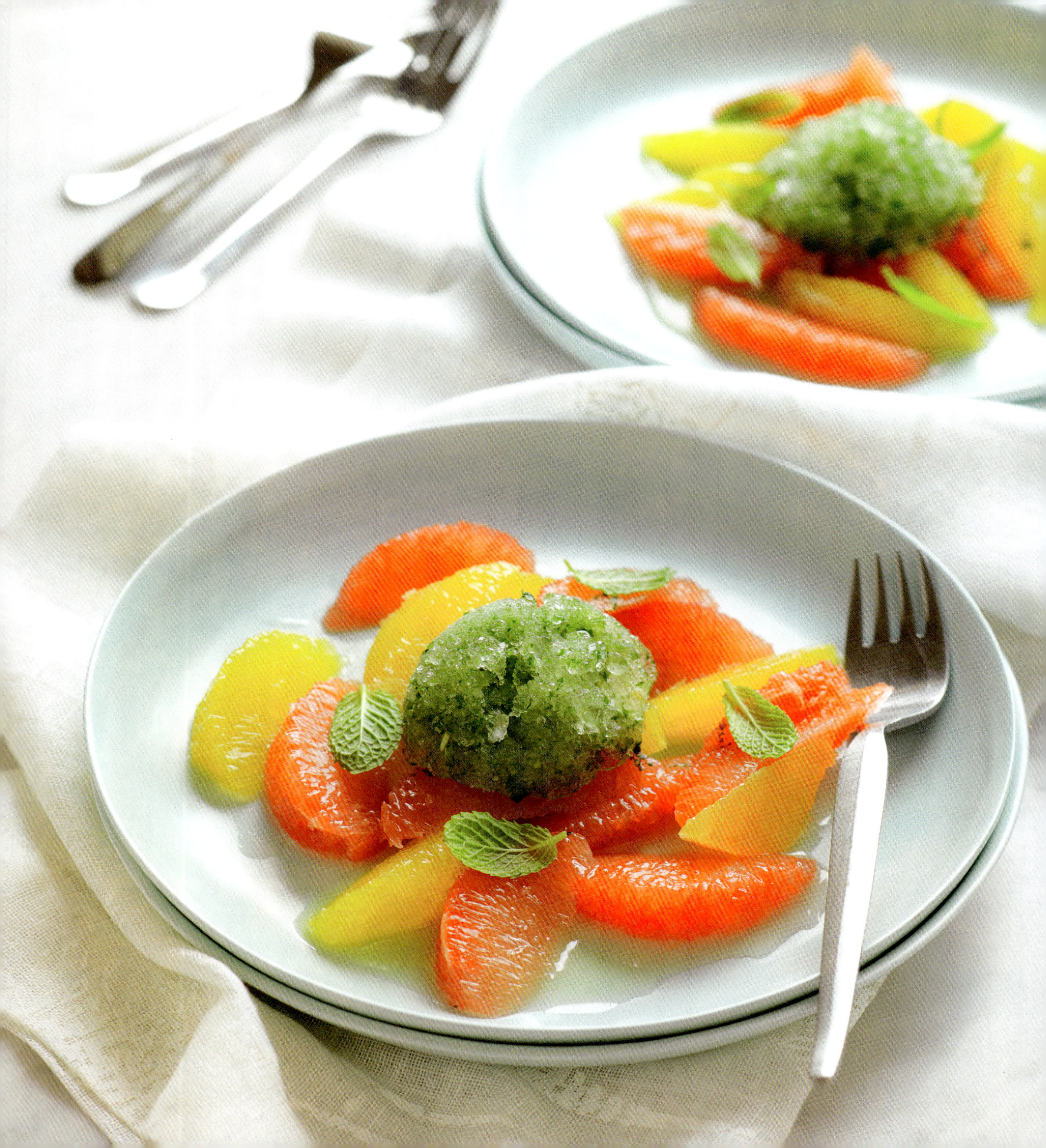

CITRUS SALAD WITH LIME AND MINT GRANITA

prep time 15 minutes ~ serves 4

2 medium oranges (480g)
2 small pink grapefruits (700g)
2 cups ice cubes
⅓ cup finely chopped fresh mint
2 tablespoons icing (confectioners') sugar
1 tablespoon lime juice

1 Segment oranges and grapefruits into medium bowl.

2 Blend or process ice, mint, sugar and juice until ice is crushed.

3 Serve fruit segments with granita; top with a few extra fresh mint leaves, if you like.

nutritional count per serving
0.4g total fat (0g saturated fat); 385kJ (92 cal); 18.1g carbohydrate; 2.1g protein; 2.7g fibre

tip Make the lime and mint granita at the last minute – it will melt quickly if left waiting.

Cut the top and bottom off each orange and grapefruit; cut down the side following the curve of the fruit, to remove the rind and white pith.

Segment the fruit over a plate or bowl, cutting between the membrane.

To make the granita, process the ice, mint, sugar and juice until the ice is crushed.

CREME CARAMEL

prep + cook time 1 hour (+ refrigeration) ~ serves 8

Also known in France as crème renversee, crème caramel is a custard that has been baked in a caramel-coated mould. When the chilled custard is turned out onto a serving plate it is automatically glazed and sauced with the caramel in the mould. In Italy it's known as crema caramella, and in Spain as flan. You can flavour it with orange, cinnamon or coffee.

¾ cup (165g) caster (superfine) sugar
½ cup (125ml) water
6 eggs
1 teaspoon vanilla extract
½ cup (75g) caster (superfine) sugar, extra
1¼ cups (310ml) thickened (heavy) cream
1¾ cups (430ml) milk

1 Preheat oven to 160°C/325°F.

2 Stir sugar and the water in medium heavy-based frying pan over heat, without boiling, until sugar dissolves. (Use pastry brush dipped in water to brush any sugar crystals down from side of pan before mixture boils.) Bring to the boil; boil, without stirring, until mixture is a deep caramel colour. Remove from heat; allow bubbles to subside. Pour toffee into deep 20cm (8-inch) round cake pan.

3 Whisk eggs, extract and extra sugar in large bowl.

4 Bring cream and milk to the boil in medium saucepan. Whisking constantly, pour hot milk mixture into egg mixture. Strain mixture into cake pan.

5 Place cake pan in baking dish; add enough boiling water to come halfway up side of pan. Bake about 40 minutes or until set.

6 Remove crème caramel from baking dish. Cover; refrigerate overnight.

7 Gently ease crème caramel from side of pan; invert onto deep-sided serving plate.

nutritional count per serving
22.3g total fat (13.3g saturated fat); 1526kJ (365 cal); 33.8g carbohydrate; 7.5g protein; 0g fibre

tips You can use just one 300ml carton cream for this recipe.

This recipe must be made a day ahead and it will keep for up to 4 days, covered, and refrigerated.

Use a heavy saucepan to make the caramel, stirring the sugar and water over medium heat. Once the sugar has dissolved and the mixture starts to boil, watch it carefully. As soon as it starts to brown, tilt the pan until the brown areas merge. Keep tilting and turning the pan until the toffee is a rich golden colour. Remove the pan from the heat, let the bubbles subside, then pour toffee over the base of the cake pan. There is no need to coat the side of the pan, or even grease it.

All the sugar needs to be dissolved when you're making caramel. Some sugar will stick to the sides of the pan – brush these off using a dampened pastry brush.

When the caramel is a deep, rich brown, pour it into the base of a deep 20cm cake pan. Tilt the pan until the base is completely covered.

Place the custard pan into a baking dish then pour in enough boiling water until it comes halfway up the side of the cake pan.

Lift pastry into pans, pressing over the base and side. Trim the excess pastry by rolling over the pan with a rolling pin. Prick the bases all over with a fork.

Pour the custard filling through a strainer into the same cleaned saucepan, then discard the vanilla bean.

Sprinkle the extra caster sugar onto the custard filling. Using a blowtorch, caramelise the sugar.

VANILLA AND RASPBERRY CREME BRULEE TARTS

prep + cook time 1 hour 45 minutes (+ refrigeration & cooling) ~ makes 8

A blowtorch is available from kitchenware and hardware stores.

1⅔ cups (250g) plain (all-purpose) flour
185g (6 ounces) cold butter, chopped
¼ cup (60ml) iced water, approximately
2 tablespoons raspberry jam
1 vanilla bean
1 cup (250ml) milk
2 egg yolks
1 tablespoon caster (superfine) sugar
1 tablespoon cornflour (cornstarch)
½ cup (110g) caster (superfine) sugar, extra

1 Sift flour into large bowl; rub in butter until crumbly. Mix in enough of the water to make ingredients just come together. Knead dough lightly on floured surface until smooth. Flatten pastry slightly, wrap in plastic wrap; refrigerate 30 minutes.

2 Grease eight 8cm (3¼-inch) round loose-based fluted flan pans. Divide pastry into eight equal portions. Roll out each portion on floured surface or between sheets of baking paper until large enough to line pans.

3 Lift pastry into pans; press over base and side, trim excess pastry. Prick bases all over with fork, place pans on oven tray; refrigerate 30 minutes.

4 Preheat oven to 200°C/400°F.

5 Line pastry with baking paper; fill with dried beans or rice. Bake 15 minutes. Remove paper and beans; bake a further 10 minutes or until browned lightly and crisp. Cool. Drop 1 teaspoon of jam into each tart shell.

6 Split vanilla bean lengthways; scrape seeds into medium saucepan, add pod and milk. Bring to the boil; remove from heat. Whisk egg yolks, sugar and cornflour in medium heatproof bowl until combined; gradually whisk in hot milk mixture. Strain into same saucepan; discard vanilla bean. Whisk over high heat until mixture boils and thickens. Remove from heat; spoon into tart shells. Cool 5 minutes; refrigerate until cold.

7 Sprinkle extra sugar onto custard. Using a blowtorch, caramelise sugar. Stand 5 minutes or until caramel cools and sets.

nutritional count per tart
24.6g total fat (15.1g saturated fat); 1914kJ (458 cal); 53.1g carbohydrate; 7.2g protein; 1.3g fibre

tips You can also make the pastry using a food processor. Process flour and butter until crumbly; with motor operating, add the water and process until ingredients just come together. Or you can use ready-made shortcrust pastry.

If you don't have a blowtorch, place the remaining sugar and 2 tablespoons water in a small heavy-based saucepan over medium heat; cook, stirring, 2 minutes, until sugar dissolves. Bring to the boil; cook, without stirring, 5 minutes, or until syrup turns deep golden. Remove from heat. Pour over cold custard and stand 1 minute or until caramel sets.

SALTED PEANUT CARAMELS

prep + cook time 30 minutes (+ standing) ~ makes 40

1½ cups (330g) caster (superfine) sugar
1¼ cups (310ml) thickened (heavy) cream
¼ cup (90g) glucose syrup
2 tablespoons golden syrup
¼ teaspoon cream of tartar
150g (4½ ounces) roasted salted peanuts, chopped coarsely
1 teaspoon sea salt flakes

1 Grease 14cm x 21cm (5½-inch x 8½-inch) loaf pan; line base and long sides with baking paper, extending paper 5cm (2 inches) over sides.

2 Stir sugar, cream, glucose, golden syrup and cream of tartar in medium saucepan, over high heat, without boiling, until sugar dissolves. Bring to the boil; boil, uncovered, without stirring, until mixture reaches 128°C/262°F on a candy thermometer. Add nuts to caramel; do not stir.

3 Pour caramel mixture into pan; sprinkle with salt. Stand at room temperature until set.

4 Use a hot oiled sharp knife to cut caramel into squares.

nutritional count per square
4.7g total fat (2.1g saturated fat); 364kJ (87 cal); 11.6g carbohydrate; 1.1g protein; 0.3g fibre

tips You can use just one 300ml carton of cream for this recipe.

Store caramels between layers of baking paper in an airtight container, in a cool dry place, for up to 1 week.

Bring the caramel mixture to the boil, uncovered, without stirring, until it reaches 128°C/262°F on a candy thermometer.

Pour the caramel and nut mixture into the greased and baking-paper-lined pan. Stand at room temperature until set.

Use a hot, oiled knife to cut the caramel into pieces.

Fold sifted icing sugar, ground almonds and blackberry puree into the beaten egg white, in two batches.

Pipe macaroons onto greased and baking-paper-lined oven trays. Tap the trays on the bench so macaroons spread slightly. Stand 45 minutes or until dry to touch.

Sandwich the macaroons together with some blackberry jam, then dust with sifted icing sugar just before serving.

BLACKBERRY FRENCH MINI-MACAROONS

prep + cook time 50 minutes (+ standing & cooling) ~ makes 16

3 egg whites
¼ cup (55g) caster (superfine) sugar
purple food colouring
70g (2½ ounces) fresh or thawed frozen blackberries
1¼ cups (200g) pure icing (confectioners') sugar
1 cup (120g) ground almonds
⅓ cup (110g) blackberry jam
1 tablespoon pure icing (confectioners') sugar, extra

1 Preheat oven to 150°C/300°F. Grease oven trays; line with baking paper.

2 Beat egg whites in small bowl with electric mixer until soft peaks form. Add caster sugar and a few drops of colouring; beat until sugar dissolves. Transfer mixture to a large bowl.

3 Push blackberries through fine sieve into small bowl; you need 1 tablespoon of blackberry puree.

4 Fold sifted icing sugar, ground almonds and puree into egg white mixture, in two batches.

5 Spoon mixture into piping bag fitted with 1cm (½-inch) plain tube. Pipe 3cm (1¼-inch) rounds, about 2.5cm (1 inch) apart, onto trays. Tap trays on bench so macaroons spread slightly. Stand 45 minutes or until macaroons feel dry to touch.

6 Bake about 15 minutes. Cool on trays.

7 Sandwich macaroons with jam. Dust with extra sifted icing sugar.

nutritional count per macaroon
4.2g total fat (0.3g saturated fat); 548kJ (313 cal); 21.8g carbohydrate; 2.3g protein; 1g fibre

tips If you don't have purple food colouring, use a few drops each of red and blue food colouring until the desired shade of purple is achieved.

Unfilled macaroons will keep, stored in an airtight container, for about a week. Fill with the jam before serving.

TURKISH DELIGHT SUNDAE

prep time 10 minutes ~ serves 6

Process raspberries and icing sugar until pureed.

Roughly chop the turkish delight bars into small pieces.

Dip an ice-cream scoop into hot water then drag across the ice-cream to make a full scoop; place in serving glasses.

150g (4½ ounces) fresh or thawed frozen raspberries
1 tablespoon icing (confectioners') sugar
1.5 litres (6 cups) vanilla ice-cream
4 x 55g (2 ounces) chocolate-coated turkish delight
½ cup (70g) coarsely chopped roasted pistachios

1 Process raspberries and icing sugar until pureed.

2 Chop the turkish delight into pieces.

3 Layer scoops of ice-cream, raspberry puree, turkish delight and nuts in six serving glasses.

nutritional count per serving
21g total fat (10.5g saturated fat); 1619kJ (387 cal); 44.2g carbohydrate; 7.3g protein; 2.5g fibre

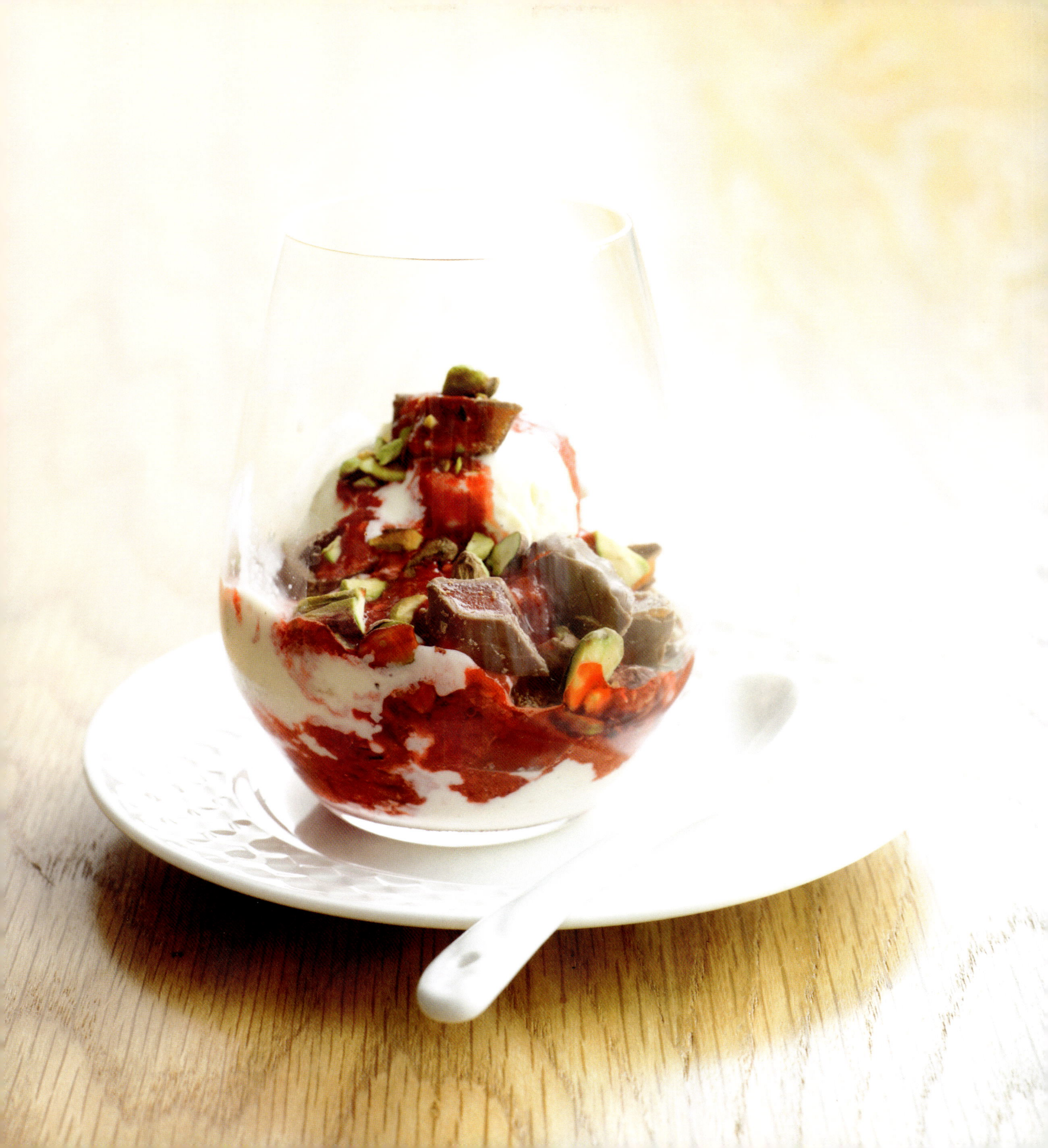

Peel and core the apples, then cut in half. Cut each half into four wedges.

Cook the apples in melted butter and brown sugar until the mixture thickens. Transfer apples to the ovenproof dish.

Pour the clafoutis batter over the apples, then bake for 40 minutes.

CARAMELISED APPLE CLAFOUTIS

prep + cook time 1 hour 5 minutes (+ cooling) ~ serves 6

Clafoutis is originally from the Limousin region of central France where, in the local dialect, it translates as "brimming over". It is one of the world's easiest desserts to make: a sweet batter is poured into a baking dish "brimming" with cherries, prunes or the fresh fruit of your choice, and baked. Traditionally, cherries native to the region were used.

6 medium apples (900g)
50g (1½ ounces) unsalted butter
½ cup (110g) firmly packed light brown sugar
80g (2½ ounces) unsalted butter, extra
⅓ cup (75g) caster (superfine) sugar
⅓ cup (50g) plain (all-purpose) flour
⅓ cup (50g) self-raising flour
4 eggs
⅔ cup (160ml) milk
⅔ cup (160ml) pouring cream
1 teaspoon vanilla extract

1 Preheat oven to 200°C/400°F. Grease shallow 2.5-litre (10-cup) ovenproof dish.

2 Peel, core and halve apples; cut each half into four wedges.

3 Melt butter in large frying pan; cook apples, stirring, 5 minutes or until browned lightly. Add brown sugar; cook 5 minutes or until mixture thickens. Transfer to dish; cool 5 minutes.

4 Melt extra butter. Combine caster sugar and sifted flours in medium bowl. Lightly beat eggs, butter, milk, cream and vanilla in small bowl. Gradually whisk egg mixture into flour mixture until smooth. Pour mixture over apples.

5 Bake clafoutis 40 minutes. Serve hot, dusted with a little sifted icing sugar, if you like.

nutritional count per serving
34.4g total fat (21.3g saturated); 2404kJ (575 cal); 57.2g carbohydrate; 8g protein; 2.9g fibre

serving suggestion Serve with whipped cream.

PEAR AND MARSHMALLOW TRIFLES

prep + cook time 45 minutes (+ cooling & refrigeration) ~ makes 6

Edible gold leaf and candy thermometers are available from kitchenware stores and cake decorating suppliers.

3 eggs
¾ cup (165g) caster (superfine) sugar
1 cup (150g) self-raising flour
3 medium pears (630g)
½ cup (110g) caster (superfine) sugar, extra
2 cups (500ml) water
1 medium orange (240g)
¼ cup (30g) coarsely chopped roasted unsalted pistachios
6 x 3cm x 4cm (1¼-inch x 1½-inch) sheets edible gold leaf

marshmallow
1 cup (220g) caster (superfine) sugar
¾ cup (180ml) water
3 teaspoons powdered gelatine
2 tablespoons water, extra

1 Preheat oven to 180°C/350°F. Grease 20cm x 30cm (8-inch x 12-inch) rectangular pan; line base and long sides with baking paper, extending paper 5cm (2 inches) over sides.

2 Beat eggs and sugar in small bowl with electric mixer until thick and creamy and sugar is dissolved. Transfer mixture to large bowl. Sift flour over egg mixture then fold ingredients together. Pour mixture into pan.

3 Bake sponge about 30 minutes. Turn sponge immediately, top-side up, onto baking-paper-covered wire rack to cool.

4 Meanwhile, peel, quarter and core pears.

5 Place extra sugar and the water in medium saucepan. Using vegetable peeler, remove 5cm (2-inch) strip of rind from orange; juice orange (you need ¼ cup juice). Add rind and juice to pan; stir over high heat, without boiling, until sugar dissolves. Bring to the boil, reduce heat; simmer, uncovered, 3 minutes. Add pear; simmer, uncovered, until pear is barely tender. Cool pear in poaching liquid.

6 Make marshmallow.

7 Cut cake into 2cm (¾-inch) cubes, divide between six serving glasses; sprinkle each with a tablespoon of pear poaching liquid, top with pears. Spoon marshmallow mixture into glasses; sprinkle with nuts. Use tweezers to lift pieces of gold leaf onto stems of pears; wrap around stems gently, being careful not to touch the gold leaf with your hands, as it will stick.

marshmallow
Stir sugar and the water in medium saucepan over high heat, without boiling, until sugar dissolves; bring to the boil. Reduce heat; simmer, uncovered, without stirring, until syrup reaches 115°C/240°F on a candy thermometer. Meanwhile, sprinkle gelatine over the extra water in small bowl; stand mixture 5 minutes. Stir gelatine mixture into hot syrup; transfer mixture to medium heatproof bowl, cool until mixture is only just warm. Beat sugar syrup with electric mixer about 8 minutes or until thick and glossy.

nutritional count per trifle
5.6g total fat (1.1g saturated fat); 2132kJ (510 cal); 108.7g carbohydrate; 8.5g protein; 3g fibre

Stir the sugar and the water in saucepan over high heat, without boiling, until sugar dissolves. Bring to the boil, then simmer, without stirring, until it reaches 115°/240°F on a candy thermometer.

Stir the sugar syrup and gelatine mixture; transfer to medium heatproof bowl. Beat warm mixture with electric mixer for about 8 minutes or until thick and glossy.

Using tweezers, lift pieces of gold leaf onto the stems of the pears, wrapping gently around the stems. Be careful not to touch the gold leaf with your fingers or hands as it will stick.

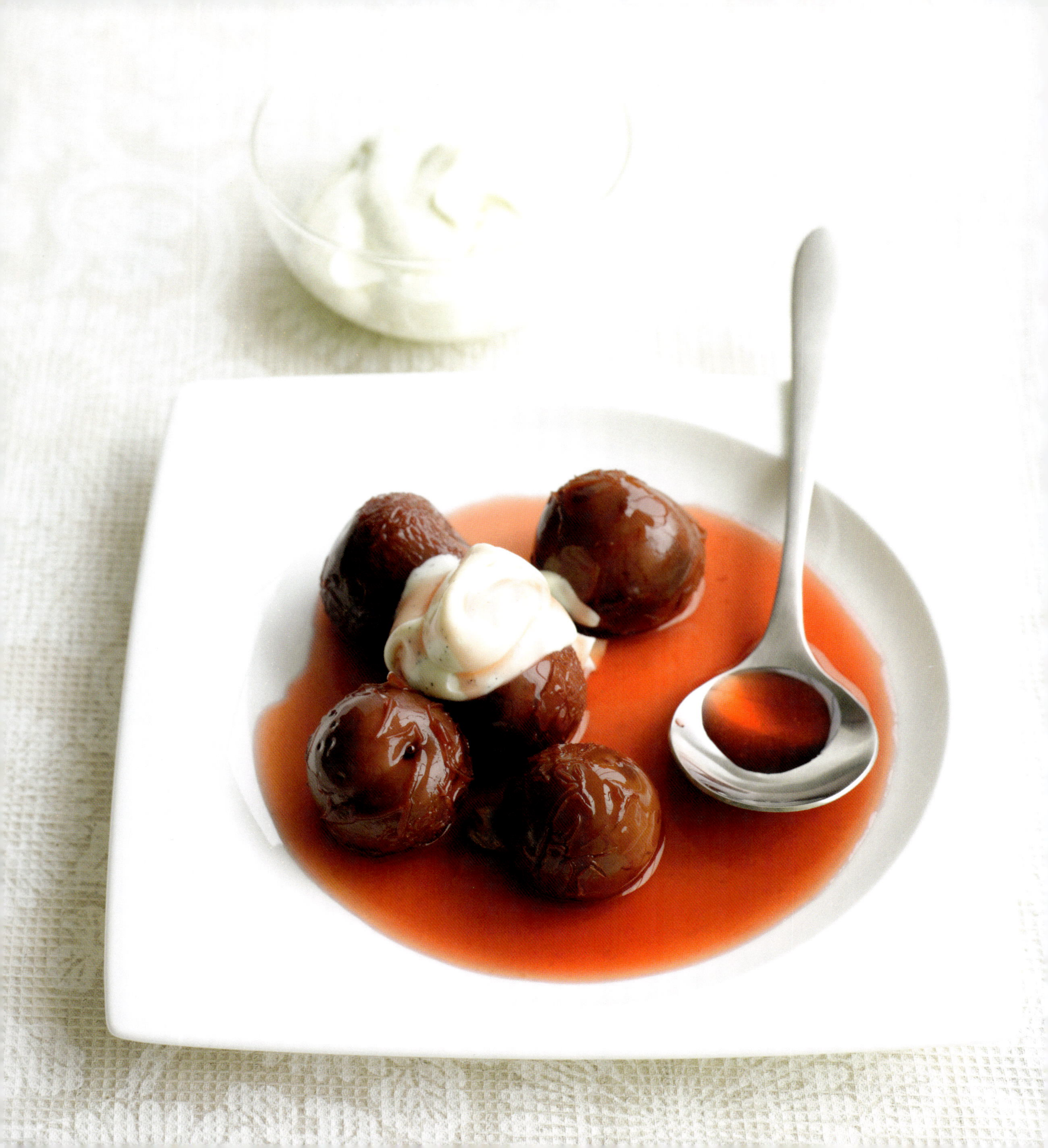

PLUMS WITH CREAMY VANILLA YOGURT

prep + cook time 15 minutes ~ serves 6

2 x 825g (1¾ pounds) canned whole plums
6 cardamom pods, bruised
2 cinnamon sticks

creamy vanilla yogurt
1 vanilla bean
½ cup (140g) Greek-style yogurt
⅓ cup (80ml) thick (double) cream
2 tablespoons sifted icing (confectioners') sugar

1 Make creamy vanilla yogurt

2 Drain juice from whole plums into medium saucepan. Add cardamom and cinnamon; bring to the boil. Reduce heat; simmer, uncovered, 3 minutes. Remove from heat. Add plums to juice mixture; cover pan, stand 10 minutes before serving.

3 Spoon warm plums and a little of the juice into serving bowls; serve with yogurt.

creamy vanilla yogurt
Split vanilla bean lengthways; scrape seeds into a medium bowl, then stir in remaining ingredients.

nutritional count per serving
6.9g total fat (4.5g saturated fat); 1170kJ (279 cal); 51.4g carbohydrate; 2.5g protein; 2.8g fibre

To bruise the cardamom pods, push down on the pods using the back of a large knife.

Drain juice from whole plums into a medium saucepan; reserve plums. Add bruised cardamom and the cinnamon sticks to the plum juice.

Cut the vanilla bean in half lengthways; scrape out the seeds, then place in a medium bowl.

MANGO, RASPBERRY AND KAFFIR LIME SORBETS

prep + cook time 1 hour (+ freezing) ~ serves 6

¾ cup (120g) pure icing (confectioners') sugar
½ cup (40g) toasted shredded coconut
½ cup (60g) ground almonds
2 egg whites
¼ cup (55g) caster (superfine) sugar

mango sorbet
425g (13½ ounces) canned mangoes, drained
1 tablespoon lemon juice
½ cup (110g) caster (superfine) sugar

raspberry sorbet
250g (8 ounces) fresh raspberries
½ cup (110g) caster (superfine) sugar
1 teaspoon finely grated orange rind
2 tablespoons orange juice

kaffir lime sorbet
½ cup (125ml) canned coconut water
8 fresh kaffir lime leaves, torn
½ cup (110g) caster (superfine) sugar
¼ teaspoon fine table salt
2 tablespoons lime juice

1 Make all three sorbets.

2 Preheat oven to 180°C/ 350°F. Grease 24cm x 32cm (9½-inch x 13-inch) swiss roll pan; line base and long sides with baking paper, extending paper 5cm (2 inches) over sides.

3 To make dacquoise: sift icing sugar into medium bowl; stir in coconut and ground almonds. Beat egg whites in small bowl with electric mixer until soft peaks form; add caster sugar, beat until sugar dissolves. Fold egg white mixture into coconut mixture. Spread mixture into pan.

4 Bake dacquoise about 10 minutes. Immediately turn onto baking-paper-lined wire rack, peel away lining paper. Cool. Cut dacquoise into twelve 4cm x 10cm (1½-inch x 4-inch) pieces; place six pieces on serving plates.

5 Spoon rounded tablespoons of each sorbet onto half the dacquoise pieces; top with remaining dacquoise. Serve immediately.

mango sorbet
Blend or process mango and juice until smooth. Combine sugar and half the mango puree in small saucepan; stir over low heat until sugar dissolves. Remove from heat; strain into small bowl. Stand small bowl inside a larger bowl filled with ice, stirring occasionally, until mixture is cold. Stir in remaining puree. Churn mixture in an ice-cream maker, following manufacturer's instructions. Spoon into deep airtight container, freeze until firm.

raspberry sorbet
Stir ingredients in small saucepan, over low heat until sugar dissolves and berries are pulpy. Remove from heat; strain into small bowl. Stand small bowl inside a larger bowl filled with ice, stirring occasionally, until mixture is cold. Churn mixture in an ice-cream maker, following manufacturer's instructions. Spoon into deep airtight container, freeze until firm.

kaffir lime sorbet
Stir ingredients in small saucepan, over low heat until sugar dissolves. Bring to the boil; remove from heat. Strain mixture into small bowl. Stand small bowl inside a larger bowl filled with ice, stirring occasionally, until mixture is cold. Churn mixture in an ice-cream maker, following manufacturer's instructions. Spoon into deep airtight container and freeze until firm.

nutritional count per serving
10.2g total fat (3.9g saturated fat); 1003kJ (240 cal); 94.3g carbohydrate; 4.9g protein; 4.7g fibre

Place the mango puree and sugar mixture in small bowl over ice inside a large bowl; stir until the mixture is cold.

To make the dacquoise, stir sifted icing sugar, coconut and ground almonds in a medium bowl until combined. Fold egg white mixture into coconut mixture.

Turn the baked dacquoise immediately onto a baking-paper-lined wire rack, then peel away the lining paper. Cool.

Cut the vanilla beans in half lengthways, then scrape the seeds into the milk and cream mixture in the saucepan. Add the vanilla pods to the pan.

Whisk the egg yolks and sugar in medium heatproof bowl until creamy.

Strain custard mixture into a medium heatproof bowl. Cover the surface of the custard with plastic wrap then refrigerate until cold.

VANILLA BEAN ICE-CREAM

prep + cook time 25 minutes (+ refrigeration, churning & freezing) ~ serves 8

1⅔ cups (410ml) milk
2⅓ cups (580ml) thickened (heavy) cream
2 vanilla beans
8 egg yolks
¾ cup (165g) caster (superfine) sugar

1 Place milk and cream in medium saucepan. Split vanilla beans in half lengthways; scrape seeds into milk mixture in pan then add the pods. Bring to the boil.

2 Meanwhile, whisk egg yolks and sugar in medium bowl until creamy; gradually whisk into hot milk mixture. Stir over low heat, without boiling, until mixture thickens slightly.

3 Strain mixture into medium heatproof bowl; discard pods. Cover surface of custard with plastic wrap; refrigerate about 1 hour or until cold.

4 Pour custard into ice-cream maker, churn according to manufacturer's instructions (or place custard in shallow container, such as an aluminium slab cake pan, cover with foil; freeze until almost firm). Place ice-cream in large bowl, chop coarsely then beat with electric mixer until smooth. Pour into deep container, cover; freeze until firm. Repeat process two more times.

nutritional count per serving
35.5g total fat (21.4g saturated fat); 1856kJ (444 cal); 25.5g carbohydrate; 6.5g protein; 0g fibre

tip You can use one 600ml carton (or two 300ml cartons) cream for this recipe.

STRAWBERRIES IN ROSEWATER SYRUP

prep + cook time 10 minutes ~ serves 6

Roughly chop the roasted pistachios.

Hull all the strawberries then thickly slice. Place all the strawberries in a medium heatproof bowl.

Pour the rosewater sugar syrup over the strawberries, then stir gently to coat in the syrup mixture.

750g (1½ pounds) strawberries
⅓ cup (80ml) water
¼ cup (55g) caster (superfine) sugar
2 teaspoons rosewater
⅓ cup (45g) coarsely chopped roasted unsalted pistachios

1 Hull strawberries; slice thickly. Place strawberries in medium heatproof bowl.

2 Stir water and sugar in small saucepan over high heat until sugar dissolves; do not boil. Remove from heat; stir in rosewater. Pour syrup over strawberries.

3 Divide strawberry mixture among six serving dishes; sprinkle with nuts.

nutritional count per serving
3.9g total fat (0.4g saturated fat); 447kJ (107 cal); 14.6g carbohydrate; 3.6g protein; 3.4g fibre

serving suggestion Serve with mini meringues or ice-cream.

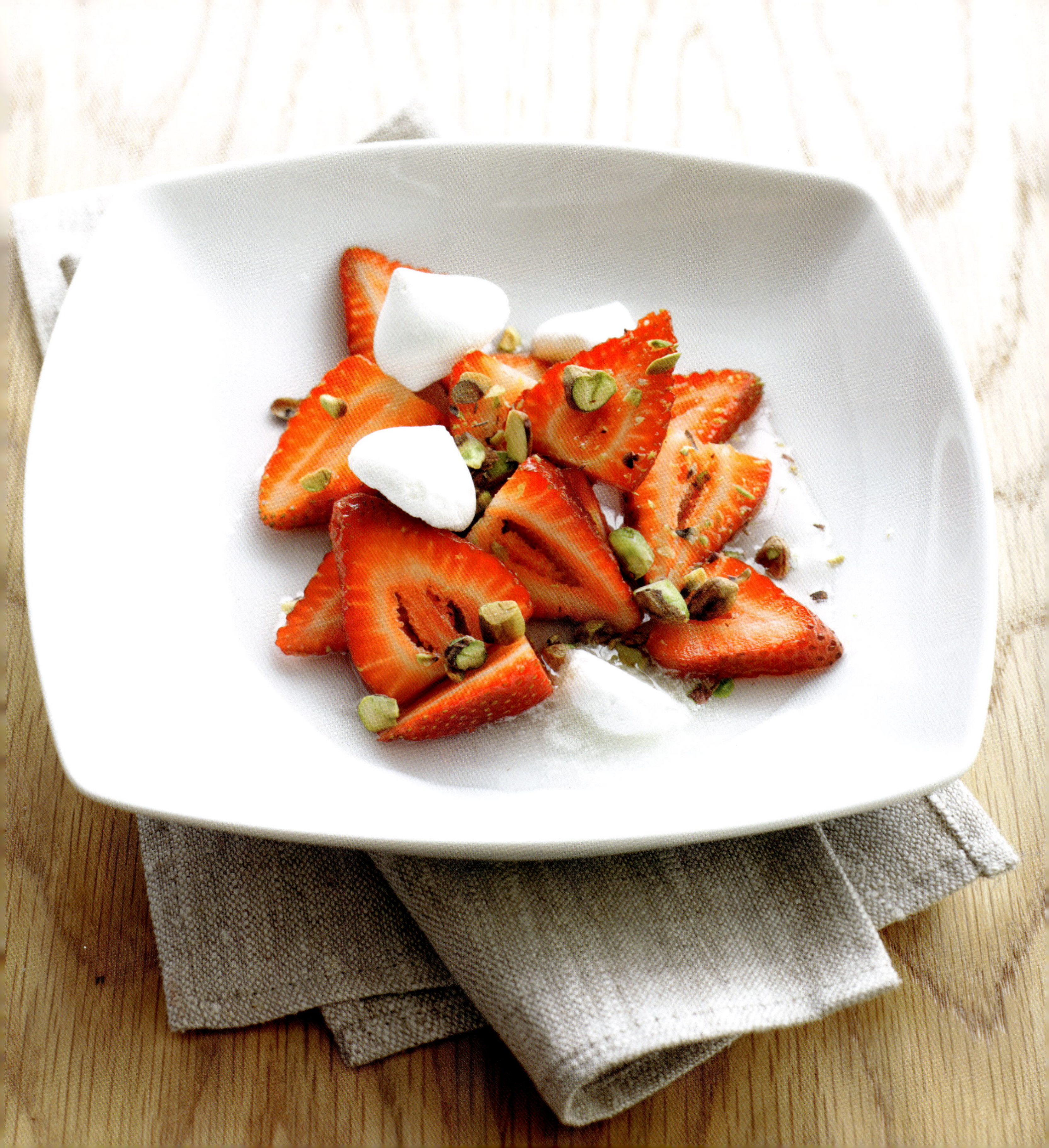

Using a sharp knife, cut the cheeks from the mangoes. Remove the skin, then roughly chop the mango flesh.

Beat egg white in small bowl with electric mixer until soft peaks form. Gradually beat in sugar until dissolved.

Fold egg white mixture into yogurt, in batches.

MANGO AND PASSIONFRUIT FOOL

prep time 15 minutes (+ refrigeration) ~ serves 2

Fruit fools are a mixture of pureed fruit and cream (or in this case, yogurt); in the past they were sometimes thickened with eggs. They are usually served in glasses or glass dishes because their soft creamy colours are part of their charm.

1 small mango (300g)
1 tablespoon passionfruit pulp
1 egg white
2 tablespoons caster (superfine) sugar
¾ cup (200g) vanilla yogurt

1 Cut cheeks from mango; remove skin, roughly chop. Blend or process mango until smooth. Combine mango puree and passionfruit in small bowl.

2 Beat egg white in small bowl with electric mixer until soft peaks form. Gradually beat in sugar until dissolved. Fold egg white into yogurt, in batches.

3 Layer mango mixture and egg-white mixture into two 1½-cup (375ml) serving glasses. Cover; refrigerate 15 minutes before serving.

nutritional count per serving
1.8g total fat (1.1g saturated fat); 491kJ (118 cal); 21g carbohydrate; 3.9g protein; 1.2g fibre

tip Frozen mango puree can be used if mangoes are out of season.

BRANDY SNAP AND RHUBARB STACKS

prep + cook time 25 minutes ~ serves 2

1½ cups (165g) coarsely chopped rhubarb
1 tablespoon water
2 tablespoons caster (superfine) sugar
10g (½ ounce) butter
1 tablespoon light brown sugar
2 teaspoons golden syrup
¼ teaspoon ground ginger
1 tablespoon plain (all-purpose) flour
2 tablespoons yogurt

1 Preheat oven to 180°C/350°F. Grease oven tray.

2 Place rhubarb, the water and caster sugar in medium saucepan; bring to the boil. Reduce heat; simmer, uncovered, stirring occasionally, about 3 minutes or until rhubarb softens. Drain rhubarb mixture through sieve over medium bowl; reserve liquid. Spread rhubarb mixture onto metal tray; cover with foil, place in freezer.

3 Meanwhile, stir butter, brown sugar, syrup and ginger in same cleaned pan over low heat until butter has melted. Remove from heat; stir in flour.

4 Drop level teaspoons of mixture about 6cm (2½ inches) apart on tray. Bake about 7 minutes or until brandy snaps bubble and become golden brown. Cool on trays 2 minutes; transfer to wire rack to cool completely.

5 Place cooled rhubarb mixture in small bowl; add yogurt, pull skewer backwards and forwards through rhubarb mixture for marbled effect.

6 Sandwich three brandy snaps with a quarter of the rhubarb mixture; repeat with remaining brandy snaps and rhubarb mixture.

7 Place stacks on serving plates; drizzle with reserved rhubarb liquid.

nutritional count per serving
7g total fat (4.5g saturated fat); 865kJ (207 cal); 31.7g carbohydrate; 3g protein; 3.4g fibre

Drain ccooked rhubarb mixture through sieve over medium bowl; reserve the liquid.

Drop level teaspoons of brandy snap mixture onto baking-paper-lined oven tray, about 6cm apart.

Bake brandy snaps until they bubble and become golden brown. Cool on trays for 2 minutes, then transfer to a wire rack to cool completely.

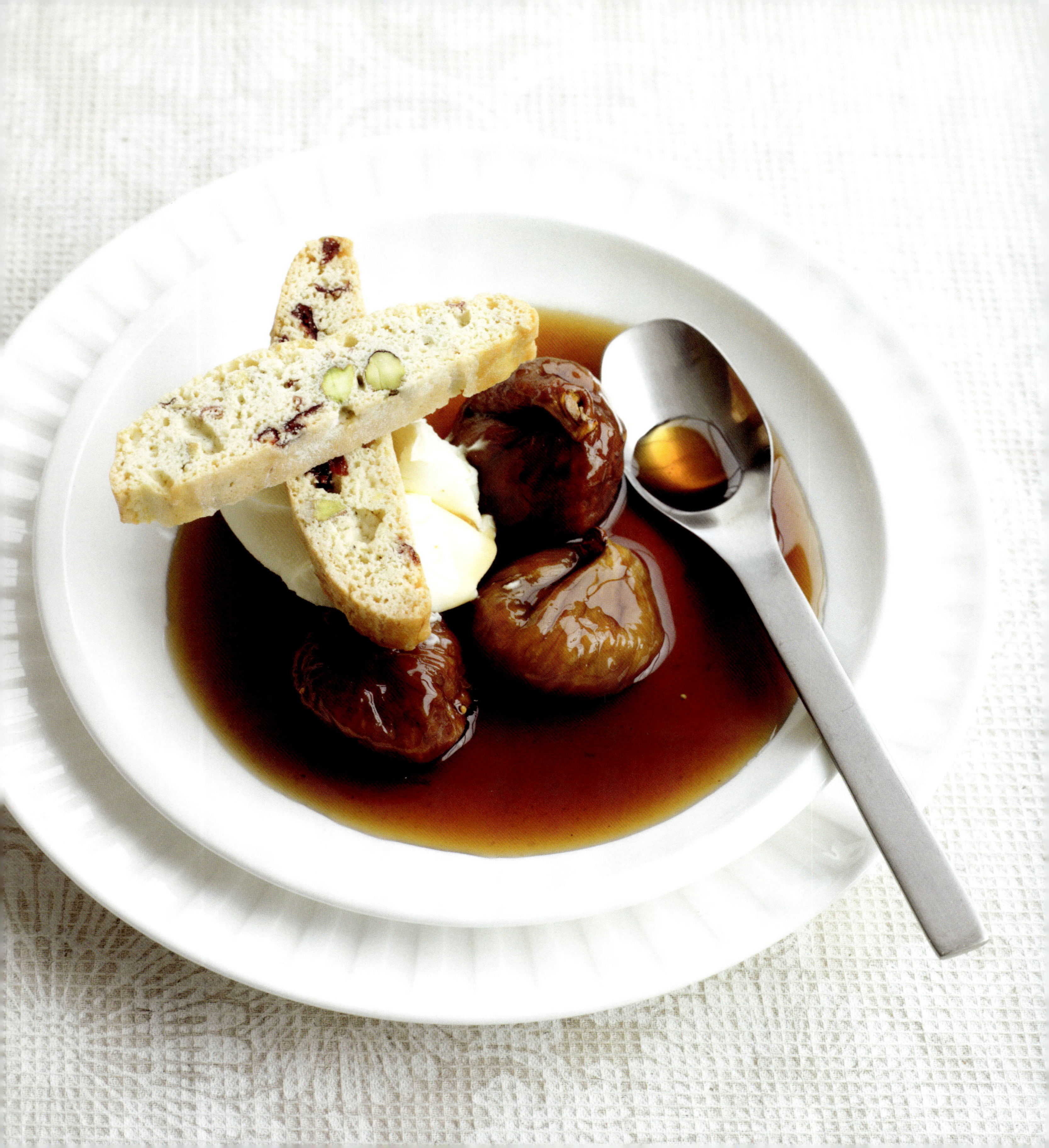

MARSALA-POACHED DRIED FIGS

prep + cook time 35 minutes ~ serves 6

1 cup (250ml) water
½ cup (110g) caster (superfine) sugar
½ cup (125ml) marsala
18 dried figs

1 Stir the water, sugar and marsala in medium saucepan, over low heat until sugar dissolves.

2 Bring syrup to the boil; add figs. Reduce heat; simmer, uncovered, without stirring, about 30 minutes or until figs soften. Serve warm.

nutritional count per serving
0.5g total fat (0g saturated fat); 1109kJ (265 cal); 57.7g carbohydrate; 2.1g protein; 8.2g fibre

serving suggestion Serve with mascarpone cheese and biscotti.

Add the marsala to the water and sugar mixture in medium saucepan over low heat until sugar dissolves.

Bring the marsala syrup to the boil, then gently add the dried figs.

Simmer figs in the syrup about 30 minutes or until the figs soften. Serve figs warm.

PAVLOVAS WITH CRUSHED STRAWBERRIES AND CREAM

prep + cook time 1 hour 15 minutes (+ cooling & standing) ~ serves 4

This dessert is our take on an eton mess, a traditional English dessert consisting of a mixture of strawberries, meringue and cream. It was served at Eton College's annual cricket game.

1 tablespoon cornflour (cornstarch)
4 egg whites
1 cup (220g) caster (superfine) sugar
½ teaspoon vanilla extract
1 teaspoon white vinegar
250g (8 ounces) strawberries
1 tablespoon icing (confectioners') sugar
1 tablespoon Grand Marnier
1¼ cups (310ml) thickened (heavy) cream

1 Preheat oven to 120°C/250°F. Line oven tray with foil; grease foil, dust with sifted cornflour, shake off excess.

2 Beat egg whites in small bowl with electric mixer until soft peaks form; gradually add caster sugar, beating until sugar dissolves. Beat in extract and vinegar.

3 Using a large serving spoon, scoop up a spoonful of pavlova mixture; using a second similar spoon, scoop under the mixture and gently push the oval-shaped scoop (quenelle) onto oven tray. Repeat to make four pavlovas.

4 Bake pavlovas about 45 minutes or until firm. Turn oven off; cool pavlovas in oven with door ajar.

5 Meanwhile, hull and coarsely chop strawberries. Combine strawberries, icing sugar and liqueur in small bowl; crush lightly with a fork. Stand 30 minutes.

6 Beat cream in small bowl with electric mixer until soft peaks form.

7 Place pavlovas on serving plates; gently break tops using the back of a dessertspoon. Top pavlovas with strawberries and cream, dust with a little extra sifted icing sugar.

nutritional count per serving
28.9g total fat (18.9g saturated fat); 1396kJ (334 cal); 66.7g carbohydrate; 6.3g protein; 1.4g fibre

tip You can use just one 300ml carton of cream for this recipe.

Beat the egg whites with an electric mixer until soft peaks form

Use a large metal spoon to scoop a spoonful of pavlova mixture; scoop under the mixture with another spoon to push quenelle onto the tray.

Place the pavlova on a serving plate then gently break the top with the back of a dessertspoon.

Process the biscuits until fine. Add the melted butter and process until combined.

Press the crumb mixture over the base and side of the tin, using a flat-bottomed, straight-sided glass to achieve an even thickness.

Pour the cheesecake filling into the biscuit crust, then bake for 1¼ hours.

BAKED SOUR CREAM CHEESECAKE

prep + cook time 1 hour 35 minutes (+ refrigeration & cooling) ~ serves 12

500g (1 pound) plain sweet biscuits
250g (4 ounces) butter, melted
600g (1¼ pounds) fresh blueberries
2 teaspoons icing (confectioners') sugar

filling
375g (12 ounces) cottage cheese
375g (12 ounces) cream cheese
3 teaspoons finely grated lemon rind
1 cup (220g) caster (superfine) sugar
4 eggs
300g (9½ ounces) sour cream
⅓ cup (80ml) lemon juice

1 Process biscuits until fine. Add butter, process until combined. Press crumb mixture over base and side of 22cm (9-inch) springform tin. Place tin on oven tray; refrigerate 30 minutes.

2 Preheat oven to 160°C/325°F.

3 To make the filling, push cottage cheese through a sieve into medium bowl. Add cream cheese, rind and sugar; beat with electric mixer until smooth. Beat in eggs, one at a time, then sour cream and juice. Pour filling into tin.

4 Bake cheesecake about 1¼ hours. Cool in oven with door ajar. Refrigerate 3 hours or overnight.

5 Before serving, top cheesecake with blueberries and dust with sifted icing sugar.

nutritional count per serving
47.4g total fat (29g saturated fat); 2866kJ (685 cal); 53.5g carbohydrate; 13.3g protein; 1.8g fibre

tips Use a flat bottomed glass with a straight side to press the crumb mixture evenly over the base and side of the tin.

Baked cheesecakes should be cooled slowly – turn the oven off after they're cooked, then prop the oven door slightly open, using a wooden spoon.

Most cheesecakes benefit from being made a day ahead, the flavours develop and the texture becomes firm.

APPLE PIE

prep + cook time 1 hour 45 minutes (+ refrigeration) ~ serves 8

Granny smiths are the traditional pie apple because they have just enough tartness to complement the sweet pastry, and they soften beautifully. For tarte tatin and other open-faced apple tarts, golden delicious are a better choice, because they keep their shape even when they're fully cooked.

10 medium apples (1.5kg)
½ cup (125ml) water
¼ cup (55g) caster (superfine) sugar
1 teaspoon finely grated lemon rind
¼ teaspoon ground cinnamon
1 egg white, beaten lightly
1 tablespoon caster (superfine) sugar, extra

pastry
1 cup (150g) plain (all-purpose) flour
½ cup (75g) self-raising flour
¼ cup (35g) cornflour (cornstarch)
¼ cup (30g) custard powder
1 tablespoon caster (superfine) sugar
100g (3 ounces) cold butter, chopped coarsely
1 egg yolk
¼ cup (60ml) iced water

1 Make pastry.

2 Peel, core and slice apples thickly. Place apple and the water in large saucepan; bring to the boil. Reduce heat; simmer, covered, 10 minutes or until apples soften. Drain; stir in sugar, rind and cinnamon. Cool.

3 Preheat oven to 220°C/475°F. Grease deep 25cm (10-inch) pie dish.

4 Divide pastry in half. Roll one half between sheets of baking paper until large enough to line dish. Lift pastry into dish; press into base and side. Spoon apple mixture into pastry case; brush edge with a little egg white.

5 Roll remaining pastry large enough to cover filling; lift onto filling. Press edges together; trim away excess pastry. Brush pastry with a little egg white; sprinkle with extra sugar.

6 Bake pie 20 minutes. Reduce oven to 180°C/350°F; bake further 25 minutes or until golden brown.

pastry
Process dry ingredients with butter until crumbly. Add egg yolk and the water; process until combined. Knead on floured surface until smooth. Wrap in plastic wrap; refrigerate 30 minutes.

nutritional count per serving
11.4g total fat (7g saturated fat); 1438kJ (344 cal); 53.9g carbohydrate; 4.3g protein; 3.7g fibre

tip Make sure the apples are drained well and cooled to room temperature before spooning into pastry case.

serving suggestion Serve with vanilla custard or ice-cream.

Knead the dough on a floured surface until smooth. Wrap in plastic, then refrigerate for 30 minutes.

Roll one half of the pastry between sheets of baking paper until large enough to line the pie dish. Lift pastry into dish, pressing into the base and side.

Roll the remaining half of pastry until large enough to cover the apples. Lift pastry onto apples and press the edges together; trim away the excess. Brush the pastry with a little beaten egg white.

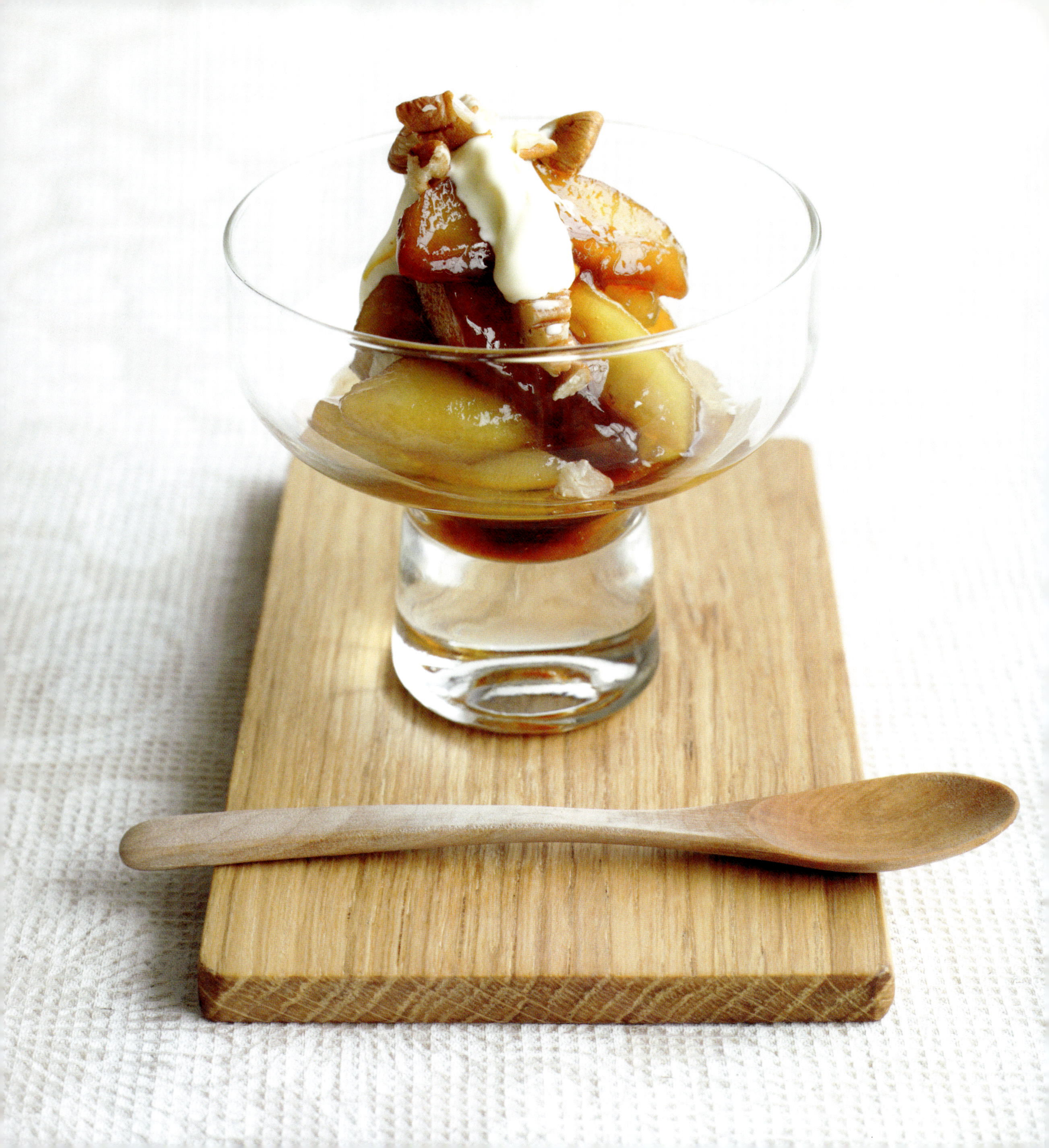

CARAMELISED APPLES

prep + cook time 25 minutes ~ serves 6

6 large apples (1.2kg)
1 tablespoon lemon juice
50g (1½ ounces) butter
⅓ cup (75g) firmly packed light brown sugar
½ cup (60g) coarsely chopped roasted pecans

1 Peel, quarter and core apples; cut each quarter into three wedges. Combine apples and lemon juice in medium bowl.

2 Melt butter in large saucepan, add apples and sugar; cook, stirring occasionally, about 10 minutes or until apples are tender.

3 Divide apple among serving bowls; sprinkle with pecans.

nutritional count per serving
14.2g total fat (5g saturated fat); 1029kJ (246 cal); 29.7g carbohydrate; 1.6g protein; 3.6g fibre

serving suggestion Serve with thick (double) cream.

Peel the apples, cut into quarters and remove the core. Cut each quarter into three wedges.

Place apples in a medium bowl, then add the lemon juice; stir until the apples are coated in juice.

Cook the apples and brown sugar in melted butter, stirring occasionally, for about 10 minutes or until the apples are tender.

APPLE CRUNCH CAKE WITH CINNAMON CUSTARD

prep + cook time 2 hours (+ refrigeration & standing) ~ serves 8

We used very small pink lady apples, the ones suitable for kids' lunchboxes.

8 small red-skinned apples (800g)
1.5 litres (6 cups) water
2 cups (440g) caster (superfine) sugar
1 cinnamon stick
185g (6 ounces) butter, softened
2 teaspoons vanilla extract
1 cup (220g) caster (superfine) sugar, extra
3 eggs
1 cup (120g) ground almonds
1½ cups (225g) self-raising flour
½ cup (125ml) buttermilk

crunch topping
30g (1 ounce) butter
2 tablespoons light brown sugar
2 tablespoons plain (all-purpose) flour

cinnamon custard
¾ cup (180ml) pouring cream
1⅓ cups (330ml) milk
1 cinnamon stick
4 egg yolks
¼ cup (55g) caster (superfine) sugar

1 Peel apples, leaving stems intact.

2 Place the water, sugar and cinnamon in a saucepan large enough to hold apples in a single layer; stir over high heat, without boiling until sugar dissolves. Bring to the boil, add apples; cover apples with a round of baking paper and a heatproof plate to keep apples submerged in syrup. Return to the boil. Reduce heat; simmer, covered, about 8 minutes or until apples are tender. Remove apples from pan with a slotted spoon. Cool 10 minutes.

3 Preheat oven to 160°C/325°F. Insert base of 26cm (10½-inch) springform pan upside down to make cake easier to remove. Grease pan, line base with baking paper.

4 Beat butter, extract and extra sugar in small bowl with electric mixer until light and fluffy. Beat in eggs, one at a time. Transfer mixture to large bowl. Stir in ground almonds, sifted flour and buttermilk, in two batches. Spread mixture into pan. Place apples, evenly spaced, around outside edge of pan, pushing apples down to base of pan.

5 Bake cake 30 minutes.

6 Meanwhile, make crunch topping.

7 Crumble topping over cake; bake cake a further 45 minutes. Stand cake in pan 15 minutes.

8 Make cinnamon custard.

9 Serve warm cake with custard.

crunch topping
Melt butter in small saucepan; stir in remaining ingredients. Refrigerate 15 minutes.

cinnamon custard
Bring cream, milk and cinnamon to the boil in medium saucepan. Remove from heat, cover; stand 20 minutes. Whisk egg yolks and sugar in medium bowl until creamy. Gradually whisk in warm milk mixture. Return mixture to pan; stir over medium heat, without boiling, until custard thickens slightly and coats the back of a spoon. Strain into medium jug; discard cinnamon stick.

nutritional count per serving
51.2g total fat (28.5g saturated fat); 4912kJ (1175 cal); 162.7g carbohydrate; 15g protein; 4.3g fibre

tip You can stir the custard in a heatproof bowl over a saucepan of simmering water to prevent the custard curdling. The custard can be served warm or cooled.

Place apples, in single layer, in suacepan of sugar syrup. Cover apples with a round of baking paper, top with a heatproof plate to keep the apples submerged in the syrup.

Evenly space the apples around the outside edge of the cake pan, pushing the apples down through the cake mixture to the base of the pan.

Stir the custard over medium heat, without boiling, until custard thickens slightly and coats the back of a spoon.

Place the caramelised apples, rounded-side down, in the pie dish. Remember, this is an upside-down pie, so be careful to arrange the apples in a decorative pattern.

Cut the pastry round to fit snugly into the pie dish and place it over the hot apples.

Tuck the pastry carefully and evenly down the sides of the dish – this will form the pastry base when the pie is inverted.

TARTE TATIN

prep + cook time 1 hour 30 minutes (+ refrigeration) ~ serves 8

Be prepared for a bit of work if you're going to make this sensational dessert. Golden delicious apples are the best apples to use, granny smith the second best.

6 large apples (1.2kg)
100g (3 ounces) unsalted butter, chopped coarsely
1 cup (220g) firmly packed light brown sugar
2 tablespoons lemon juice

pastry
1 cup (150g) plain (all-purpose) flour
2 tablespoons caster (superfine) sugar
80g (2½ ounces) cold unsalted butter, chopped coarsely
2 tablespoons sour cream

1 Peel apples; core and quarter. Melt butter in large heavy-based frying pan; add apples, sprinkle evenly with sugar and juice. Cook, uncovered, over low heat, about 40 minutes, turning apples as they caramelise.

2 Meanwhile, make pastry.

3 Preheat oven to 200°C/400°F.

4 Place apples, rounded-sides down, in 24cm (9½-inch) pie dish, packing tightly to ensure there are no gaps; drizzle with 1 tablespoon of the caramel in pan. Reserve remaining caramel.

5 Roll pastry between sheets of baking paper until large enough to cover apples. Peel away one sheet of baking paper; cut pastry to fit dish. Remove remaining paper. Place pastry carefully over hot apples; tuck pastry around apples.

6 Bake tarte tatin about 30 minutes or until pastry is browned. Carefully turn onto serving plate, apple-side up; drizzle apple with reheated reserved caramel. Serve warm.

pastry
Process flour, sugar, butter and sour cream until ingredients just come together. Knead on floured surface until smooth. Wrap in plastic wrap; refrigerate 30 minutes.

nutritional count per serving
21.1g total fat (13.7g saturated fat); 1860kJ (445 cal); 59.5g carbohydrate; 2.7g protein; 2.9g fibre

CHOCOLATE AND ROAST ALMOND TORTE

prep + cook time 1 hour 15 minutes (+ cooling) ~ serves 12

1¼ cups (200g) blanched almonds, roasted
185g (6 ounces) butter, chopped
200g (6½ ounces) dark eating (semi-sweet) chocolate, chopped coarsely
6 eggs, separated
1 cup (220g) caster (superfine) sugar
1 cup (250g) thick (double) cream

almond praline
⅔ cup (50g) flaked almonds
1 cup (220g) caster (superfine) sugar
⅓ cup (80ml) water

chocolate glaze
½ cup (125ml) pouring cream
200g (6½ ounces) dark eating (semi-sweet) chocolate, chopped coarsely

1 Preheat oven to 180°C/350°F. Grease 24cm (9½-inch) round springform pan; line base and side with baking paper, extending paper 5cm (2 inches) above side.

2 Blend or process nuts until fine.

3 Place butter and chocolate in medium saucepan, stir over low heat until smooth. Cool.

4 Beat egg yolks and sugar in large bowl with electric mixer until combined. Beat egg whites in medium bowl with electric mixer until soft peaks form.

5 Fold chocolate mixture and nuts into egg-yolk mixture; fold in egg-white mixture, in two batches. Pour mixture into tin.

6 Bake cake about 40 minutes. Stand cake in pan 10 minutes before transferring to wire rack over tray to cool.

7 Meanwhile, make almond praline then chocolate glaze.

8 Spread glaze over top and side of cake; sprinkle with crushed praline. Serve with praline shards and cream.

almond praline
Preheat oven to 180°C/350°F. Place nuts on baking-paper-lined oven tray; roast about 5 minutes or until browned lightly. Meanwhile, stir sugar and the water in small saucepan over medium heat without boiling, until sugar dissolves; bring to the boil. Boil, uncovered, without stirring, until mixture is caramel in colour. Pour toffee over nuts on tray; stand at room temperature until set. Break about one-third of the praline into pieces; place in snap lock bag, seal tightly. Smash praline with a rolling pin or meat mallet until finely crushed. Break remaining praline into large shards.

chocolate glaze
Bring cream to the boil in small saucepan. Remove from heat, add chocolate; stir until smooth.

nutritional count per serving
51.6g total fat (28.7g saturated fat); 3014kJ (721 cal); 57.4g carbohydrate; 9.5g protein; 3.4g fibre

Fold the chocolate mixture and nuts into the egg yolk mixture. Fold the egg white mixture into the chocolate mixture, in two batches.

Sprinkle the nuts over a baking-paper-lined oven tray. Pour the caramel over the nuts, then stand at room temperature until set.

Pour the chocolate glaze on the cake; spread the glaze over the top and side to cover.

Lift pastry into pans, pressing over the base and side. Trim the excess pastry by rolling over the pan with a rolling pin. Prick the bases all over with a fork.

Spoon the cooked caramel mixture into the pastry cases.

Spoon meringue onto caramel filling, then bake about 5 minutes or until the meringue has browned lightly.

SALTY CARAMEL MERINGUE PIES

prep + cook time 1 hour (+ refrigeration) ~ makes 8

395g (12½ ounces) canned sweetened condensed milk
30g (1 ounce) butter
¼ cup (90g) golden syrup or treacle
2 teaspoons sea salt flakes
¼ cup (60ml) pouring cream

pastry
1 cup (150g) plain (all-purpose) flour
⅓ cup (55g) icing (confectioners') sugar
90g (3 ounces) butter, chopped
1 egg yolk
1 tablespoon iced water, approximately

meringue
4 egg whites
1 cup (220g) caster (superfine) sugar

1 Make pastry.

2 Divide pastry into eight portions. Roll one portion at a time between sheets of baking paper until large enough to line eight 8cm (3-inch) loose-based flan tins. Ease pastry into tins, pressing into base and side; trim edges. prick bases with fork. Place on oven tray; refrigerate 20 minutes.

3 Meanwhile, preheat oven to 180°C/350°F.

4 Line pastry with baking paper, fill with dried beans or rice. Bake 10 minutes. Remove paper and beans; bake about 5 minutes or until browned. Cool.

5 Stir condensed milk, butter, syrup and salt in small heavy-based saucepan over medium heat about 12 minutes or until caramel-coloured. Stir in cream. Spoon filling into pastry cases.

6 Make meringue; spoon onto tarts.

7 Bake tarts about 5 minutes or until browned lightly.

pastry
Process flour, icing sugar and butter until crumbly. Add egg yolk and enough of the water, processing until ingredients just come together. Knead pastry on floured surface until smooth. Wrap in plastic wrap; refrigerate 30 minutes.

meringue
Beat egg whites in small bowl with electric mixer until soft peaks form. Gradually add sugar, beating until dissolved between each addition.

nutritional count per pie
17.9g total fat (11.4g saturated fat); 2195kJ (525 cal); 85.2g carbohydrate; 9.1g protein; 0.7g fibre

SWEET LIME MANGOES
prep + cook time 15 minutes ~ serves 4

Using a sharp knife, cut the cheeks from the mangoes. Score the flesh on each cheek in a shallow criss-cross pattern.

Sprinkle the brown sugar evenly over each mango cheek.

Cook mangoes, cut-side down, in heated frying pan until browned lightly and sugar caramelises.

4 small mangoes (1.2kg)
1 tablespoon finely grated lime rind
1 tablespoon lime juice
1 tablespoon light brown sugar
½ cup (140g) yogurt

1 Cut cheeks from mangoes; score each in shallow criss-cross pattern.

2 Combine rind and juice; drizzle over each mango cheek. Sprinkle with sugar.

3 Cook mangoes, cut-side down, in heated large frying pan (or on grill plate or barbecue) until browned lightly.

4 Serve mango with yogurt.

nutritional count per serving
1.7g total fat (0.7g saturated fat); 798kJ (191 cal); 35.8g carbohydrate; 4.1g protein; 4.1g fibre

ends ~ 284 ~ ends

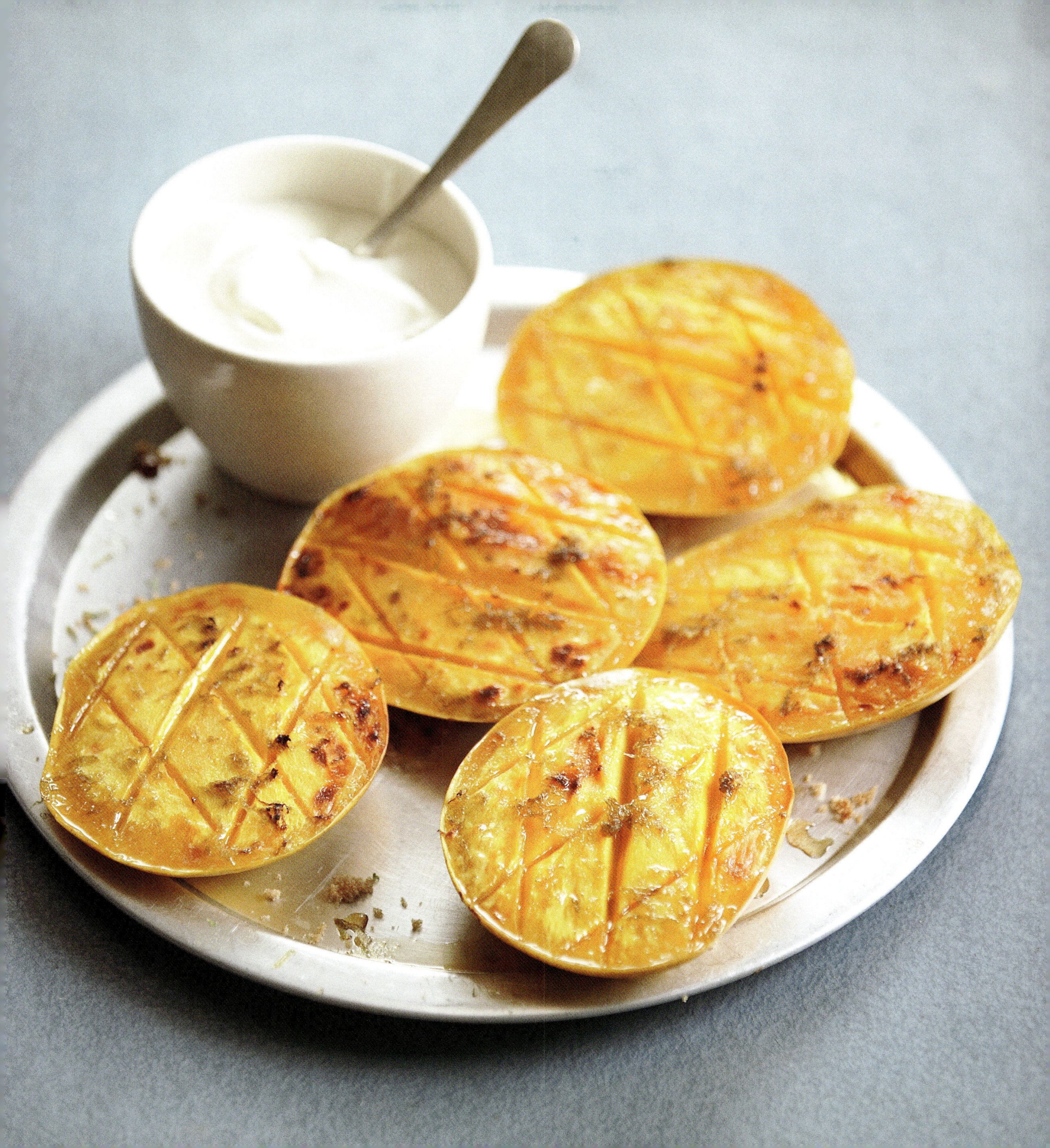

Use a rolling pin to carefully lift the pastry into a loose-based flan tin. Press the pastry into the base and side of the tin, then trim the excess pastry.

Line the pastry case with baking paper and fill with dried beans. Bake 15 minutes. Remove the paper and beans, then bake for 10 minutes or until lightly browned.

Pour the lemon filling into the cooled pastry case. Bake the tart for about 30 minutes or until the filling has just set.

LEMON TART

prep + cook time 1 hour 25 minutes (+ refrigeration) ~ serves 8

Lemon tart appears on almost every restaurant menu, with varying degrees of quality. We guarantee this recipe is as good, if not better, than any lemon tart you've ever tasted. Don't overcook the filling. The custard should feel firm around the outside of the tart, but still a bit wobbly in the middle – it will set as the tart cools.

1¼ cups (185g) plain (all-purpose) flour
⅓ cup (55g) icing (confectioners) sugar
¼ cup (30g) ground almonds
125g (4 ounces) cold butter, chopped coarsely
1 egg yolk
2 tablespoons iced water

lemon filling
3 teaspoons finely grated lemon rind
⅓ cup (80ml) lemon juice
3 eggs
½ cup (110g) caster (superfine) sugar
⅔ cup (160ml) pouring cream

1 Process flour, icing sugar, ground almonds and butter until crumbly. Add egg yolk and the water; process until combined. Knead dough on floured surface until smooth. Wrap in plastic wrap; refrigerate 30 minutes.

2 Roll pastry between sheets of baking paper until large enough to line shallow (2cm/¾-inch deep) 24cm (9½-inch) round loose-based flan tin. Lift pastry into tin; press into side, trim edge. Cover; refrigerate 30 minutes.

3 Meanwhile, preheat oven to 200°C/400°F.

4 Place flan tin on oven tray. Line pastry case with baking paper, fill with dried beans or rice. Bake, uncovered, 15 minutes. Remove paper and beans; bake a further 10 minutes or until browned lightly.

5 Meanwhile, make lemon filling.

6 Reduce oven to 180°C/350°F.

7 Pour lemon filling into pastry case; bake about 30 minutes or until filling has set slightly, cool. Refrigerate until cold. Just before serving, dust with a little extra sifted icing sugar.

lemon filling
Whisk ingredients in medium bowl; stand 5 minutes.

nutritional count per serving
25.3g total fat (14.3g saturated fat); 1714kJ (410 cal); 38.5g carbohydrate; 6.7g protein; 1.3g fibre

tip This tart is best made a day ahead and stored in the fridge.

serving suggestion Serve with whipped cream.

WARM STRAWBERRY RHUBARB CRUMBLES

prep + cook time 45 minutes ~ serves 6

500g (1 pound) rhubarb
250g (8 ounces) strawberries
¼ cup (55g) caster (superfine) sugar
2 teaspoons vanilla extract
2 eggs
¼ cup (55g) caster (superfine) sugar, extra
1 tablespoon cornflour (cornstarch)
1¼ cups (310ml) pouring cream
1 cup (250ml) milk
2 teaspoons vanilla extract, extra

crumble
½ cup (75g) self-raising flour
¼ cup (55g) demerara sugar
60g (2 ounces) cold butter, chopped finely
½ cup (60g) coarsely chopped pecans

1 Preheat oven to 180°C/350°F.

2 Cut rhubarb into 5cm (2-inch) pieces; hull strawberries. Combine rhubarb, strawberries, sugar and extract in shallow baking dish. Bake 20 minutes or until rhubarb softens.

3 Meanwhile, make crumble.

4 Whisk eggs, extra sugar and cornflour in medium saucepan until combined; gradually whisk in cream and milk. Cook, whisking, until mixture boils and thickens. Remove from heat; stir in extra extract.

5 Pour custard into six heatproof serving glasses. Top with rhubarb mixture, then crumble.

crumble
Line oven tray with baking paper. Combine sifted flour and sugar in medium bowl; rub in butter until crumbly, stir in nuts. Spoon mixture in a thin layer onto tray. Bake about 15 minutes or until mixture is browned lightly. Cool 10 minutes before coarsely crumbling mixture.

nutritional count per serving
39.5g total fat (20.3g saturated fat); 2391kJ (572 cal); 44.7g carbohydrate; 9.1g protein; 4.2g fibre

tip You can use just one 300ml carton of cream for this recipe.

Trim rhubarb, then cut the sticks into 5cm pieces.

Bake the rhubarb, strawberries, sugar and extract in a shallow baking dish for 20 minutes or until the rhubarb softens.

Rub the butter into the sifted flour and sugar until the mixture is crumbly.

Grease the soufflé dishes with butter, sprinkle inside the dish with caster sugar to coat the base and side. Shake out any excess sugar.

Place lemon curd ingredients in a heatproof bowl over a medium saucepan of simmering water; stir until the mixture is thick enough to coat the back of a wooden spoon.

Beat the egg whites and caster sugar in small bowl until the sugar dissolves. Transfer egg white mixture to a large bowl; fold in the lemon curd.

LEMON CURD SOUFFLES

prep + cook time 40 minutes (+ cooling) ~ serves 4

40g (1½ ounces) butter, melted
2 tablespoons caster (superfine) sugar
4 egg whites
¾ cup (165g) caster (superfine) sugar, extra
2 teaspoons icing (confectioners') sugar

lemon curd
2 eggs
¾ cup (165g) caster (superfine) sugar
¼ cup (60ml) fresh lemon juice
1 teaspoon finely grated lemon rind

1 Make lemon curd.

2 Preheat oven to 200°C/400°F. Grease four 1¼-cup (310ml) soufflé dishes well with the melted butter; refrigerate 5 minutes. Sprinkle inside of dishes with caster sugar; shake out excess. Place dishes on oven tray.

3 Beat egg whites and extra caster sugar in small bowl with electric mixer until sugar dissolves. Transfer to large bowl; lightly fold in lemon curd. Spoon mixture into dishes.

4 Bake soufflés about 12 minutes or until puffed and top is browned lightly. Serve soufflés immediately dusted with sifted icing sugar.

lemon curd
Beat eggs lightly with a fork in small jug; strain eggs into medium heatproof bowl. Add sugar and strained juice; place bowl over medium saucepan of simmering water. Stir about 10 minutes or until mixture thickly coats the back of a wooden spoon; stir in rind. Remove from heat. Stand bowl inside a larger bowl filled with ice, stirring occasionally, about 10 minutes or until curd is cold.

nutritional count per serving
10.8g total fat (6.2g saturated fat); 2015kJ (482 cal); 93g carbohydrate; 7.1g protein; 0g fibre

serving suggestion Serve with vanilla ice-cream.

SUMMER PUDDING

prep + cook time 35 minutes (+ refrigeration) ~ serves 6

Mix and match the berries and the jam to suit your tastes. You can use fresh berries instead of frozen, if you like. A combination of fresh and frozen is good too.

⅓ cup (75g) caster (superfine) sugar
½ cup (125ml) water
300g (9½ ounces) frozen blackberries
500g (1 pound) frozen mixed berries
10 thick slices stale white bread (760g)
¼ cup (80g) blackberry jam

1 Bring sugar and the water to the boil in medium saucepan. Stir in berries; return to the boil. Reduce heat; simmer, uncovered, until berries soften. Strain over medium bowl; reserve syrup and berries separately.

2 Line 1.25-litre (5-cup) pudding bowl with plastic wrap, extending wrap 10cm (4 inches) over side of bowl. Remove crusts from bread. Place two slices of bread on top of each other, then cut into a rounded wedge shape (see step pic 1); repeat with another two slices of bread. Cut a round from another slice of bread to fit the base of the bowl. Cut remaining bread into 10cm (4-inch) long strips.

3 Place small bread round in base of pudding bowl; use bread strips to line side of bowl.

4 Pour ⅔ cup of the reserved syrup into small jug; reserve. Fill pudding bowl with berries; cover with remaining syrup, top with rounded wedge shapes of bread. Cover pudding with overhanging plastic wrap, weight pudding with a plate; refrigerate 3 hours or overnight.

5 Before serving, stir jam and 2 tablespoons of the reserved syrup in small saucepan until heated through. Turn pudding out onto serving plate, remove plastic; brush with remaining reserved syrup then jam mixture.

nutritional count per serving
3.5g total fat (0.5g saturated fat); 1856kJ (444 cal); 84.6g carbohydrate; 12.8g protein; 8.9g fibre

serving suggestion Serve with fresh berries and whipped cream or ice-cream.

Line the base and side of the basin with the bread slices, overlapping slightly and making sure there are no gaps for the filling to leak out.

Fill the bread-lined basin with fruit then pour the syrup over it. Top with bread slices until completely covered.

Cover the pudding with a saucer that will fit inside the pudding basin and place weights (cans of food are good) on top.

Line the pastry case with baking paper; fill with dried beans or rice. Bake 10 minutes. Remove the paper and beans; bake a further 8 minutes or until pastry is browned lightly.

Carefully pour the custard over the fig filling.

Use a blowtorch to caramelise the top of the custard.

FIG CUSTARD TART

prep + cook time 1 hour 30 minutes (+ refrigeration & cooling) ~ serves 8

A blowtorch is available from kitchenware and hardware stores.

250g (8 ounces) dried figs, chopped finely
½ cup (125ml) boiling water
2 tablespoons brandy
1 cup (250ml) pouring cream
3 eggs
⅔ cup (150g) caster (superfine) sugar
1 teaspoon vanilla extract
⅔ cup (200g) thick (double) cream

pastry
1¼ cups (175g) plain (all-purpose) flour
⅓ cup (55g) icing (confectioners') sugar
¼ cup (30g) ground almonds
125g (4 ounces) cold butter, chopped
1 egg yolk
1 teaspoon iced water

1 Make pastry.

2 Grease 24cm (9½-inch) round loose-based flan tin. Roll pastry between sheets of baking paper until large enough to line tin. Lift pastry into tin; press into side, trim edge. Refrigerate 20 minutes.

3 Preheat oven to 200°C/400°F.

4 Place tin on oven tray, line pastry case with baking paper; fill with dried beans or rice. Bake 10 minutes. Remove paper and beans; bake about 8 minutes or until pastry is browned lightly. Cool. Reduce oven to 150°C/300°F.

5 Meanwhile, place figs and the water in small saucepan; bring to the boil. Reduce heat; simmer, uncovered, about 5 minutes or until mixture is thick and pulpy. Remove from heat; stir in brandy. Blend or process fig mixture until smooth; spread into pastry case.

6 Bring pouring cream to the boil in small saucepan; remove from heat. Whisk eggs, sugar and extract in medium bowl until combined. Gradually whisk hot cream mixture into egg mixture; pour custard into pastry case.

7 Bake tart about 20 minutes or until custard sets. Cool 10 minutes. Using a blowtorch, caramelise top of tart. Cool in tin.

8 Serve tart dusted with a little sifted icing sugar, if you like, and thick cream.

pastry
Process flour, sugar, ground almonds and butter until crumbly. Add egg yolk and the water; process until ingredients come together. Knead dough gently on floured surface until smooth. Wrap in plastic wrap; refrigerate 30 minutes.

nutritional count per serving
43.9g total fat (26.3g saturated fat); 2826kJ (676 cal); 60g carbohydrate; 8.2g protein; 5.6g fibre

LEMON SYRUP CAKE

prep + cook time 50 minutes ~ serves 10

Lemon syrup cake is probably the most well-known and popular of all. We love this recipe for its tangy taste and velvety texture.

A baba pan has a pretty fluted base, which becomes the top of the cake. Grease it well with softened butter.

Beat the butter, lemon rind and sugar in a small bowl with an electric mixer until it is light and fluffy.

Place the hot cake on to a wire rack set over an oven tray (to catch the drips). Pour the hot syrup over the hot cake.

125g (4 ounces) butter, softened
3 teaspoons finely grated lemon rind
⅔ cup (150g) caster (superfine) sugar
2 eggs
⅔ cup (160ml) buttermilk
2 tablespoons lemon juice
1½ cups (225g) self-raising flour

lemon syrup
⅓ cup (80ml) lemon juice
¼ cup (60ml) water
¾ cup (165g) caster (superfine) sugar

1 Preheat oven to 180°C/350°F. Grease 24cm (9½-inch) baba pan or deep 22cm (9-inch) round cake pan.

2 Beat butter, rind and sugar in small bowl with electric mixer until light and fluffy. Beat in eggs, one at a time. Transfer mixture to large bowl; fold in buttermilk, lemon juice and sifted flour, in two batches. Spread mixture into pan.

3 Bake cake about 30 minutes if using baba pan or about 40 minutes if using round pan. Stand cake 5 minutes; turn onto wire rack set over tray.

4 Meanwhile, make lemon syrup.

5 Pour hot syrup over hot cake; serve warm.

lemon syrup
Stir ingredients in small saucepan over heat, without boiling, until sugar dissolves. Simmer, uncovered, without stirring, 5 minutes.

nutritional count per serving
11.9g total fat (7.3g saturated fat); 1350kJ (323 cal); 48.8g carbohydrate; 4.4g protein; 0.9g fibre

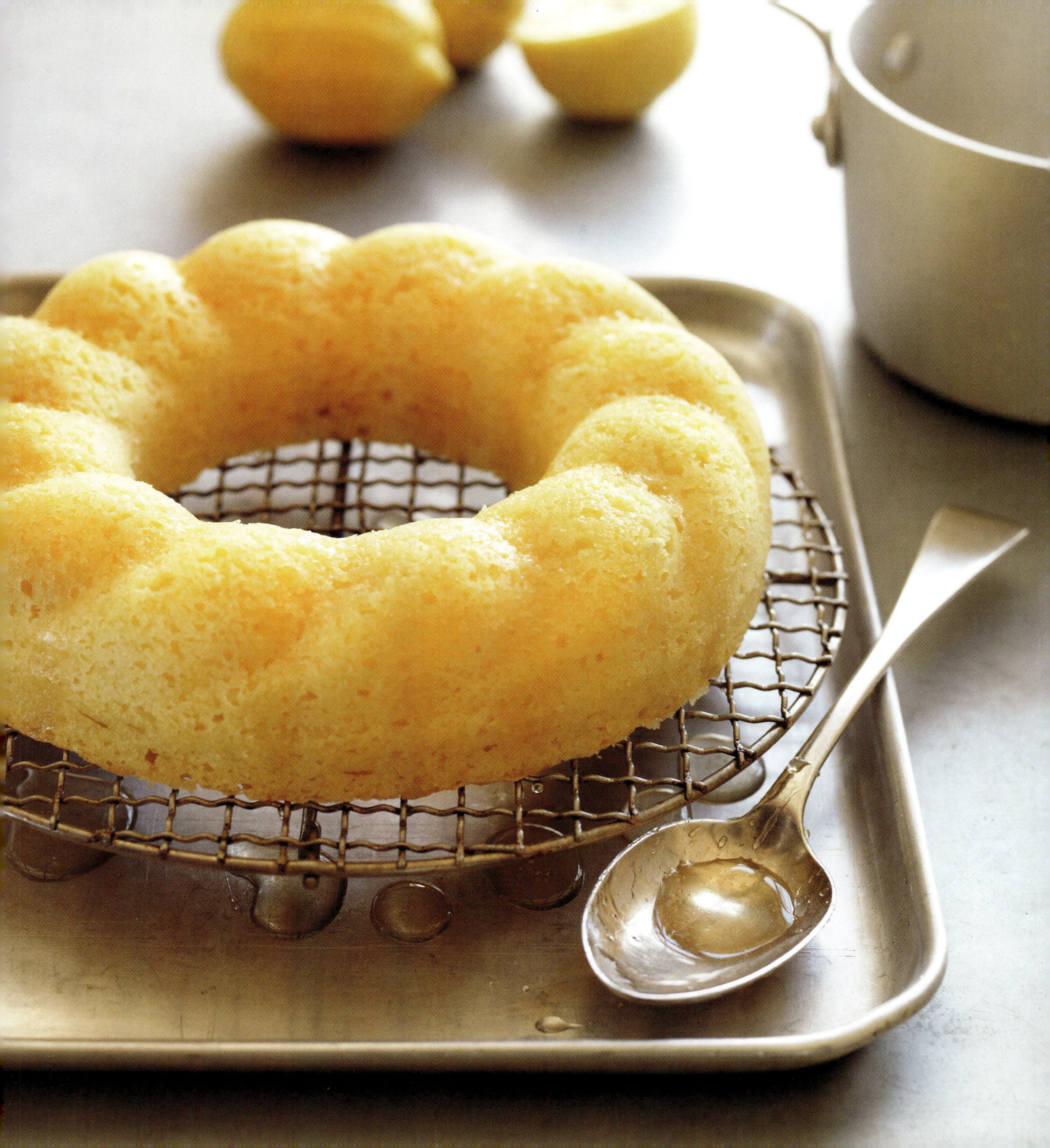

CHOCOLATE, PEAR AND HAZELNUT SELF-SAUCING PUDDING

prep + cook time 1 hour 40 minutes ~ serves 6

100g (3 ounces) dark eating (semi-sweet) chocolate, chopped coarsely
50g (1½ ounces) butter
⅔ cup (160ml) milk
⅔ cup (100g) roasted hazelnuts, chopped coarsely
¼ cup (25g) ground hazelnuts
1 cup (220g) firmly packed brown sugar
1 cup (150g) self-raising flour
1 egg, beaten lightly
2 medium pears (460g)

fudge sauce
½ cup (50g) cocoa powder
1 cup (220g) firmly packed light brown sugar
1¾ cups (430ml) water
100g (3 ounces) butter, chopped

1 Preheat oven to 180°C/350°F. Grease shallow 3-litre (12-cup) baking dish.

2 Stir chocolate, butter and milk in small saucepan over low heat until smooth. Transfer to large bowl. Stir in nuts, ground hazelnuts and sugar, then sifted flour and egg. Spoon mixture into dish.

3 Peel and core pears; slice thinly. Place pear slices, slightly overlapping, on top of chocolate mixture in dish.

4 Make fudge sauce; pour over pears.

5 Bake pudding about 1 hour. Stand pudding 10 minutes before serving.

fudge sauce
Sift cocoa and sugar into small saucepan, stir in water and butter. Stir over medium heat until smooth; do not boil.

nutritional count per serving
41.9g total fat (20.4g saturated); 3624kJ (867 cal); 109g carbohydrate; 10.4g protein; 5.5g fibre

serving suggestion Serve with whipped cream or ice-cream.

Stir nuts, ground hazelnuts and sugar into chocolate mixture, then stir in sifted flour and the egg.

Spoon the chocolate pudding mixture into the baking dish. Place pear slices, slightly overlapping, on top of mixture.

Gently pour the fudge sauce over the pears.

Stand dates, the water and bicarbonate of soda in covered processor for 5 minutes.

Process butter and sugar with date mixture until pureed. Add flour and eggs, then process until combined.

Stir ingredients for butterscotch sauce in small saucepan over low heat until smooth and sauce has thickened slightly.

STICKY DATE PUDDING WITH BUTTERSCOTCH SAUCE

prep + cook time 1 hour 10 minutes (+ standing) ~ serves 6

1¼ cups (275g) seeded dried dates
1¼ cups (310ml) boiling water
1 teaspoon bicarbonate of soda (baking soda)
50g (1½ ounces) butter, chopped
½ cup (110g) firmly packed light brown sugar
1 cup (150g) self-raising flour
2 eggs

butterscotch sauce
¾ cup (165g) firmly packed light brown sugar
1¼ cups (310ml) pouring cream
80g (2½ ounces) butter

1 Preheat oven to 180°C/350°F. Grease deep 20cm (8-inch) round cake pan; line base with baking paper.

2 Place dates and the water in food processor. Stir in soda; cover with lid, stand 5 minutes.

3 Add butter and sugar to processor; process until pureed. Add flour and eggs; process until just combined. Pour mixture into pan.

4 Bake pudding about 1 hour. Stand pudding in pan 10 minutes; turn onto serving plate.

5 Meanwhile, make butterscotch sauce.

6 Serve warm pudding with sauce.

butterscotch sauce
Stir ingredients in small saucepan over low heat until sauce is smooth and thickened slightly.

nutritional count per serving
41.5g total fat (26.6g saturated); 2993kJ (716 cal); 77g carbohydrate; 6.7g protein; 5.4g fibre

tips You can use just one 300ml carton cream for this recipe.

Both the pudding and sauce can be made a day ahead and stored, separately, covered, in the fridge.

You can freeze the pudding for up to 3 months. Defrost and warm the pudding in a microwave oven while making the butterscotch sauce. Or, freeze wedges of the pudding and thaw in the microwave for about 30 seconds – an instant dessert to have with whipped cream or ice-cream, with or without the sauce.

SNOW EGGS WITH BLACKBERRY FOOL

prep + cook time 1 hour 20 minutes ~ serves 8

We used two ½-cup (125ml) silicone egg poacher moulds at a time, for this recipe – they are available in specialty kitchenware and chef supply stores.

35g (1 ounce) unsalted butter
2 tablespoons light brown sugar
1½ tablespoons golden syrup or treacle
¼ cup (35g) plain (all-purpose) flour
½ teaspoon lemon juice
4 egg whites
1 cup (160g) icing (confectioners') sugar
2 tablespoons icing (confectioners') sugar, extra

blackberry fool
300g (9½ ounces) blackberries
1 cup (250ml) thickened (heavy) cream
1 cup (230g) thick vanilla custard

1 Preheat oven to 180°C/350°F.

2 Grease three oven trays. Trace eight 11cm (4¼-inch) rounds, about 5cm (2 inches) apart, onto three sheets baking paper to use as a guide; line trays with paper, marked-side down.

3 To make snaps, stir butter, brown sugar and golden syrup in small saucepan, over low heat, until smooth. Remove from heat; stir in sifted flour and juice. Using a wet, thin metal spatula, spread mixture into marked rounds on trays.

4 Bake snaps about 12 minutes or until they bubble and are golden brown. Slide a thin metal spatula under each snap to loosen; working quickly, shape one snap over back of silicone egg poacher mould. Transfer to wire rack to cool. Repeat with remaining snaps.

5 To make snow eggs, half fill a large frying pan with water; bring to the boil. Reduce heat to gentle simmer. Beat egg whites in small bowl with electric mixer until soft peaks form. Gradually add icing sugar, about one tablespoon at a time; beat about 5 minutes, or until mixture is thick. Spoon ½ cup of the meringue mixture into greased silicone egg poacher moulds; smooth surface. Place moulds in simmering water about 5 minutes or until meringue is firm. Using slotted spoon carefully remove moulds from pan; stand 1 minute. Transfer snow eggs onto baking-paper-lined tray; gently turn moulds inside out to release the snow eggs. Repeat with remaining meringue mixture.

6 Make blackberry fool.

7 Divide blackberry fool into serving glasses; top with snow eggs and snaps. Dust with sifted extra icing sugar.

blackberry fool
Roughly mash blackberries in small bowl with fork. Beat cream in another small bowl with electric mixer until soft peaks form; fold in custard, then blackberries for a marbled effect.

nutritional count per serving
16.2g total fat (10.6g saturated fat); 1350kJ (323 cal); 40.6g carbohydrate; 4.5g protein; 2.5g fibre

tip If using frozen blackberries, ensure they are thawed and drained well on absorbent paper before mashing with a fork.

Working quickly, shape the snap over the back of a silicone egg poacher mould; cool on wire rack. Bake snaps one at a time to give you enough time to handle and shape each one before they harden.

Carefully place the meringue-filled silicone egg poaching moulds into a large wide shallow pan of simmering water. We cooked two at a time, but more can be cooked together.

Carefully lift the moulds from the water, turn them upside-down onto a baking-paper-lined tray. Gently turn the moulds inside out to release the snow eggs. These can be cooked several hours before you need them.

GLOSSARY

ANCHOVY FILLETS fillets of this small oily fish are preserved and packed in oil or salt in small cans or jars, and are strong in flavour. Fresh anchovies are much milder in flavour.

ARTICHOKE HEARTS tender centre of the globe artichoke; can be harvested from the plant after the prickly choke is removed. Cooked hearts can be bought from delicatessens or canned in brine.

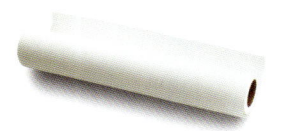

BAKING PAPER also called parchment paper or baking parchment – is a silicone-coated paper primarily used for lining baking pans and oven trays so cakes and biscuits won't stick.

BAY LEAVES aromatic leaves from the bay tree available fresh or dried; adds a strong, slightly peppery flavour.

BEETROOT (BEETS) also known as red beets; firm, round root vegetable.

BREADCRUMBS, PANKO (JAPANESE) have a lighter texture than Western-style breadcrumbs. Gives a crunchy texture with a delicate, pale golden colour. Can be found at Asian grocery stores and most major supermarkets.

BURGHUL also called bulghur wheat; hulled steamed wheat kernels that, once dried, are crushed into various sized grains. It is not the same as cracked wheat.

CAPSICUM (BELL PEPPER) also called pepper. They are available in a variety of colours – green, yellow, red, orange and purplish-black. Discard seeds and membranes before use.

CHEESE

bocconcini walnut-sized, baby mozzarella, a delicate, semi-soft, white cheese traditionally made from buffalo milk. Sold fresh, it spoils rapidly so will only keep, refrigerated in brine, for 1 or 2 days at the most.

goat's made from goat's milk; has an earthy, strong taste. Available in soft and firm textures, in various shapes and sizes and rolled in ash or herbs.

gruyère a swiss cheese having small holes and a nutty, slightly salty, flavour.

haloumi a Greek Cypriot cheese with a semi-firm, spongy texture and very salty sweet flavour. Ripened and stored in salted whey; best grilled or fried. Eat while still warm as it toughens on cooling.

mascarpone an Italian fresh cultured-cream product made similarly to yogurt. Whiteish to creamy yellow in colour, with a buttery-rich, luscious texture. It is soft, creamy and spreadable.

CHICKPEAS (GARBANZO BEANS) also called hummus or channa; an irregularly round, sandy-coloured legume. Firm texture even after cooking, a floury mouth-feel and robust nutty flavour; available canned or dried (soak for several hours in cold water before use).

CHILLI use rubber gloves when handling fresh chillies as they can burn your skin. We use unseeded chillies because the seeds contain the heat; use fewer chillies rather than seeding the lot.

green any unripened chilli; also some varieties that are ripe when green, such as jalapeño, habanero or poblano.

long red (also green, yellow) available fresh and dried; a generic term used for any moderately hot, long, thin chilli.

CHOCOLATE

dark eating (semi-sweet) also known as luxury chocolate; made of a high percentage of cocoa liquor and cocoa butter, and little added sugar. Unless stated otherwise, we use dark eating chocolate in this book as it's ideal for use in desserts and cakes.

white contains no cocoa solids but derives its sweet flavour from cocoa butter. Very sensitive to heat.

CHOY SUM also known as pakaukeo or flowering cabbage, a member of the buk choy family; easy to identify with its long stems, light green leaves and yellow flowers. Stems and leaves are both edible, steamed or stir-fried.

CINNAMON available both in the piece (called sticks or quills) and ground into powder; one of the world's most common spices.

COCONUT

cream obtained commercially from the first pressing of the coconut flesh alone, without the addition of water; the second pressing (less rich) is sold as coconut milk. Available in cans and cartons at most supermarkets.

desiccated concentrated, dried, unsweetened and finely shredded coconut flesh.

flaked dried flaked coconut flesh.

milk not the liquid inside the fruit (coconut water), but the diluted liquid from the second pressing of the white flesh of a mature coconut. Available in cans and cartons at most supermarkets.

shredded unsweetened thin strips of dried coconut flesh.

glossary ~ 305 ~ glossary

CORIANDER (CILANTRO) also called pak chee or chinese parsley; bright-green-leafed herb with both pungent aroma and taste. Used as an ingredient in a wide variety of cuisines. Often stirred into or sprinkled over a dish just before serving for maximum impact as its characteristics diminish with cooking. Coriander seeds are dried and sold either whole or ground, and neither form tastes remotely like the fresh leaf.

CORNICHON French for gherkin, a very small variety of cucumber. Pickled, they are a traditional accompaniment to pâté; the Swiss always serve them with fondue (or raclette).

COUSCOUS a fine, grain-like cereal product made from semolina; from the countries of North Africa. A semolina flour and water dough is sieved then dehydrated to produce minuscule even-sized pellets of couscous; it is rehydrated by steaming or with the addition of a warm liquid and swells to three or four times its original size; eaten like rice with a tagine, as a side dish or salad ingredient.

CUMIN also known as zeera or comino; resembling caraway in size, cumin is the dried seed of a plant related to the parsley family. Has a spicy, almost curry-like flavour and is available dried as seeds or ground.

DAIKON also called white radish; long, white horseradish with a wonderful, sweet flavour. After peeling, eat it raw in salads or shredded as a garnish; also great when sliced or cubed and cooked in stir-fries and casseroles. The flesh is white but the skin can be either white or black; buy those that are firm and unwrinkled from Asian food shops.

EGGPLANT also called aubergine. Ranging in size from tiny to very large and in colour from pale green to deep purple.

EGGS if a recipe calls for raw or barely cooked eggs, exercise caution if there is a salmonella problem in your area, particularly in food eaten by children and pregnant women.

FENNEL also called finocchio; a crunchy green vegetable slightly resembling celery that's eaten raw in salads; fried as an accompaniment; or used as an ingredient in soups and sauces.

FISH SAUCE called naam pla if Thai-made, nuoc naam if Vietnamese. Made from pulverised salted fermented fish (most often anchovies); has a pungent smell and strong taste. Available in varying degrees of intensity, so use according to your taste.

GELATINE we use dried (powdered) gelatine; it's also available in sheet form called leaf gelatine. The two types are interchangable.

GHEE a type of clarified butter; milk solids are cooked until golden brown (in clarified butter they are not), which imparts a nutty flavour and sweet aroma; it can be heated to a high temperature without burning. Use clarified butter if you can't get ghee.

glossary ~ 306 ~ glossary

GINGER

fresh also called green or root ginger; the thick gnarled root of a tropical plant. Can be kept, peeled, covered with dry sherry in a jar and refrigerated, or frozen in an airtight container.

pickled pink or red coloured; available, packaged, from Asian food shops. Pickled paper-thin shavings of ginger in a mixture of vinegar, sugar and natural colouring; used in Japanese cooking.

GLUCOSE SYRUP also known as liquid glucose, made from wheat starch; used in jam and confectionery making. Available at health-food stores and supermarkets.

HOISIN SAUCE a thick, sweet and spicy Chinese barbecue sauce made from salted fermented soybeans, onions and garlic; used as a marinade or baste, or to accent stir-fries and barbecued or roasted foods. From Asian food shops and supermarkets.

KAFFIR LIME also called magrood, leech lime or jeruk purut. The wrinkled, bumpy-skinned green fruit of a small citrus tree originally grown in South Africa and South-East Asia. As a rule, only the rind and leaves are used.

KAFFIR LIME LEAVES also called bai magrood and looks like two glossy dark green leaves joined end to end, forming a rounded hourglass shape. Used fresh or dried in many South-East Asian dishes, they are used like bay leaves or curry leaves, especially in Thai cooking. Sold fresh, dried or frozen, the dried leaves are less potent so double the number if using them as a substitute for fresh; a strip of fresh lime peel may be substituted for each kaffir lime leaf.

KUMARA (ORANGE SWEET POTATO) the Polynesian name of an orange-fleshed sweet potato often confused with yam; good baked, boiled, mashed or fried similarly to other potatoes.

LEMON GRASS a tall, clumping, lemon-smelling and tasting, sharp-edged aromatic tropical grass; the white lower part of the stem is used, finely chopped. Can be found, fresh, dried, powdered and frozen, in supermarkets, greengrocers and Asian food shops.

LENTILS dried pulses often identified by and named after their colour. Lentils have high food value.

MAPLE SYRUP distilled from the sap of sugar maple trees found in Canada and some states of the USA. Maple-flavoured syrup is not an adequate substitute for the real thing.

MIRIN a Japanese champagne-coloured cooking wine, made of glutinous rice and alcohol. It is used expressly for cooking and should not be confused with sake. A seasoned sweet mirin called manjo mirin is also available.

MUSHROOMS

chanterelle also called girolles or pfifferling; a trumpet-shaped wild mushroom, ranging in colour from yellow to orange. It has a delicate flavour and a chewy texture. Also available dried.

chestnut are cultivated mushrooms with a firm texture and strong flavour. They are available only irregularly.

oyster also known as abalone; grey-white mushrooms shaped like a fan. Prized for their smooth texture and subtle, oyster-like flavour.

porcini (dried) the richest-flavoured mushrooms, also known as cèpes. Expensive but, because they are so strongly flavoured, only a small amount is required for any particular dish.

shiitake also called Chinese black, forest or golden oak mushrooms. Although cultivated, they have the earthiness and taste of wild mushrooms. Large and meaty, they can be used as a substitute for meat in some Asian vegetarian dishes. Dried shiitake must be rehydrated before use.

swiss brown also called roman or cremini. Light to dark brown mushrooms with full-bodied flavour; suited for use in casseroles or being stuffed and baked.

MUSTARD

dijon also called french. Pale brown, creamy, distinctively flavoured, fairly mild French mustard.

wholegrain also known as seeded. A French-style coarse-grain mustard made from crushed mustard seeds and dijon-style french mustard.

NOODLES, HOKKIEN also called stir-fry noodles; fresh wheat noodles that look like thick, yellow-brown spaghetti, needing no pre-cooking before use.

NUTMEG a strong and pungent spice ground from the dried nut of an evergreen tree native to Indonesia. Usually found ground but the flavour is more intense from a whole nut, available from spice shops, so it's best to grate your own. Used often in baking but also works nicely in savoury dishes. Found in mixed spice mixtures.

OLIVE OIL made from ripened olives. Extra virgin and virgin are the first and second press, respectively; "extra light" or "light" refers to taste not fat levels.

ONIONS

green (scallions) also known, incorrectly, as shallots; an immature onion picked before the bulb has formed, having a long, bright-green edible stalk.

red also known as spanish, red spanish or bermuda onion; a sweet-flavoured, large, purple-red onion.

shallots also called french shallots or eschalots. Small and elongated, with a brown skin, they grow in tight clusters.

OYSTER SAUCE thick, richly flavoured brown sauce made from oysters and their brine, cooked with salt and soy sauce, and thickened with starches.

PANCETTA an Italian unsmoked bacon, pork belly cured in salt and spices then rolled into a sausage shape and dried for several weeks.

PINE NUTS also known as pignoli; not a nut but a small, cream-coloured kernel from pine cones. They are best roasted before use to bring out the flavour.

POLENTA also called cornmeal. A flour-like cereal made of dried corn (maize). Also the name of the dish made from it.

POMEGRANATE dark-red, leathery-skinned fresh fruit about the size of an orange filled with hundreds of seeds, each wrapped in an edible lucent-crimson pulp having a unique tangy sweet-sour flavour.

PRESERVED LEMON whole or quartered salted lemons preserved in a mixture of olive oil and lemon juice and occasionally spices. A North African specialty, they are added to casseroles and tagines, as well as salad dressings or chopped and stirred into yogurt. Available from delis and specialty food shops. Use the rind only and rinse well under cold water before using.

PRESERVED TURNIP also called hua chai po or cu cai muoi, or dried radish because of its similarity to daikon. Sold packaged whole or sliced, is very salty and must be rinsed and dried before use.

PROSCIUTTO a kind of unsmoked Italian ham; salted, air-cured and aged, it is usually eaten uncooked.

QUINOA pronounced keen-wa, is a gluten-free grain. It has a delicate, slightly nutty taste and chewy texture.

RHUBARB a plant with long, green-red stalks; becomes sweet and edible when cooked.

RICE

arborio small, round grain rice well-suited to absorb a large amount of liquid; the high level of starch makes it especially suitable for risottos, giving the dish its classic creaminess.

wild not a member of the rice family but the seed of an aquatic grass. Has a strong nutty taste and can be pricy, so is best mixed with brown and white rices.

glossary ~ 309 ~ glossary

ROCKET (ARUGULA) peppery green leaf eaten raw in salads or used in cooking.

ROSEMARY pungent herb with long, thin pointy leaves.

ROSEWATER extract made from crushed rose petals; used for its aromatic quality in many sweetmeats and desserts.

SAFFRON stigma of a member of the crocus family, available ground or in strands; imparts a yellow-orange colour to food once infused. The quality can vary greatly; the best is the most expensive spice in the world.

SASHIMI fish sold as sashimi has to meet stringent guidelines regarding its handling. Seek local advice from authorities before eating raw seafood.

SEAFOOD

oysters available in many varieties, including pacific, bay/blacklip, and Sydney or New Zealand rock oyster.

prawns (shrimp) varieties include, school, king, royal red, Sydney harbour, tiger. Can be bought cooked (as pictured) or uncooked (green), with or without shells.

salmon red-pink firm fleshed fish with few bones; moist delicate flavour.

scallops should smell sweetly briny rather than fishy when fresh. They are very perishable so fresh scallops should be used within 1 to 2 days of purchase.

squid also called calamari; a type of mollusc. Buy squid hoods to make preparation and cooking faster.

SESAME SEEDS black and white are the most common of this small oval seed, however there are also red and brown varieties. Roast the seeds in a heavy-based frying pan over low heat.

SILVER BEET (SWISS CHARD) also known as, incorrectly, spinach; has fleshy stalks and large leaves, both of which can be prepared as for spinach.

SNOW PEAS also called mangetout; a variety of garden pea, eaten pod and all. Used in stir-fries or eaten raw in salads. Snow pea sprouts are available from supermarkets or greengrocers and are usually eaten raw in salads or sandwiches.

SOY SAUCE, JAPANESE an all-purpose low-sodium soy sauce made with more wheat content than its Chinese counterparts; fermented in barrels and aged. The best soy to choose if you only want one variety.

SPINACH also known as english spinach and incorrectly, silver beet. Baby spinach leaves are best eaten raw in salads; the larger leaves should be added last to soups, stews and stir-fries, and should be cooked until barely wilted.

SPONGE FINGER BISCUITS also known as savoiardi, savoy biscuits or lady's fingers; Italian-style crisp fingers made from sponge cake mixture.

STAR ANISE a dried star-shaped pod whose seeds have an astringent aniseed flavour; commonly used to flavour stocks and marinades.

SUGAR

caster (superfine) finely granulated table sugar.

demerara small-grained golden-coloured crystal sugar.

icing (confectioners') also known as powdered sugar; pulverised granulated sugar crushed together with a small amount of cornflour (cornstarch).

light brown a very soft, finely granulated sugar retaining molasses for its characteristic colour and flavour.

palm also called nam tan pip, jaggery or jawa; made from the sap of the sugar palm tree. Light brown to black in colour and usually sold in rock-hard cakes; use light brown sugar instead.

SUGAR SNAP PEAS sugar snap peas, also known as honey snap peas, are fresh plump small peas which are eaten whole, pod and all, similarly to snow peas. They are equally good served raw in salads or, as we suggest here, steamed or microwaved until just tender and eaten as a vegetable accompaniment for a main course.

SUMAC a purple-red, astringent spice ground from berries growing on shrubs that flourish wild around the Mediterranean; adds a tart, lemony flavour to dips and dressings and goes well with barbecued meat. Can be found in Middle Eastern food stores.

TAHINI sesame seed paste available from Middle Eastern food stores and health food stores.

TAMARIND the tamarind tree produces clusters of hairy brown pods, each of which is filled with seeds and a viscous pulp, that are dried and pressed into the blocks of tamarind found in Asian food shops. Gives a sweet-sour, slightly astringent taste to marinades, pastes, sauces and dressings.

TAMARIND CONCENTRATE (or paste) the commercial result of the distillation of tamarind juice into a condensed, compacted paste.

TOMATOES

canned peeled tomatoes in natural juices; available crushed, chopped or diced. Use undrained.

cherry also known as tiny tim or tom thumb tomatoes, they are small (bite-sized) and round.

roma (egg) also known as plum; are smallish, oval-shaped tomatoes much used in Italian cooking or salads.

semi-dried partially dried tomato pieces in olive oil; softer and juicier than sun-dried, these are not a preserve thus do not keep as long as sun-dried.

truss small vine-ripened tomatoes with vine still attached.

VANILLA BEAN dried, long, thin pod from a tropical golden orchid; the minuscule black seeds inside the bean are used to impart a luscious flavour.

WASABI also called wasabe; an Asian horseradish used to make the pungent, green-coloured sauce traditionally served with Japanese raw fish dishes; sold in powdered or paste form.

WATERCRESS one of the cress family, a large group of peppery greens used raw in salads, dips and sandwiches, or cooked in soups. Highly perishable, so it must be used as soon as possible after purchase.

WITLOF (BELGIAN ENDIVE) related to and often confused with chicory. A versatile vegetable, it tastes good cooked and raw. Grown in darkness like white asparagus to prevent it becoming green; looks somewhat like a tightly furled, cream to very light-green cigar.

WRAPPERS wonton and gow gee wrappers or spring roll pastry sheets, made of flour, egg and water, are found in the refrigerated or freezer section of Asian food shops and many supermarkets. These come in different thicknesses and shapes.

YEAST (dried and fresh), a raising agent used in dough making. Granular (7g sachets) and fresh compressed (20g blocks) yeast can almost always be substituted one for the other when yeast is called for.

YOGURT, GREEK-STYLE plain yogurt that has been strained in a cloth (muslin) to remove the whey and to give it a creamy consistency. It is ideal for use in dips and dressings.

ZUCCHINI also known as courgette; small, pale- or dark-green or yellow vegetable of the squash family. Harvested when young, its edible flowers can be stuffed and deep-fried or used in salads.